Uncompensated Hospital Care

also of interest in this series

The Effectiveness of Medical Care: Validating Clinical Wisdom
Barbara Starfield, M.D., M.P.H., and Others

The Hospital Power Equilibrium: Physician Behavior and Cost Control
David W. Young and Richard B. Saltman

Uncompensated Hospital Care

Rights and Responsibilities

Edited by Frank A. Sloan,
James F. Blumstein, and
James M. Perrin

The Johns Hopkins University Press
Baltimore and London

© 1986 The Johns Hopkins University Press
All rights reserved
Printed in the United States of America

The Johns Hopkins University Press,
701 West 40th Street,
Baltimore, Maryland 21211
The Johns Hopkins Press Ltd, London

The paper in this book is acid-free and meets the guidelines for
permanence and durability of the Committee on Production Guidelines
for Book Longevity of the Council on Library Resources.

Library of Congress Cataloging in Publication Data
Main entry under title:

Uncompensated hospital care.

   (The Johns Hopkins series in contemporary medicine
and public health)
   Based on a conference held at Vanderbilt
University on Apr. 5–6, 1984.
   Includes bibliographies and index.
   1. Hospitals—United States—Rates—Congresses.
2. Poor—Hospital care—United States—Finance—
Congresses.   3. Hospitals—United States—Business
management—Congresses.   4. Medical economics—
United States—Congresses.   I. Sloan, Frank A.
II. Blumstein, James F., 1945–   .   III. Perrin,
James M. (James Marc)   IV. Series.   [DNLM: 1. Economics,
Hospital—United States—congresses.   2. Health Policy—
economics—United States—congresses.   3. Health Services
Accessibility—economics—United States—congresses.
4. Medical Assistance—economics—United States—
congresses.   WX 157 U54 1984]
RA981.A2U45   1985   338.4'336211'0973   85-45045
ISBN 0-8018-2867-8

Contents

Contents

Ten
Conclusion
Frank A. Sloan

Contents

Tables

Figures

Preface

The chapters in this book were originally presented as papers at a conference entitled "Uncompensated Hospital Care: Assigning Rights and Defining Responsibilities," held at Vanderbilt University on April 5 and 6, 1984. The topic was selected because it raises basic questions about individual rights to health care services and about how services provided to those who cannot afford them should be financed. While public officials, private health insurers, health care providers, and interested citizens have become acutely aware of this issue, they lack pertinent factual information and an adequate evaluation of the available public policy options for financing such uncompensated care.

We have defined "uncompensated hospital care" as the value of charity care and bad debts owed by patients to hospitals. Two other forms of nonpayment are excluded from our definition of uncompensated care: service discounts to patients as a professional courtesy or as compensation to dissatisfied patients, and contractual adjustments obtained by public and private insurers using a cost-based reimbursement method.

Chapter 1, by Uwe Reinhardt, places current concern about uncompensated health care in an historical context. Reinhardt points out that among industrialized nations only the United States has been so bold as to attempt to accommodate both egalitarian and libertarian theories of justice simultaneously. Adherence to the former has led public programs to guarantee the disadvantaged access to health care services. Belief in libertarian principles, on the other hand, has made government a guarantor of individual freedom for health care providers and even allowed them to protect their economic turf. Although, in principle, it may be desirable to achieve equality in the distribution of health services, freedom for providers, and budgetary control, in fact, one can obtain, at most, only two of these at once. In this important sense, uncompensated hospital care involves much larger social questions than may first appear to be raised.

Chapter 2, by Frank Sloan, Joseph Valvona, and Ross Mullner, addresses these issues. In most cases, the empirical findings provided in this chapter are the first of their kind. How much uncompensated care do hospitals provide in the aggregate? Is there any evidence that the amount of uncompensated care has risen in recent years? Which types of hospitals provide disproportionate amounts of uncompensated care? If a hospital desired to reduce its uncompensated care burden, which actions does the statistical analysis reported in this chapter suggest it should take? What types of actions are hospitals actually taking to reduce their free care burdens? To what extent can "financial distress" that particular hospitals are experiencing be attributed to high free care burdens at these institutions? Have an appreciable number of hospitals closed because they had large amounts of charity care and bad debts? What are the health characteristics of patients who do not have an identifiable source of third-party payment at the time of discharge from the hospital? Such patients are much less likely to pay the hospital bill in part or in full.

In Chapter 3, James Perrin further documents the characteristics of patients likely to receive uncompensated care, with emphasis on patients with high-cost illnesses. Until now, the extent to which nonpaying hospital patients have high-cost illnesses has not been known. Perrin's data from one tertiary care center and from a national hospital discharge survey suggest that there may be a group of patients, though inconsequential in terms of numbers, who do incur a considerable expense measured in terms of dollars spent on hospital care. This interface between high-cost illness and uncompensated hospital care is particularly apparent for low-birthweight newborns. Assuming that a few instances of a relationship between high-cost illness and uncompensated care can be identified, Perrin asks whether such patients should be treated in specific centers for such care as opposed to general hospitals. The advantages of several delivery options are evaluated from standpoints of both efficiency and quality of care.

Chapter 4, by Peter Schuck, is the first of several chapters on alternative mechanisms for financing uncompensated hospital care. Schuck identifies several types of subsidies which have been used to subsidize hospital care and assesses their advantages and deficiencies. One important choice is between explicit and implicit subsidies. To many—economists and moralists, for example—concealed subsidies are objectionable. To politicians, however, hidden subsidies have certain attractive features. An alternative to public subsidization is a requirement imposed by government that hospitals provide minimum amounts of free care. If there is to be a public subsidy, a decision must be made about the appropriate level of government to be charged with the responsibility of operating the program. There are pros and cons regarding each level, but Schuck concludes that arguments for a federal program are stronger on balance. If a public subsidy is desired, there must be a choice between an entitlement program and a closed-ended subsidy. Schuck suggests several conditions under which entitlements are justified but discusses why, as a practical and a constitutional matter, free hospital care is not yet recognized as an entitlement. During the 1980s, entitlement programs, such as Medicaid, have been subjected to new controls. In this sense, the difference between entitlement and closed-ended subsidy programs, Schuck argues, are now less than they once were. Finally, if there is to be a new public subsidy program for hospital care, who should be eligible? Schuck establishes no hard-and-fast rules but, rather, discusses criteria that ought to inform such a judgment.

The Hill-Burton Act was passed by Congress in 1946 with the objective of filling a then-perceived need for additional and more modern hospital facilities. As James F. Blumstein's discussion of the program in Chapter 5 explains, as the program was originally administered, hospitals that received Hill-Burton funds were required to give assurances that indigent patients as a group would have access to a reasonable volume of services at funded institutions. After several rounds of litigation, the uncompensated care provision of Hill-Burton has moved in the direction of an entitlements approach. Whereas the initial requirement was more or less a general exhortation to hospitals, specific quantitative standards evolved over time. As currently structured, the program provides the best working example of a government requirement that hospitals offer charity care without simultaneously providing an operating subsidy to pay for such care. At the same time, the program requires that hospitals provide a fixed amount of uncompensated care to indigent patients during a given period. It therefore has a closed-ended feature that serves as a limit on overall program cost. Blumstein points out the irony that the more recent individual entitlements approach is at odds with the societal obligation approach to health care endorsed in 1983 in the report of the President's Commission for the Study of Ethical Problems in Medicine and Biomedical and Behavioral Research.

A substantial part of the free care hospitals provide is subsidized by hospital patients who pay full charges. This pattern of cross-subsidization in the hospital industry is called "cost-shifting," or perhaps more appropriately, "charge-shifting." Chapter 6, by Charles Phelps, discusses why this practice has arisen in this industry. To explain this phenomenon, he presents a simple model of hospital behavior in which there are several competing parties within the hospital with different views about how hospital resources should be allocated. These parties face forces exogenous to the hospital—for example, stringent cost containment measures imposed by third-party payers with large numbers of insured persons. Such exogenous changes cause stresses and strains among the competing parties within the hospital. In response to a cost containment measure, for instance, the competing parties would have to decide how the remaining profit is to be reallocated. Free care to indigents is only one potential use of such funds. Phelps discusses problems in measurement of cross subsidies. In evaluating the desirability of cross subsidies, Phelps notes some of economists' suspicions of the practice. Yet in conclusion, he cautions that at least some of the cross subsidies undertaken by the hospital arise at the implicit or explicit request of society. Policymakers should be cautious about requiring hospitals to eliminate such practices.

Medicaid was enacted in the mid-1960s to finance medical care for certain categories of poor people. In an important sense, widespread concern for uncompensated care in the 1980s represents a failure of Medicaid to cover all types of persons with low income. Medicaid is only one source of financing medical care for indigents, albeit an important one. In Chapter 7, Beverlee Myers documents how care for the indigent is currently financed and assesses effects of alternative public policies involving indigent care. To accomplish this objective, she first formulates a concept of medical indigency. She then summarizes sources of payment for indigent hospital care during the early 1980s, using national data but focusing on California. Although the sources of financing are generally common to all states, there are important differences in particulars. For example, Medicaid programs differ among states in important dimensions. She illustrates this variation by comparing policies in Texas and Maryland with those in California. She concludes the paper by discussing options for a national indigent hospital-care policy. She views a universal national health insurance program as a long-run solution to the inequities she finds in the current system. Lacking a comprehensive solution of this type, several alternative partial solutions may address some aspects of the larger problem: decategorizing and federalizing some of the Medicaid programs, mandatory state regulation of hospital prices and revenues, targeting subsidies for high-risk populations and hospitals, and using vouchers to permit indigents to purchase private insurance.

Policy options for providing financing that is external to the hospital for uncompensated hospital care are developed in further detail in Chapter 8, by Gail Wilensky. She categorizes programs into three groups: those that target providers, those that target individuals, and those that provide grants to local governments to purchase indigent and uncompensated care. Programs that target providers include direct reimbursement via all-payer rate-setting (an option considered in greater depth in the following chapter, by Jack Meyer) and revenue pools under which the state establishes a system for taxing hospital revenue and disburses funds from the pool to hospitals for provision of uncompensated care. Programs that target individuals range from insurance programs to protect persons and families from the cost of catastrophic illness, insurance risk-sharing pools to provide access to insurance coverage for high-risk individuals who would otherwise have trouble obtaining insurance coverage, insurance for the unemployed, and insurance for the uninsured (vouchers). A program that targets local governments would establish a matching or bloc grant program to provide funding to local governments for the purchase of indigent or uncompensated care.

Wilensky also assesses several options for raising revenue for programs in the above three categories: general revenue, excise taxes, and a tax cap (taxing employer contributions to health insurance above a pre-set contribution level). Although all of the programs have advantages and deficiencies, in the end, Wilensky recommends a two-pronged approach: grants to state governments with funds passing through to local governments; and risk pools, subsidized by federal and state governments, for individuals who, though not poor, cannot afford insurance because of a preexisting health condition. The two programs should be financed by a combination of tax caps and excise taxes.

A few states have adopted all-payer rate regulation of hospitals as a method for constraining the rise in expenditures for hospital care and reducing the differential amounts various insurers pay for such care. Chapter 9, by Jack Meyer, provides an in-depth description and analysis of the ways these state-run programs channel funds to hospitals that render substantial amounts of charity and bad debt care. Uncompensated care aspects of programs in four states with all-payer rate regulation—Massachusetts, Maryland, New York, and New Jersey—are described and compared. The comparisons focus on risk pools versus adjustment to allowable revenue increases, methods used to allocate monies from revenue pools, and the desirability of including bad debts in the reimbursement of uncompensated hospital care. In the concluding section, Meyer proposes an alternative solution, an explicit financing scheme based on issuing vouchers to low-income persons for the purchase of private insurance.

Chapter 10, by Frank Sloan, provides concluding commentary on reasons for widespread policy interest in uncompensated care during the mid-1980s, on the larger societal issues involved in uncompensated hospital care, on the policy options described in earlier chapters, and on a future research agenda.

Acknowledgments

Several organizations and persons were important in making this book possible. We thank Hospital Corporation of America for a grant to hold three Health Policy Symposiums at Vanderbilt University. First drafts of the chapters in this book were presented at the first of these symposiums. The Office of the Vice Chancellor for Health Affairs at Vanderbilt is providing additional financial support for the symposiums. We appreciate the advice and counsel of the Vice Chancellor, Roscoe R. Robinson, as well as several senior officials at HCA in planning these symposiums. The views expressed in this book are those of the authors and do not reflect official positions at Vanderbilt University, Hospital Corporation of America, or the authors' employers.

The book benefited from discussion and comment at the symposium. Over thirty persons in addition to the authors attended the symposium. The National Conference of State Legislatures published a summary of the results of the symposium, "Twelve Questions: What Legislators Need to Know about Uncompensated Hospital Care," and also produced a short film which presents the issues in concise form to state legislators. The summary and the film are available from NCSL.

Joanne Bennett provided careful editorial assistance. Sharon Stanley helped run the symposium and typed several drafts of the manuscript. We appreciate her patience. Andrea McNiel coordinated the logistical aspects.

Uncompensated Hospital Care

ONE
Uncompensated Hospital Care

Uwe E. Reinhardt

Strictly construed, the term *uncompensated care* reflects the perspective of health care providers. It refers to health services for which providers are somehow "inadequately" compensated. The situation arises when providers voluntarily render charity care for which neither patients nor a third party is directly billed. It also occurs when patients who have been billed for services fail to pay these bills. One might call the latter case one of involuntary charity care.

To assess the magnitude of uncompensated hospital care, one may employ at least three distinct monetary yardsticks. The first of these is the incremental cost occasioned by the delivery of uncompensated care; the second, the full accounting cost of such care (the incremental cost of uncompensated care plus whatever overhead the accountant has allocated to that care); and the third, the charges the provider would normally have billed to paying patients or third parties for that care.

Because the incremental cost of particular hospital services is typically much below fully allocated accounting costs, and because the latter may be below charges, monetary estimates of the magnitude of uncompensated care will, of course, be sensitive to the selection of the underlying yardstick.[1] As is shown in the following chapter by Sloan, Valvona, and Mullner, however, at the aggregate national level, the magnitude of uncompensated care seems relatively moderate regardless of the monetary yardstick one uses to estimate it. From the provider's perspective, the problem warrants the attention of policymakers mainly because the incidence of uncompensated care is distributed quite unevenly among hospitals, a point also brought out clearly in Sloan, Valvona, and Mullner's chapter. Coupled with the current shift away from retrospective full-cost reimbursement of hospitals toward prospective compensation, the heavy load of uncompensated care borne by some hospitals may easily push these towards the brink of fiscal ruin. A way must be found to share more sensibly the fiscal burden represented by uncompensated care.

Yet, rescuing hospitals burdened by heavy loads of uncompensated care is only part of the challenge represented by that phenomenon. From a wider social perspective, the problem of uncompensated care is but the tip of an iceberg, namely, the problem of providing "adequate" health care to all members of our society, including members of the lower-income groups who may not be able to pay for such care or who can do so only with hardship. Indeed, from this perspective the term *uncompensated care* becomes a code word that covers even care which was never sought and rendered, but should have been, on medical grounds.

Within this wider context, the problem of uncompensated care has two facets. First, society must somehow reach a political consensus on the range of services to which every citizen, rich or poor, is deemed entitled as a matter of "right." Next, there is the question of how best to implement the guarantees implicit in that right. Although our debate on national health policy during the last decade may make it appear that the issue of rights to health care has long been settled, leaving only the process of implementation to be determined, in fact both facets of the problem are still subject to debate.

The following chapters generally adopt the wider social perspective on the problem of uncompensated care, treating the provider's narrower fiscal concern simply as one facet of that problem. For the most part, these papers do not dwell on the question of rights, Chapter 5 by Blumstein being the notable exception. The emphasis is appropriate for policy analysis, because the policy analyst's comparative advantage lies not in the definition of entitlements, but in defining strategies for their implementation.

In this introductory chapter the issues of rights and responsibilities receive somewhat greater emphasis to furnish a backdrop for the subsequent chapters. The section below offers some thoughts on the locus of fiscal responsibility for the cost of uncompensated care. The issue of entitlements is taken up in the following section, where it is argued that one of the major shortcomings of American health policy has been its attempt to offer both patients *and* health care providers too many entitlements all around. The final section calls for a pragmatic redefinition of an ethical foundation for our health care sector.

Responsibility for Uncompensated Hospital Care

In seeking to assign financial responsibility for the cost of uncompensated care, one must distinguish between care rendered to bona fide, uninsured indigents and the uncollectible accounts of patients who could, in principle, have paid their bills, but failed to do so. As discussed by Sloan, Valvona, and Mullner (Chap. 2), by Perrin (Chap. 3), and by Wilensky (Chap. 8), not all uncompensated care actually represents indigent care; some of it represents the bad debts left on the hospitals' books by middle-income families. The question arises to what extent the burden of such bad debts should be socialized.

One's visceral reaction to this question is that providers should be able to shift to others the cost of their own poor credit management. On further thought, however, the answer becomes less straightforward, because the bad debt left behind by a middle-class family may not always reflect poor accounts-receivable management on the part of the hospital.

The cost of a sufficiently complex medical case can devastate the budget and lifestyle of even a middle-class family. It is not clear that society welcomes that outcome, even if the family has been careless by remaining uninsured. Nor is it clear that the courts would force such an outcome, or that the media would report it with a balanced perspective. Without probing the reasons that some middle-class families fail to purchase adequate helath insurance (and, according to data included in Chapter 8 by Wilensky, a good many of them fail to do so), one wonders what admissions policies hospitals should follow when they suspect, *ex ante*, that an uninsured middle-class patient may generate uncollectible bills *ex post*. Will society permit the hospital to deny that patient treatment, or will our so-called Judeo-Christian ethic make us compel the hospital to treat the patient anyhow? And if the latter be the case, should the hospital be made to bear the cost of our ethical precepts or should that burden be socialized? Indeed, do not our ethical precepts in this area effectively make one person's failure to adequately insure himself or herself a so-called "externality," that is, a situation in which one person's conduct visits spillover costs on his or her fellow citizens? And if one accepts the proposition implicit in that question, does there perhaps arise a case for compulsory catastrophic health insurance, just as many states now mandate liability insurance for motorists?

There arises, next, the question of who should be responsible for providing and financing health care for bona fide uninsured indigents. Prior to World War II, when health care was technically simple and thus relatively inexpensive, our nation relied heavily on private individuals and institutions to care for the indigent. Some of that tradition has carried over into the postwar period. Although the Medicare and Medicaid programs were specifically designed to shift fiscal responsibility for much of that care to the public sector, such uncovered indigent care as remained was left to the good offices of physicians and of hospitals.

The hospitals, of course, have been helped along in their thinking by the Hill-Burton program (more fully described in James F. Blumstein's perceptive chapter on that program). Although one might argue that the Hill-Burton program was really a form of precompensation for what hospitals subsequently reported as government-mandated uncompensated charity care, the program was not formally set up in a way that provided a separate account for Hill-Burton grants against which the cost of subsequent charity could be amortized;[2] nor were these funds managed in a way that would have yielded the actual funds for such care. Funds for the cost of such care have instead been procured by apportioning its cost to the bills of whatever payers were feeble or inattentive enough to absorb them. This process, known in the trade by the code phrase "cost-shifting," is really a game of pinning the tail on the donkey. Traditionally, the donkeys have been those American business firms (and their customers) that have offered their employees company-paid health insurance plans.

These business firms have been served by a commercial health insurance industry that has been literally ruled by health-care providers under the age-old principle of *divide et impera*. There are so many of these commercial insurers that each of them typically accounts for only a small proportion of the individual provider's revenue stream. Consequently, the industry has lacked the countervailing market power to resist the practice of cost-shifting.[3] Absent this countervailing market power, however, the industry's only feasible response to the practice has been to wail and to pay, and wailed and paid it has, both in generous doses.

But while the insurance industry and its business clients may have deplored cost-shifting, that practice has actually served as a fig leaf of sorts over a rather unseemly part of the American body politic: its inability thus far to fold every American into at least a catastrophic health insurance program. However capricious and unfair its ultimate incidence may have been, the game of pinning the (cost) tail on the (business) donkey did help to preserve America's membership in the community of civilized nations, and therein surely lies some virtue.

It must be asked whether this capricious approach to the financing of indigent care makes sense for the future, whatever appeal it may have for budget-minded politicians and for social thinkers who now seek to "reprivatize" America's social obligations. Several factors seem to work against this approach.

First, the technical content of routine medical practice is becoming ever more complex, and at a rapid pace. One thinks most commonly in this connection of the technical progress in life-saving interventions at both extremes of the age distribution. These interventions, while saving many life-years, often entail costly medical support thereafter. One also thinks of modern medicine's ability to enhance the quality of life through artificial replacement of sundry parts of the human body. And, finally, one thinks of the ever new, highly productive, and yet costly breakthroughs in internal diagnostic imaging. Application of these costly techniques is rapidly becoming routine even in routine medical cases. We may not wish to withhold them from uninsured indigents.

Barring any major legislative initiative to fold the currently uninsured indigents into public insurance programs, we should not expect their number to fall in the future. We therefore should not expect the cost of indigent care to dwindle either. To saddle providers of that indigent care with the dual responsibility, first, of treating the uninsured indigents and, second, of casting about for a private source that can be forced to pay for such care strikes one as dubious social policy, particularly when the burden of that care is so unevenly distributed among hospitals.

Second, the practice of cost-shifting is likely to become ever more difficult in the changing market for hospital care. Not only has the government decided to confront the hospital sector with prospectively fixed, administered prices per diagnosis-related group (DRG), but the business community also is seeking to create countervailing market power vis-à-vis health care providers by taking the insurance function out of the hands of commercial insurers and forming self-funded "preferred provider" arrangements. To the extent that the private sector's demand for hospital care will become more price-sensitive, it will be increasingly difficult to pin cost (tails) on private-business (donkeys).

Third, an increasing proportion of hospital care in the United States is likely to be rendered by investor-owned hospitals. Under the rather open-ended reimbursement practices of the past, these hospitals have found it either good business, good public relations, or just plain decent to render charity care, for their shareholders were not among the donkeys on whom the cost of that charity needed to be pinned. One is, therefore, not surprised to find that these hospitals have hitherto rendered about the same proportion of charity care as have their similarly situated peers in the not-for-profit sector. The question is whether that generosity can survive in a highly competitive, price-sensitive market environment. Not-for-profit hospitals, too, will be hard pressed in that environment, but they differ from their for-profit peers in at least two respects. First, in a pinch, they can appeal to charitable sources of funds not readily accessible to for-profit enterprises. Second, not-for-profit hospitals are not scrutinized on a quarterly basis by a stock market whose analysts regard the maximization of shareholders' wealth as the sole social responsibility of a business firm, and who have therefore no compunction to let nice guys finish last. Worse still, many shareholders in investor-owned hospitals will be distant institutional investors who may be hard-pressed themselves by their own boards of trustees to produce high portfolio returns, regardless of social responsibility. To rely, in such an environment, on investor-owned hospitals as a significant source of "free" charity care is not only imprudent; it is also manifestly unfair.

To sum up, it is improbable that the hospital care of the nation's uninsured indigents can continue to be left to the noblesse oblige of hospital care providers, be they for-profit or not-for-profit. A way must be found to relieve providers of this financial burden and to socialize that burden. As Gail Wilensky points out in her far-ranging review of this problem in Chapter 8, one could do so by means of state-regulated all-payer reimbursement systems or through special revenue pools to which hard-pressed hospitals can look for relief. Alternatively, one could endow the indigents themselves with adequate health insurance coverage. Beverlee Myers reminds us in Chapter 7 that one should not forget national health insurance as one solution, although the political prospects of so ambitious an approach seem slim. Some of the more modest options reviewed by Wilensky, on the other hand, do seem eminently feasible.

Whatever approach is ultimately adopted, however, it will be necessary to debate more openly precisely what rights society should accord both patients and providers of health care. That question hinges, of course, on one's perception of a just society.

Entitlements in American Health Care

The Search for an Enduring Theory of Justice

Probably any thoughtful person has wondered at some point whether it is possible to rank alternative distributions of economic privilege in society by their inherent degree of "justice."[4] Such a ranking would be helpful in normative policy analysis and in the actual forging of policy, particularly in the realm of health care. The ranking might suggest, for example, what a nation aspiring to be a just society need and need not do for members at the bottom of the income ladder. The ranking might also suggest what individual liberties (for example, those of health care providers) may be curtailed for the sake of justice.

Any particular individual may conceivably offer such a ranking, but that is not helpful in policy analysis. The question is whether there exist some unquestioned, universally valid, and enduring ethical precepts—say, a divine set of rules—from which one may deduce an equally universally valid and enduring theory of distributive justice.

Economists have long ago despaired of this possibility. Those who seek to rank alternative distributions of privilege typically do so with appeal to Utilitarian doctrine, according to which a nation's resources should be distributed so as to maximize a "societal happiness." The problem is that not once in the century and a half since John Stuart Mill first proposed this maxim has anyone been able to develop a universally acceptable measure of societal happiness. As a theory of justice, Utilitarianism therefore strikes one as vacuous, as does most normative policy analysis flowing from it. The truth is that economists have little worthwhile to say on this issue.

While honest economists long ago despaired of developing an overarching theory of distributive justice, political philosophers continue to hammer away at the problem. The several distinct theories of distributive justice emerging from these efforts are elegant in their internal logic, and eminently stimulating even to a skeptic. In the end, however, that literature fails as a guide towards a universally acceptable principle of justice. On the contrary, it persuades one that there cannot possibly be such a principle. For however tight the internal logic of any particular philosopher's theory of justice may be, that logic is ultimately anchored on some overarching value for which that author claims primacy on purely subjective grounds. Collectively, the political philosophers writing on the subject teach us that justice, like beauty, rests in the eye of the beholder.

Libertarian philosophers, for example, elevate individual liberty to the status of the single, overriding social value to which all other values are subordinate, and which can never justly be traded off against any subordinate value. Implicit in the libertarian's concept of "liberty" is the tenet that the individual is entitled to dispose of his or her possessions as he or she sees fit. Extreme versions of the theory—articulated, for example, in Robert Nozick's *Anarchy, State, and Utopia* (1974)—hold that any governmental infringement on this presumed property right is *ipso facto* unjust. Thus, to tax one person's wealth in order to finance another person's health care is unjust, as is a policy that compels physicians or privately owned facilities to render health care to designated individuals. In the libertarian's credo, it is the health care provider's right to determine whom to serve and whom not to serve, and also what price to exact for health services rendered. Health care providers must find this a comforting credo.

Diametrically opposed to the libertarian credo are the various theories of distributive justice espoused by egalitarian philosophers. Egalitarian philosophers elevate "equal respect for all individuals" or "equality of opportunity" to the overriding value of a just society to which all other values—among them individual liberty—are deemed subordinate.[5] Equality of opportunity, argue these philosophers, requires as a minimum that all members of society have equal access to certain basic commodities, access to which determines an individual's range of opportunities and measure of self-respect. Health care, along with food, shelter, and education, is among these basic commodities.

The entitlements implicit in the egalitarian tenet seem rather open-ended, and as recent history in this country has shown, they certainly are. Egalitarians, however, do not glibly ignore resource constraints. They merely argue that, in the face of such constraints, need, rather than ability to pay, should be the basis for rationing. Clearly this theory of justice implies redistribution of the sort libertarians consider coercive and hence unjust.

One's own predilections aside, it is certainly no more logically compelling to let equal opportunity triumph completely over individual liberty than it is to do the reverse. Indeed, outside the ivory tower any prevailing sense of justice is apt to be an amalgam in which each of the pure theories is somewhat compromised. While purist philosophers may deplore such compromises, policymakers must not only countenance them but actively lead in forging the amalgam.

Concepts of Justice in American Health Care

A remarkable and unique feature of American health policy has been its attempt to accommodate simultaneously both the egalitarian and the libertarian theories of justice in their extreme purity. No other nation in the industrialized West has been quite so bold, or quite so naive, as to attempt that feat. Ironically, no other nation finds itself, in the mid-1980s, with the unsolved problem of uncompensated indigent care at the center stage of its health policy debate. There appears to be a causal link between schizoid thinking on the ethical plane and impotence at the level of policy.

Throughout the postwar period, and possibly even earlier, our policies on the distribution of health care have been firmly rooted in the egalitarian credo: it has been a widely shared notion that health care in the United States should be distributed on the basis of medical need rather than ability to pay. Furthermore, with appeal to the overarching principle of "equal respect for all individuals," it has generally been held (at least in public debate) that the nation should aim for equality in the *process* of health care—that there should be equality in the so-called amenities accompanying the delivery of health care, including the travel and wait time during access and the degree of free choice among providers.[6] Politicians of all ideological stripes have supported these tenets (at least none has openly questioned them), and health care providers have endorsed them as well.

Cynics may argue that no one seriously entertained these lofty maxims and that they were recited by politicians mainly for public consumption. Some glaring remaining inequalities in access to health care may be cited to buttress that case. But a fair reading of health legislation during the 1960s and 1970s should persuade even a skeptic that public policy in those years was motivated by a genuine desire to move the country closer to an egalitarian distribution of health care. By the end of the 1970s, few policy analysts and even fewer public officials still questioned the proposition that access to all medically necessary and technically feasible health care on equal (process) terms is one of an American citizen's basic rights.

The pursuit of an egalitarian health care system is, of course, not a uniquely American phenomenon. Most other industrialized nations have shared that goal, and some of them seem to have been rather more successful than have we in approaching it. A uniquely American phenomenon, however, has been the endeavor to extract an *egalitarian* distribution of health care from a delivery system still firmly grounded in *libertarian* principles.

To be sure, our health care delivery system does not measure up in all respects to a libertarian's dream. Some individual liberties are being compromised by government for the sake of quality control, and even the staunchest defenders of the libertarian credo, America's physicians, have from time to time enlisted the government's coercive power to protect their economic turf

Uwe E. Reinhardt

through occupational licensing. We share such infringements with other modern societies. But in no other modern society espousing egalitarian principles for the distribution of health care have physicians and hospitals been quite so free as they have in the United States to organize their facilities as they see fit, to practice medicine as they see fit, and to price their services as they see fit. In these realms, libertarian principles have prevailed, and every legislative attempt to compromise them for the sake of cost control or greater equity in distribution has, until very recently, been beaten back successfully, with overt appeals to the libertarian credo. "If you want an egalitarian distribution of health care," providers have said, "we endorse it heartily, and we shall do our best to bring it about—but for a fee, and we want that fee to be reasonable as we define that term."

Libertarian and egalitarian purists wrestle with one another in any democratic society. The politician's task, as noted earlier, is to fashion from this struggle a sustainable social compromise. It is on that count that American health policy has performed poorly relative to other democracies. For, in seeking to cater to both extremes among notions of distributive justice, American policymakers have bestowed upon the nation a maze of public health programs that make a Rube Goldberg contraption appear streamlined by comparison.

There has been extraordinarily generous public health insurance coverage for some services and for some individuals—replete with completely free choice of providers by patients and with virtually open-ended reimbursement formulas for providers. One would be hard put, for example, to identify another Western democracy in which the government reimbursed as passively as has ours the synthetic depreciation expenses created by the mere swapping of hospital ownership.[7] Yet, attempts to curb that flow of public funds into private treasuries have always been decried and, until very recently, rejected as an intolerable, regulatory infringement on private liberties.

Congressional respect for this peculiar conception of "liberty" naturally carried the danger of turning any federal health program into a fiscal hemorrhage. Too timid to prevent that outcome through controls on providers, our politicians have pursued the next logical policy to contain public health budgets: they simply have left glaring gaps in health insurance coverage, particularly for the near poor and the unemployed (whose health insurance coverage typically ceases with employment). As the *Medical Tribune* reported in 1982 under the headline "Food Budget Paying Doctor":

> One of the hardest things about the current recession is facing patients who have lost jobs and can't pay their medical bills. "I experience a feeling of guilt [reports a family physician]; I've got groceries and my home. Some of our patients no longer have money for either." . . . A survey by this newspaper at the American Association of Family Practitioners annual meeting suggests that this experience reflects those of many—and perhaps most—primary physicians today in this country as they con-

front the impact of a nationwide 10% unemployment rate, peaking at 15% and 20% in some localities. (November 10, 1982, pp. 1, 15)

One may protest the injection of anecdotal evidence into august policy analysis and quibble over the aggregate statistical significance of such stories. But the fact remains, once again, that one would be hard put to identify any other industrialized society today that would still visit upon an unemployed worker's family, already down on its luck in so many material and emotional ways, the added anxiety and potential real hardship of going without health insurance coverage. It happens only in America.

It has become fashionable to attribute our long-standing failures in this area to a streak of meanness in the American character. Having lived both outside and inside this nation, I do not accept that interpretation. The special genius of nations who have long settled these problems lies not in their citizens' superior character, but lies, as noted, in a political process capable of forging a more stable ethical foundation for their health care systems. In all of these nations, the providers of health care enjoy fewer liberties than do their American counterparts. But in addition, a good many of these countries—for example, the United Kingdom, West Germany, France, Switzerland, and Holland—have been rather more tolerant of some degree of tiering in their health systems than have the champions of egalitarianism in the United States.

Perhaps the time has come for Americans, too, to debate more openly—and without the customary rancor and slander[8]—just what are the essential ingredients of a just health care system. That debate forms part of the health-policy agenda for the 1980s.

Potential Trade-Offs between Equity, Freedom, and Budgetary Control

Ideally, one would like our health care system to achieve three distinct goals at once: first, to distribute health care equitably; second, to afford the providers of health care a maximum of freedom; and third, to permit budgetary control *ex ante* and to guarantee economic efficiency in the course of health care delivery. The gist of the preceding section has been that one cannot reasonably expect to attain all three goals at once. One can attain, at most, any two of them in their purest form or, alternatively, all three of them in some compromised form.

Persistent political efforts to secure for Americans an extreme form of egalitarianism in health care probably have hurt the very individuals they were intended to help: the poor and the near poor. The nation simply does not seem ready to pay the price of so ambitious a policy: either uncontrollable budgets or, alternatively, the kind of stringent controls other nations have seen fit to impose on their health care providers. Egalitarians who would like to do well by the poor would probably do well to retreat a bit from their present position.

Uwe E. Reinhardt

To begin with, it would be enormously helpful in future discourse if those calling for greater equity in American health care articulated more clearly just what they mean by equity. Most Americans, for example, would probably not want to see the probability of recovering from a given medical condition, and the extent of that recovery, vary by income or class for want of appropriate medical care. To guarantee equality in these terms, however, is a far cry from guaranteeing also equality in the *process* of securing appropriate care where "process," as already noted, is meant to include the amenities accompanying the delivery of health care, including the degree of free choice among providers. As Norman Daniels argues in his thoughtful essay "Equity of Access to Health Care" (1982, p. 63), "An [egalitarian] argument that grants health care services a very special status because of their primary function of meeting health care needs does not by itself seem powerful enough to justify the concern . . . that the equal distribution of amenities is also a necessary condition for equity of access."

Daniels points out (p. 64) that a good case for equality in amenities can be made with appeal to the overarching principle of "equal respect for all persons," a principle that seems particularly applicable when individuals are ill. Still, there remains the challenge of identifying just which amenities are the essential ingredients of that respect. For example, is the completely free choice of providers now built into the Medicare program a *sine qua non* of that respect? And must all hospitals in America be equally luxurious? These questions were boldly raised in the recently published report of the President's Commission for the Study of Ethical Problems in Medicine and Biomedical and Behavioral Research (1983), and the commission answered them, boldly, in the negative. Its reasoning deserves respectful debate.

From the perspective of economics, these questions are important, as they bear directly on the government's ability to act as a prudent purchaser. A solution to the problem of uncompensated indigent care necessarily implies the use of collective funds for the purchase of such care. If our notions of equity require that every collectively financed indigent must have completely free choice of provider, then those who administer the collective funds have only limited market power. More adequate countervailing power could be put into their hands if, where technically feasible, the care of the indigents could be procured under competitive bids from competing health maintenance organizations (HMOs), so-called primary care networks (PCNs), or other forms of preferred provider organizations (PPOs). These innovative approaches to health care procurement, now actively pursued in a number of states, may eventually falter if they are ceaselessly stigmatized as "two-tier" health care. The champions of the poor, and the poor themselves, must recognize that, in the political and budgetary climate of the 1980s, pursuit of the maxim "for the poor, nothing but the best" may leave the poor with nothing.

One suspects, however, that the main thrust against such choice-constrained arrangements may ultimately be launched, not by the champions of the poor, but by the self-proclaimed champions of liberty, health care providers prominent among them. First, we must grant these providers—especially physicians—that one part of their professional ethos *is* deeply rooted in egalitarian doctrine and that many of them sincerely hold the patient's freedom of choice to be an essential ingredient of equity. At the same time, it must also occur to many of them that, in connection with collectively financed health care, the patients' freedom of choice works hand in glove with the principle of *divide et impera*, which, in turn, has contributed so well to the providers' "prosperity and good repute."[9] If choice-restricted programs for the poor constrain collective budgets, they will do so by constraining the incomes of health care providers collectively. Why would sane providers welcome that? With a burgeoning supply of physicians, the latter in particular will look askance at closed-panel delivery systems that can effect cost-reductions by substituting nonmedical for medical personnel.

Along with physicians, other actors in health care and in the business community may have misgivings about choice-constrained procurement of health care by public programs. After all, the separate exertion of market power on the part of government would quite probably invite price discrimination on the part of hospitals; but what economists call "price discrimination" is nothing other than the much bemoaned practice of cost-shifting.

Herein, then, lies a truly taxing intellectual challenge for the champions of libertarian thought in both health care and the wider business community. In effect, the American hospital sector currently stands at a crossroads, not only in connection with indigent care, but in the entire realm of hospital compensation. In the long run, the nation can come to grips with the problem of hospital compensation only by either (1) converting the hospital sector into a network of rate-regulated public utilities, or (2) permitting as a matter of policy a multi-tier hospital industry, replete with widespread price discrimination vis-à-vis public and private payers.

The former approach, the utility model, will be necessary if the nation wishes to preserve at least the semblance of a one-tier hospital sector, avoid price discrimination, and yet control the secular growth of hospital costs. It is the approach apparently preferred by the Health Insurance Association of America (HIAA), which has gone on record as favoring so-called "state regulated, uniform all-payer hospital compensation rates" applicable to all public and private payers in a given state. At least some segments of the business community seem to favor this approach as well.[10] Under these state-regulated, uniform rates, the cost of indigent care would presumably be reapportioned by the regulators on a "fair" basis. It is an approach with surface appeal, but with some problems as well, as Meyer's Chapter 9 emphasizes.

The second approach, widespread price discrimination, contains the normal features of those price-competitive market systems in which sellers provide a nontransferable service produced with high fixed costs and relatively low incremental (variable) costs. Such a health care market would be a close cousin of the contemporary market for airline travel, in which cost-shifting is the order of the day. In such a market environment, the government, and other major procurers separately, would presumably negotiate prospective prices with hospitals, or extract such prices by means of competitive bids (as described earlier). These prices would not necessarily be "fair" in the current sense of that term—that is, they would not necessarily cover the hospital's full costs, let alone a so-called fair rate of return to the equity of investor-owned hospitals.[11] A hospital might nevertheless find such prices attractive, as long as it had excess capacity, and as long as the negotiated or bid prices yielded at least some positive margin towards overhead and profits, that is, as long as these prices covered at least variable costs. Such a system need not imperil the economic viability of individual hospitals if the latter were free to extract the desired overall rate of return from other privately financed patients, whatever discriminatory pricing scheme that may require. Hospitals would price their beds as, say, TWA prices its seats on a 747 plane.

It remains to be seen what the libertarian school of thought in health care will make of such an arrangement. It just might call the arrangement "unfair." But no one has ever claimed that price-competitive markets are invariably fair, nor can it be argued that the exertion of market power by large purchasers is invariably unfair.

Conclusion

In its best aspects, the American health care system is arguably the best in the world. In its worst aspects, it is arguably among the worst, certainly in the industrialized world. One manifestation of the worst is the perennial problem of uncompensated indigent care, a hot potato no one seems willing to hold any longer. That problem is uniquely American.

It has been the central thesis of this essay that the problem of uncompensated indigent care springs not so much from meanness in the American spirit as from our ill-fated attempts during the past several decades to guarantee too many entitlements to too many actors in health care. In this connection, one thinks instinctively of the entitlements granted individuals in their role as patients. There may have been, indeed, a few too many of those. But one should also think of the extraordinary entitlements American policymakers have traditionally granted the providers of health care, entitlements that have, on occasion, bordered on handing providers the key to the public treasury.

As policy analysts and policymakers address themselves to the problem of uncompensated indigent care, they would do well to fold into their deliberations a review of the nation's presumed health care entitlements *all around.* A useful first step will be to articulate ethical precepts more clearly, and to debate them without rancor.

Notes

1. To assess the fiscal impact of uncompensated care on health care providers, one should measure such care by its *opportunity cost*. In a hospital with excess capacity, these opportunity costs would be represented by the incremental cost of uncompensated care as long as such care used fixed facilities and manpower that would otherwise have been idle. In a hospital faced with excess demand, these opportunity costs would be more appropriately measured by charges if patients receiving uncompensated care displaced potential patients who would have paid full charges.

2. Technically, one could have accounted for a hospital's Hill-Burton grants by having it credit the grants to a "Deferred Credit" account. The cost of subsequent charity care, including an allocation for overhead costs, could then have been debited to that account.

3. The individual client of a grocery store, of course, also represents but a small fraction of the grocery's revenues. In that market, however, customers choose stores on the basis of price. By contrast, in the hospital sector, the individual client (the patient and his or her physician) have hitherto been spared the need to choose hospitals on the basis of price, and therein is rooted the health insurer's lack of market power.

4. In thinking about this section and composing it, the author has benefited greatly from conversations with Joshua Lewis, a Princeton undergraduate whose senior thesis, "Considerations on Distributive Justice," contains an excellent survey of alternative theories of distributive justice and their relevance to the allocation of expensive, life-saving medical technology. See also Gutman (1981).

5. See, for example, Williams (1971) and Rawls (1971).

6. Surprisingly to those who know the authors, Sloan and Bentkover (1979) are cited by Daniels (1982) as advocates of this more extreme brand of egalitarianism.

7. When a group of investors, A, purchase a privately owned hospital from investor group B, the former can, of course, reasonably claim that the purchase price is the appropriate depreciation base for both tax and reimbursement purposes. It is to group B that the windfall gains accrued. After all, what economic incentive did hospital group A have to drive a hard bargain with the owners, B, when hospital group A was assured of full-cost retrospective reimbursement plus a guaranteed rate of return to the equity of owners A. The formula created numerous instant health care millionaires at taxpayers' expense.

8. To illustrate, not long ago I was severely chastised by the American Dental Association (ADA) for suggesting that Americans now eclipsed from proper dental care for want of money might be treated for minor problems cost effectively by paradental personnel. That approach was decried by the ADA as "two-tier" health care at variance with the ADA's ethical precepts. How the ADA lives with the large number of currently untreated patients is, of course, an intriguing question. In the ADA's view of the world, no care at all is presumably not a "tier."

9. Interestingly, while the Hippocratic oath contains no explicit reference to equity in the distribution of health care, it does include the passage, "may prosperity and good repute ever be yours."

Uwe E. Reinhardt

10. As was reported in the *American Medical News* (November 25, 1983), the chief executives of several large business corporations in Arizona recently issued a report calling for full-fledged regulation of the state's hospital system, including comprehensive state and local planning and state-regulated reform, and all-payer rates per case.

11. Incidentally, the accounting procedures by which fixed overhead is allocated to individual product lines are known to be rather arbitrary. It is therefore not technically possible to determine "fair" profit margins for particular services (or cases) within a multiproduct firm, such as a hospital.

References

Daniels, Norman. 1982. "Equity of Access to Health Care: Some Conceptual and Ethical Issues." *Milbank Memorial Fund Quarterly Health and Society* 60, no. 1 (Winter): 51–81.

Gutman, Amy. 1981. "For and Against Equal Access to Health Care." *Milbank Memorial Fund Quarterly Health and Society* 59, no. 4 (Fall): 542–60.

Lewis, Joshua. 1984. "Considerations on Distributive Justice: The Allocation of Expensive, Life-Saving Medical Technology and Theories of Distributive Justice." Senior thesis, Princeton University, April 13.

Nozick, Robert. 1974. *Anarchy, State, and Utopia.* New York: Basic Books.

President's Commission for the Study of Ethical Problems in Medicine and Biomedical and Behavioral Research. 1983. *Securing Access to Health Care.* Vol. 1, *Report.* Washington, D.C., March.

Rawls, John. 1971. *A Theory of Justice.* Cambridge: Harvard University Press.

Sloan, Frank, and John D. Bentkover. 1979. *Access to Ambulatory Care and the U.S. Economy.* Lexington, Mass.: Lexington Books.

Williams, Bernard. 1971. "The Idea of Equality." In *Justice and Equality.* Ed. H. A. Bedan. Englewood Cliffs, N.J.: Prentice Hall.

TWO

Identifying the Issues: A Statistical Profile

*Frank A. Sloan, Joseph Valvona,
and Ross Mullner*

Because uncompensated hospital care is an important social concern, there has been much discussion about it in the media, in various political forums, and in such regulatory hearings as certificate-of-need review. Often, no data are presented, and when data are made available, they often pertain to a limited number of patients or hospitals. For policymaking purposes, a broader statistical perspective—the city, the state, and/or the nation as a whole—is needed.

The objective of this chapter is to provide a statistical overview of uncompensated hospital care from a national perspective. Uncompensated care is defined as the sum of "charity care" and "bad debts." Charity care arises when patients who are judged by the hospital as unable to pay do not pay, and bad debt applies to patients who presumably can but do not pay the hospital bill in part or in full. If so designated at the time of admission, charity care may be applied to satisfy a hospital's Hill-Burton obligation. In practice, it is doubtful that many hospitals make a rigorous distinction between charity care and bad debts. For this reason, it is advisable to consider the two together. We exclude the following from uncompensated care: contractual adjustments, which represent the difference between hospital charges and the amount actually paid by a third-party payer on the basis of costs; and discounts for professional courtesy or to patients who express dissatisfaction with the hospital care they received.

These issues will be addressed in this chapter:

1. How much uncompensated care do hospitals provide in the aggregate?
2. Is there any evidence that the amount of uncompensated care has risen in recent years?
3. Which types of hospitals provide disproportionate amounts of uncompensated care? By "type," we refer to hospital ownership, teaching status, metropolitan versus nonmetropolitan location, and affiliation or nonaffiliation with a multihospital system.

4. If a hospital desired to reduce its uncompensated care burden, which actions do our statistical analysis indicate it should take? What types of actions are hospitals actually taking to reduce their free-care burdens?
5. To what extent can the "financial distress" that particular hospitals are now experiencing be attributed to high free-care burdens at these institutions?
6. Have an appreciable number of hospitals closed because they provided too much uncompensated care? More generally, how does the uncompensated care burden of hospitals immediately prior to closure compare with those of other community hospitals?

Unfortunately, there are no data available nationally or for individual states on hospitalized patients who incur bad debts or are treated by the hospital on a charity basis. For this reason, our analysis of patient data is more limited. We do ask:

7. What are the diagnoses of patients classified by hospitals as "self-pay" and "no charge" at the time the patient is discharged from the hospital? From previous research, we know that a much higher proportion of self-pay patients do not pay their hospital bills in full than is the case for insured patients. What types of surgical procedures are performed on self-pay and no-charge patients? What are the diagnoses of no- and partial-pay patients at one major teaching hospital?

Methods

Data

The data herein come from a number of sources. Information on the amount of uncompensated care provided and hospital financial status comes from the Annual Surveys of Hospitals for 1978 through 1982 taken by the American Hospital Association (AHA). Data on actions hospitals have taken to reduce the amount of free care they provide come from the AHA's "Survey of Medical Care for the Poor and Hospitals' Financial Status—1983." The analysis is limited to nonfederal, short-term general and other special hospitals.

Both types of surveys were sent to all U.S. hospitals. The overall response rate to the Annual Surveys was high, especially for a mail survey (90% in 1982—American Hospital Association 1983, p. v.) However, there was substantial item nonresponse to the revenue and balance sheet questions.

We estimate that only two-fifths of the hospitals provided complete responses to these questions. Small and investor-owned hospitals were overrepresented among hospitals with missing or incomplete revenue and balance sheet information. The AHA uses an algorithm for filling in missing data; all statistics published by the AHA from the Annual Survey are based partly on imputed data. When possible, the AHA uses values from previous years from the hospital to fill in the missing value. Otherwise, it uses a prediction equation based on regression analysis. Although the AHA's replacement techniques are probably adequate for many purposes, given our reliance on certain items from hospital income statements and balance sheets, we confine some of our analysis to hospitals which provided complete financial data.

Data on hospital closings come from an unpublished file on closed hospitals compiled by the American Hospital Association. We have matched data on hospitals which closed during 1980–82 and those which remained open during these years with responses to the 1978 and 1979 Annual Surveys from the same hospitals.

The national information on the distribution of patients by payer source, diagnosis, surgical procedures performed, and characteristics of the discharged patient used in this study comes from the 1981 Hospital Discharge Survey (HDS), conducted by the National Center for Health Statistics. The 1981 survey contains data on 227,000 discharges. Our analysis focuses on patients who were under age sixty-five at the time of discharge (160,000 discharges). The survey asked the hospital to indicate the anticipated primary and secondary payment sources at the time of discharge. The expected payment source undoubtedly differs from the actual source in some cases, but such changes were not recorded by the HDS.

Estimates were obtained of the amount of uncompensated care by service for fiscal years 1981 and 1982 from Vanderbilt Hospital. In 1982, Vanderbilt provided $16 million in uncompensated care to inpatients, which represented 13 percent of gross inpatient revenue. The data are illustrative of the no-pay and reduced-pay patient mix in a major teaching center with a high free-care burden in the early 1980s. Since 1982, Vanderbilt has adopted explicit limits on the amount of such care it provides.

Statistical Approach

To assess why uncompensated care burdens vary among hospitals and determine the extent to which a high burden contributes to hospital financial distress, we have specified and estimated regressions with bad debt and charity care as a fraction of hospital gross patient revenue, and several financial ratios as dependent variables. The latter include two indicators of liquidity—the current ratio (current assets/current liabilities) and a modified current ratio (which excludes receivables from current assets); two profitability measures— total margin (net income/total revenue) and return-on-fund balance (net income/fund balance); and a capital structure ratio—long-term debt to assets (long-term debt/total assets). Regression analysis allows the investigator, using retrospective data, to isolate the contribution of individual influences on the dependent variable.

All discharges of patients listing "self-pay" or "no-charge" as the primary source of payment have been extracted from the 1981 HDS. Information on hospital charges was not collected. To estimate the distribution of self-pay and no-charge patients by major diagnosis and by type of surgery, each self-pay and no-charge discharge has been weighted by the product of the length of stay and the mean 1981 charge by hospital bed-size category (six categories) and Census Division (nine divisions).

To further describe characteristics of patients likely to receive uncompensated care, a discriminant analysis was performed with discharges of patients under age sixty-five as the observational unit and the following principal expected sources of payment as the dependent variable: self-pay/no-charge; Medicaid or other state-local government payer; private insurance (mainly Blue Cross and fee-for-service commercial insurance); and workmen's compensation.

Discriminant analysis is a statistical technique used to "discriminate" between groups of cases and predict into which group a particular case will fall, based on values of the predictor variables. The technique might be used by a bank, for example, to predict whether or not a potential borrower falls in the category of people most likely to default on the bank's loan. To determine how self-pay/no-charge patients differ from other patients under age sixty-five who have some form of third-party coverage, discriminant analysis has been used on the data.

Results

Aggregate Amount of Uncompensated Care Provided

Community hospitals provided $6.2 billion of uncompensated care in 1982, which is equivalent to 5 percent of charges and 6 percent of total payments to such hospitals. In 1982, contractual adjustments and other discounts amounted to almost $18 billion (Fig. 2.1 and American Hospital Association 1983).

The uncompensated care burden has increased in real terms, but the rate of increase is highly sensitive to the deflator used to construct a time series in constant dollars. With a gross national product deflator, the dollar amount of such care grew from $4.2 billion in 1978 to $6.2 billion in 1982 (based on 1982 dollars). However, using the consumer price index and an index based on hospital prices (net hospital revenue per adjusted patient day), the 1978 figures are higher, when expressed in 1982 dollars: $4.5 and $5.2 billion, respectively. Expressed in terms of hospital prices, real uncompensated care was the same in 1980 as in 1982 and was higher in 1981 than in either of the other years.

Of the $6.2 billion provided in 1982, about $1.7 billion was for charity care (Fig. 2.1). Some types of hospitals provided virtually no charity care. For example, investor-owned hospitals classified 97 percent of the uncompensated care they rendered as "bad debt."

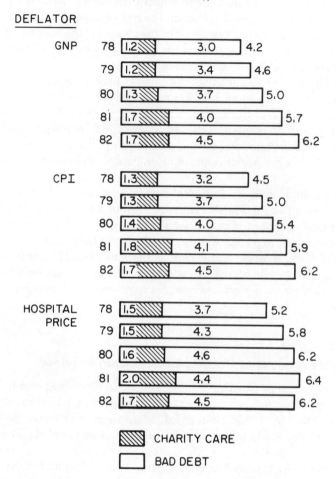

Fig. 2.1. Volume of uncompensated care (billions of 1982$)

DEFLATOR

GNP
78 1.2 3.0 4.2
79 1.2 3.4 4.6
80 1.3 3.7 5.0
81 1.7 4.0 5.7
82 1.7 4.5 6.2

CPI
78 1.3 3.2 4.5
79 1.3 3.7 5.0
80 1.4 4.0 5.4
81 1.8 4.1 5.9
82 1.7 4.5 6.2

HOSPITAL PRICE
78 1.5 3.7 5.2
79 1.5 4.3 5.8
80 1.6 4.6 6.2
81 2.0 4.4 6.4
82 1.7 4.5 6.2

CHARITY CARE

BAD DEBT

Uncompensated Care by Hospital Type

Variations among hospitals in the amount of uncompensated care provided are far more remarkable than the aggregate estimates, expressed with levels or as rates of growth. In 1982, teaching hospitals, defined by membership in the Council of Teaching Hospitals (COTH), provided 36 percent of the $6.2 billion of total uncompensated care, but they accounted for only 27 percent of total charges (Fig. 2.2). This differential is totally accounted for by the disproportionate share of uncompensated care provided by COTH hospitals operated by state and local governments. These eighty-one public hospitals provided $1.1 billion of such care in 1982. Nonteaching public hospitals also have a

Frank A. Sloan, Joseph Valvona, and Ross Mullner

Fig. 2.2 Volume of uncompensated care versus charges by hospital type, 1982 (percentage distribution)

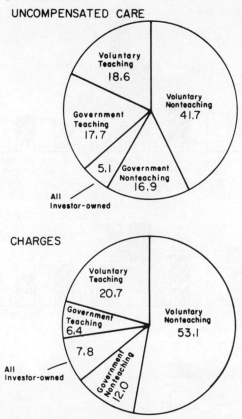

UNCOMPENSATED CARE

Voluntary
Teaching
18.6

Voluntary
Nonteaching
41.7

Government
Teaching
17.7

5.1 Government
Nonteaching
16.9

All
Investor-owned

CHARGES

Voluntary
Teaching
20.7

Government
Teaching
6.4

Voluntary
Nonteaching
53.1

7.8

All
Investor-owned

Government
Nonteaching
12.0

substantial burden, providing 17 percent of the uncompensated care, but accounting for only 12 percent of total charges. In contrast, both nonteaching voluntary and investor-owned hospitals had substantially larger slices of the charge than of the uncompensated care pie.

Comparisons of the distribution of the uncompensated care burden by hospital ownership, payer mix, and metropolitan versus nonmetropolitan location in 1978 and 1982 show these distributions to be virtually identical in both years.

These impressions are confirmed with data based on the 2,260 hospitals which provided complete financial information on the 1982 Annual Survey. Charity care and bad debt represented 4.4 percent of charges in this sample. The percentages were the same in metropolitan and nonmetropolitan hospitals (Fig. 2.3), but because of their relative size, the metropolitan hospitals provided much more of such care. The percentages were much higher for public hospitals (8.6% for metropolitan and 5.3% for nonmetropolitan) than for

Identifying the Issues   **21**

Fig. 2.3. Uncompensated care as a percentage of charges by hospital location, ownership, and bed size, 1982

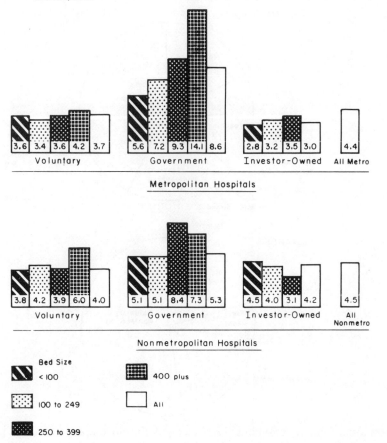

voluntary and investor-owned hospitals. It is noteworthy, however, that whereas the percentage for metropolitan voluntary hospitals was higher than for metropolitan investor-owned hospitals (3.7% for voluntaries versus 3.0% for investor-owned), the pattern is reversed for nonmetropolitan hospitals (4.0% for voluntaries versus 4.2% for investor-owned).

The data are consistent with a contention of several investor-owned hospitals that they often provide more uncompensated care when they are the sole hospital in the community. Except for public hospitals, there is no apparent relationship between the charity care–bad debt percentage and hospital bed size. Uncompensated care seems to be a much higher burden for the metropolitan public hospital than for the nonmetropolitan public hospital. In fact, the uncompensated care percentages for the latter were only slightly higher in 1982 than for nonmetropolitan voluntary and investor-owned hospitals.

Frank A. Sloan, Joseph Valvona, and Ross Mullner

When the sample is further subdivided into teaching versus nonteaching hospital groups (Fig. 2.4), one sees that large public hospitals (those over 400 beds) affiliated with COTH have substantial uncompensated care burdens. While charity care–bad debt as a percentage of charges was 18.4 percent for such hospitals and 15.0 percent for public COTH hospitals overall, voluntary COTH hospitals had a corresponding uncompensated care percentage of 4.6. Of course, these are mean values, and there is considerable variation among hospitals within some of these groups.

Regression analysis on the sample of 2,260 hospitals with the uncompensated care percentage as the dependent variable allows consideration of the roles of a much larger set of potential determinants of variations among hospi-

Fig. 2.4. Uncompensated care as a percentage of charges by hospital teaching status, ownership and bed size, 1982
(metropolitan hospitals only)

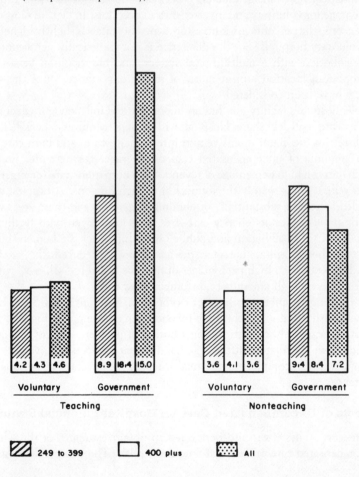

tals in the charity care–bad debt burden. Regression analysis enabled us to answer these questions: Are the differences among hospital types statistically significant? Does the relationship between teaching, ownership, and the dependent variable disappear when other factors such as facility mix, payer mix, affiliation or nonaffiliation with a multihospital system, and region are considered?

The main conclusions of our regression analysis of variations in the uncompensated care burdens among hospitals are as follows:

1. COTH and public hospitals have a higher charity care–bad debt share, and these differences are statistically significant. Adding additional explanatory variables produces no appreciable changes on the estimated effect of teaching or public ownership on provision of uncompensated care. In contrast, holding other variables, including teaching status, constant, there is generally no statistically significant difference between the charity care and bad debt percentage for voluntary and investor-owned hospitals. In fact, in most of the regressions, the percentage for investor-owned hospitals is slightly higher than for voluntary hospitals, but the difference is not statistically significant. Bed size, affiliation with a multihospital system, and metropolitan versus nonmetropolitan location are, at most, of minor importance, once the above factors have been considered.

2. A hospital's facility mix has an important and independent effect on its charity care–bad debt share. Hospitals with high percentages of beds dedicated to obstetrics, neonatal intensive and intermediate care, and burn care have high amounts of uncompensated care on average. Furthermore, hospitals which derive a high percentage of revenue from outpatient care (emergency or other outpatient—mainly the former) have high burdens. A hospital which decided to reduce substantially or eliminate its activity in these areas would substantially reduce its charity care–bad debt load. Even with facility mix included, COTH affiliation and public ownership affect the burden, but the effects of these hospital characteristics are somewhat reduced.

3. Hospitals with high percentages of revenue billed to "self-pay" patients have relatively high amounts of uncompensated care.

4. Holding a number of other factors constant, hospitals in the South have a higher charity care–bad debt share (about 3 percentage points higher). Since our statistical method holds the distribution of payment sources by hospital constant, we speculate that the regional difference reflects relative per capita income and the completeness of health insurance coverage of persons with insurance.

Effects of Uncompensated Care on Hospital Financial Status

Regression analysis was also performed to obtain estimates of the effect of uncompensated care on hospital financial health. The independent variable for uncompensated care burden was defined as the ratio of charity care and bad debt to charges. The financial ratios considered, these being the dependent variables, are listed in Table 2.1.

With one exception, it was found that the financial ratios fall as the amount of uncompensated care rises. The strongest relationships were between uncompensated care and profitability. Based on regression results, we estimate that, as the hospital's uncompensated care as a percentage of charges rises from 2 to 12 percent, total margin falls from 40 (a "low" bound on the effect) to 51 percent (a "high" bound). At the same time, the return-on-fund balance declines an average of 21 to 38 percent.

Corresponding effects of the uncompensated care on the two liquidity ratios are smaller. We estimate that a change in the uncompensated care percentage from 2 to 12 percent would reduce the current ratio by 1 to 5 percent on average. If a hospital has a history of high bad debts, the book value of its accounts receivable may substantially overstate the amount of revenue it will actually collect from these pending accounts. Thus, we also assessed determinants of variation among hospitals in the current ratio less receivables. Raising the hospital's charity care–bad debt percentage from 2 to 12 percent is estimated to lower the modified current ratio from 7 to 12 percent on average.

A high uncompensated care burden has two offsetting effects on hospital leverage. First, to the extent that it is more difficult to raise funds internally because of reduced profit margins, the hospital seeks additional funds from external sources. Second, low profitability raises the cost of such externally generated capital to the hospital, and as a consequence, the hospital borrows less. Our results suggest that the second effect dominates. The hospital with an uncompensated care percentage of 12 has a long-term-debt-to-total-asset ratio

Table 2.1. Selected hospital financial ratios: hospitals with low versus hospitals with high uncompensated care burden

	Difference in financial ratio (%)
Liquidity	
Current ratio	1–5
Current ratio less receivables	7–12
Profitability	
Total margin	40–51
Return on fund balance	21–38
Capital structure	
Long-term debt to total assets	8–10

Note: A low-burden hospital is one whose charity care and bad debt amounts to 2% of gross patient revenue; the corresponding ratio for a high-burden hospital is 12%. All other hospital characteristics are assumed to be at the sample means.

8 to 10 percent lower on average than its counterpart with an uncompensated care percentage of 2.

Relationship of Uncompensated Care to Hospital Closings

A total of 189 hospitals closed between 1980 and 1982. Of these, 111 were nonfederal, short-term general hospitals. The vast majority of the 111 had fewer than 100 beds at the time they closed (Table 2.2); almost half were investor-owned; they were about evenly divided between metropolitan and nonmetropolitan locations.

Closed hospitals and others were almost identical in terms of the volume of charity and bad debt care they provided in 1978 and 1979 as a percentage of gross patient revenue (Table 2.3). Ratios of net to gross revenue, a measure which includes contractual allowances as well as charity care and bad debts, were also similar between the two groups of hospitals. From these data it does not appear that uncompensated care per se was a major factor in the closings. Nor does it seem likely that uninsured and low-income people were placed at a particular disadvantage by hospital closings.

Several items calculated from hospital balance sheets suggest that the hospitals which closed experienced some difficulty in obtaining payment from patients prior to closing. This may reflect poor management practices rather than a high indigent population in the market area. The uncollectible ratio (the ratio of uncollectibles to accounts receivable) was 0.24 in both 1978 and 1979,

Table 2.2. General characteristics of community hospitals that closed in 1980–82

Characteristic	Percentage distribution
Bed size	
6– 24	26.1
25– 49	28.9
50– 99	21.6
100–199	16.2
200–299	3.6
300–399	0.9
400–499	1.8
500+	0.9
	100.0
Location	
Metropolitan	52.2
Nonmetropolitan	47.8
	100.0
Ownership	
State/local government	17.1
Voluntary	37.8
Investor-owned	45.1
	100.0

Table 2.3. Financial status in 1978–79 of hospitals that closed in 1980–82 compared with other hospitals

Indicator	1978		1979	
	Closed	Other	Closed	Other
Uncompensated care				
Charity and bad debt as % of gross patient revenue	3.60	3.65	3.80	3.87
Net to gross revenue ratio	83.48	85.71	84.45	87.18
Other indicators				
Current ratio	3.33	3.59	2.93	3.43
Accounts receivable ratio	0.89	0.78[b]	0.74	0.76
Uncollectible ratio	0.24	0.18[b]	0.24	0.18[b]
Return-on-fund balance	−0.01	0.05	−0.01	0.06
Total margin	−0.03	0.02[b]	−0.03	0.02[b]
Long-term debt to total assets ratio	0.11	0.24[a]	0.14	0.24[a]
Debt to equity ratio	1.69	1.33	1.01	1.16
Age of plant	0.41	0.35[b]	0.44	0.35[a]

[a] = Statistically significant difference at 1% level (two-tail test)
[b] = Statistically significant difference at 5% level (two-tail test)

versus 0.18 for hospitals that remained open. The accounts receivable ratio (accounts receivable to current assets) for the closed hospitals was higher than for other hospitals in 1978, but there was no difference between the two groups in 1979.

Closed hospitals tended to be less profitable in the base period, 1978 and 1979 (see especially "Total margin" in Table 2.3), older (see "Age of plant"), and less highly levered (see "Long-term debt to total assets ratio") than hospitals which remained open during 1980–82. As seen above, uncompensated care has an independent effect on profitability and leverage.

Hospital Actions to Reduce Their Uncompensated Care Burdens

Hospitals may take several preventive actions to avoid or at least postpone financial stress arising from a high amount of uncompensated care. Unfortunately, the data on such actions are fragmentary and at best yield preliminary indications about the extent such preventive measures are now being implemented.

About 15 percent of hospitals adopted explicit limits on the amount of charity care they provided in 1981 and 1982 (Table 2.4). Hospitals that have traditionally provided large amounts of such care (for instance, hospitals with major commitments to teaching) are well-represented among those adopting explicit limits (Fig. 2.5). In particular, 26 percent of public hospitals which are members of the Council of Teaching Hospitals adopted such ceilings. Hospitals which established limits before 1981 are included in the 85 percent of hospitals which did not establish a limit in 1981 and 1982.

Table 2.4. Management measures taken by hospitals in 1981 and 1982 to respond to or prevent fiscal stress

Measure	Percentage adopting
1. Adopt explicit limits on amount of charity care	14.6
2. Increase billing and collection efforts	84.0
3. Reduce hours of operation or staffing in the outpatient department	9.6
4. Reduce hours of operation or staffing in the emergency room	5.9
5. Transfer ownership of the hospital to a controlling organization which also owns nonhospital enterprises	4.7

Source: American Hospital Association, Survey of Medical Care for the Poor and Hospitals' Financial Status, 1983.

The vast majority (84%) increased their billing and collection efforts in 1981–82. It is impossible to ascertain the extent to which this response to the survey question merely reflects attempts to "try to do better" or a *real* change in billing and collection procedures. In contrast, relatively few hospitals took other actions which would lower uncompensated care levels indirectly, such as

Fig. 2.5. Percentage of hospitals adopting explicit limits on charity care in 1981 or 1982

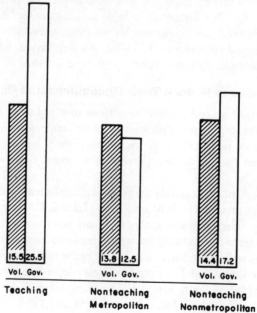

15.5 25.5
Vol. Gov.
Teaching

13.8 12.5
Vol. Gov.
Nonteaching Metropolitan

14.4 17.2
Vol. Gov.
Nonteaching Nonmetropolitan

Frank A. Sloan, Joseph Valvona, and Ross Mullner

reducing hours of operation or staffing in the outpatient department or the emergency room.

Characteristics of Patients Likely to Receive Uncompensated Care

As previously mentioned, there is a significant relationship between the percentage of total hospital charges to self-pay patients and the amount of uncompensated care the hospital provides. On average, hospitals received 82 percent of charges from all sources in 1981 (Ginsburg and Sloan 1984). The discrepancy between charges and receipts was primarily because of contractual allowances obtained by Medicare and other cost-based insurers. Hospitals received payment for only 72 percent of total charges from self-pay patients, and none of the 28 percent gap can be explained by contractual allowances. A study of thirty Massachusetts hospitals concluded that, in 1982, three-fifths of total bad debt was attributable to self-pay patients (Center for Health Policy Studies 1984). The relationship between self-pay as the primary source of payment and nonpayment enables us to use information from the 1981 Hospital Discharge Survey to make inferences about the characteristics of patients who receive uncompensated care from community hospitals.

Table 2.5 shows that patients with a primary payment source of self-pay or no-charge are very likely to be maternity or accident cases. These two types of primary diagnoses represented 53 percent of all such patients and 42 percent of the estimated charges incurred by all self-pay/no-charge patients in 1981. Adding three major diagnostic categories (digestive disorders, mental disorders, and complicated pregnancies) to these, one can account for approximately 70 percent of self-pay/no-charge discharges and over 60 percent of estimated total charges with five major diagnostic categories. Among the most frequent detailed diagnoses for this payment group were normal deliveries, concussions, fracture of face bones, gastroenteritis and colitis, acute appendicitis, alcohol dependence syndrome, schizophrenia, abortions, and early labor.

The distribution of self-pay/no-charge patients who had surgery performed is presented in Table 2.6. The most prevalent surgical category was obstetrics, which represented approximately 25 percent of the discharges and 18 percent of total estimated charges in 1981. Obstetrical procedures and operations on the male and female genital organs, digestive system, and musculoskeletal system composed 72 percent of discharges and 64 percent of charges. Ninety-four percent of the operations on male genitals were for circumcision. This, and the high incidence of maternity-related procedures, indicate that young mothers with young children are likely to be self-pay or no-charge hospital patients. Other frequent operations on self-pay/no-charge patients in 1981 were dilation and curettage, episiotomy, appendectomy, cholecystectomy, and repair of fractured bones using metallic substances.

Table 2.5. Percentage distribution of self-pay and no-charge patients by major diagnosis

Diagnostic group	Discharges		Total estimated charges	
Delivery	39.7		26.1	
Accidents	12.8		15.7	
		52.5		41.8
Digestive system	7.3		9.0	
Mental disorders	5.8		9.3	
Respiratory system	5.3		5.5	
Circulatory system	5.0		8.8	
Complications in pregnancy	4.8		2.1	
Genitourinary system	4.5		4.6	
		85.2		81.1
Other[a]	14.8		18.9	
		100.0		100.0

[a] Includes infectious and parasitic diseases, neoplasms, endocrine, nutritional, and metabolic diseases, diseases of the blood and blood-forming organs, diseases of the nervous system, diseases of the skin, diseases of the musculoskeletal system, congenital anomolies, conditions of the perinatal period, and miscellaneous conditions.

Table 2.7 compares characteristics of patients and their hospitals with four different expected sources of payment: self-pay/no-charge, Medicaid and other government insurance (except Medicare), private insurance, and workmen's compensation. The data pertain to patients from the 1981 HDS who were under age sixty-five at the time of discharge.

Table 2.6. Percentage distribution of self-pay and no-charge patients by major surgical classifications

Surgical group	Discharges		Total estimated charges	
Obstetrics	25.1		18.3	
Male genital organs	14.0		10.6	
Female genital organs	12.1		9.2	
Digestive system	12.1		15.5	
Musculoskeletal system	8.2		10.7	
		71.5		64.3
Integumentary system	5.9		6.5	
Cardiovascular system	3.3		5.7	
Nervous system	2.9		4.2	
		83.6		80.7
Other[a]	16.4		19.3	
		100.0		100.0

[a] Includes operations on the endocrine system, eye, ear, nose, mouth and pharynx, respiratory system, lymphatic system, urinary system, and miscellaneous operations.

Frank A. Sloan, Joseph Valvona, and Ross Mullner

Table 2.7. Frequency distributions: selected characteristics by source of payment

	Self-pay / no-charge	Medicaid/ other gov.	Private insurance	Workmen's comp.	All payment sources
Surgery	0.363	0.382	0.493	0.627	0.466
Delivery	0.372	0.288	0.223	0.008	0.243
Cesarean	0.024	0.023	0.022	0.001	0.022
Accident	0.132	0.069	0.079	0.414	0.089
Burn	0.005	0.003	0.002	0.026	0.003
Mental Disorder	0.062	0.076	0.044	0.008	0.051
Investor-owned	0.045	0.057	0.089	0.118	0.081
Voluntary, church	0.140	0.157	0.209	0.268	0.195
Government	0.404	0.321	0.188	0.167	0.230
Voluntary, nonchurch	0.411	0.465	0.513	0.446	0.495
Northeast	0.172	0.256	0.220	0.220	0.222
North Central	0.182	0.270	0.310	0.225	0.290
West	0.215	0.166	0.138	0.207	0.151
South	0.430	0.308	0.332	0.348	0.337
Bed size 0– 99	0.181	0.160	0.156	0.164	0.159
Bed size 100–299	0.299	0.310	0.339	0.352	0.331
Bed size 300–499	0.206	0.248	0.250	0.248	0.247
Bed size 500+	0.314	0.282	0.255	0.235	0.264
Single female over 24	0.074	0.115	0.069	0.055	0.084
White	0.738	0.541	0.852	0.848	0.789
Black	0.173	0.357	0.121	0.119	0.165
Male	0.425	0.347	0.398	0.804	0.400
Surgery with length of stay greater than 21 days	0.019	0.020	0.016	0.027	0.017
No surgery and length of stay greater than 21 days	0.015	0.018	0.015	0.012	0.016
Discharged against medical advice	0.016	0.019	0.007	0.005	0.010
Discharged dead	0.013	0.010	0.009	0.002	0.009
Newborn	0.203	0.143	0.107	0.000	0.120
Age 0–14	0.116	0.184	0.111	0.000	0.122
Age 45–64	0.142	0.168	0.287	0.302	0.254
Surgery on day of admission	0.161	0.119	0.134	0.123	0.134

Twenty-four percent of total cases in the sample were deliveries, but 37 percent of all self-pay/no-charge patients had a delivery during the stay. In fact, for all medical diagnoses and surgical procedures examined, deliveries had the highest incidence of self-pay/no-charge. We examined characteristics of mothers for whom self-pay/no-charge was the primary expected payment source. The mothers were slightly younger than mothers who gave birth over-all (U.S. Department of Commerce 1984), but, contrary to conventional wisdom, only 18 percent were under age nineteen, only 24 percent were unmarried, and only 14 percent were black.

A much higher percentage of accidents was covered by workmen's compen-sation than by the other payment sources. Forty-one percent of all workmen's compensation patients were hospitalized for accidents. Although workmen's compensation was dominant for accidents, self-pay/no-charge was also an overrepresented source of payment; 13 percent of the self-pay/no-charge pa-tients had accidents as the primary reason for admission.

Investor-owned and church-operated voluntary hospitals had a rather small representation of self-pay/no-charge patients; in contrast, government hospi-tals had a strong overrepresentation from this group. Discharges from investor-owned hospitals composed 8 percent of the sample, but had less than 5 percent of the self-pay/no-charge patients. Church-operated hospitals accounted for 20 percent of the sample but had 14 percent of the self-pay/no-charge patients. Secular voluntary hospitals had 50 percent of the total but 41 percent of self-pay/no-charge patients. In contrast, government hospitals provided 40 per-cent of the discharges designated as self-pay/no-charge but had only 23 percent of the total sample.

Among bed-size categories, hospitals with more than 500 beds had the greatest self-pay/no-charge load. Hospitals in the Northeast and North Cen-tral Census Areas treated proportionately fewer patients classified as self-pay/no-charge, while those in the West and South treated a substantially greater proportion. The greatest discrepancy was in the South, where 34 percent of total patients in the sample were treated, representing 43 percent of the self-pay/no-charge patients.

According to the discriminant analysis, the best predictors that a case will be classified as "self-pay" or "no-charge" are the following:

1. A nonsurgical delivery.
2. A newborn.
3. Race. White patients are more likely to be self-pay/no-charge than blacks, since black patients are more likely than whites to be covered by Medicaid and other government programs.
4. Hospital ownership. Government hospitals have the highest proportion of self-pay/no-charge patients, and investor-owned hospitals have the lowest.

Frank A. Sloan, Joseph Valvona, and Ross Mullner

5. Hospital bed size. Hospitals with more than 500 beds are the most likely to treat self-pay patients.
6. Regional location. Hospitals in the West and South have a higher incidence of self-pay/no-charge cases than those in the North Central states or the Northeast.
7. Day of surgery. Surgery on the day of admission leads to a greater probability that the patient will be self-pay.

To illustrate the numerical importance of the above factors, we have developed a set of scenarios. Each scenario is based on a set of assumed patient and hospital characteristics which, when used in combination with the classification functions from the discriminant analysis, yield probabilities that the patient will be in each of the four payment categories. For example, in scenario 1 in Table 2.8, we have assumed that the patient is a white female between the ages of fifteen and forty-four who has a nonsurgical delivery in a government hospital in the South with a bed size over 500. Under these assumptions, the probability that she will have self-pay/no-charge as the primary source of payment is 0.66. Keeping all the characteristics the same, but varying race (scenario 2) reduces the probability to 0.42.

As just demonstrated, nonsurgical delivery is a strong predictor that the patient will be self-pay. The probabilities of self-pay/no-charge for a white and black mother delivering at a secular voluntary hospital are 0.47 and 0.31, respectively (scenarios 3 and 4); the corresponding predicted probability for a white who delivers at an investor-owned hospital is 0.35 and for a black is 0.23 (scenarios 7 and 8). Deliveries through surgical intervention do not distinguish self-pay or no-charge from the other payment sources.

A newborn child is very likely to be classified as self-pay/no-charge. A white female newborn treated at a large government hospital in the South has a 65 percent likelihood of being self-pay or no-charge. The same child in the West has a 64 percent chance of being in this category and in the North Central Area, only a 48 percent chance (scenarios 10–12).

Scenarios 21 and 22 (Table 2.8) show the difference between a patient who has surgery and one who has surgery on the day he or she is admitted to the hospital. Same-day surgery is interpreted to signify an emergency or urgency. The predicted probability is 0.34 that the patient who has surgery on the day of admission is self-pay, but 0.27 if surgery is performed on a later day than the date of admission.

Hospital ownership has an important bearing on the likelihood of self-pay status. Predicted probabilities from several scenarios are summarized in Table 2.9.

Several characteristics are unimportant as predictors of self-pay status. Particularly noteworthy is the lack of predictive value of a long stay (greater than 21 days), a measure of illness severity.

Table 2.8. Scenarios based on discriminant analysis

	1	2	3	4	5	6	7	8	9	10
Female	1	1	1	1	1	1	1	1	1	1
Male	0	0	0	0	0	0	0	0	0	0
Age 15–44	1	1	1	1	1	1	1	1	1	0
Newborn	0	0	0	0	0	0	0	0	0	1
White	1	0	1	0	1	0	1	0	1	1
Black	0	1	0	1	0	1	0	1	0	0
North Central	0	0	0	0	0	0	0	0	0	0
South	1	1	1	1	1	1	1	1	1	1
West	0	0	0	0	0	0	0	0	0	0
Delivery	1	1	1	1	1	1	1	1	1	0
Accident	0	0	0	0	0	0	0	0	0	0
Mental disorder	0	0	0	0	0	0	0	0	0	0
Surgery	0	0	0	0	0	0	0	0	0	0
Voluntary, church	0	0	0	0	1	1	0	0	0	0
Voluntary, nonchurch	0	0	1	1	0	0	0	0	0	0
Government	1	1	0	0	0	0	0	0	1	1
Investor-owned	0	0	0	0	0	0	1	1	0	0
Surgery on day of admission	0	0	0	0	0	0	0	0	0	0
Bed size 100–299	0	0	0	0	0	0	0	0	1	0
Bed size over 500	1	1	1	1	1	1	1	1	0	1
P (self-pay/ no charge)	0.66	0.42	0.47	0.31	0.43	0.28	0.35	0.23	0.59	0.65

Uncompensated Care at Vanderbilt Hospital

Much of the care rendered at Vanderbilt Hospital on a charity or bad debt basis during 1982–83 was to patients in nursery, pediatrics, and obstetrics-gynecology and to patients on the larger services—medicine and general surgery (Table 2.10). The mean unpaid bill was $2,884, which was much smaller than the mean charge per case in the same year at Vanderbilt Hospital, $5,826. The vast majority of patients who received charity care or incurred bad debts had small unpaid bills. However, 2 percent of such patients had unpaid bills of $25,000 or more, and these patients accounted for 35 percent of total uncompensated care at the hospital.

Almost half of these high-cost patients were newborns. Of the major service categories listed in Table 2.10, nursery had the highest average unpaid charge ($6,185). This service accounted for 27 percent of the total uncompensated care bill at the hospital in 1982–83, but only 13 percent of the uncompensated care cases. As a group, normal newborns were fairly numerous among uncompensated care patients (6%) but not expensive (1% of the total unpaid bill).

Frank A. Sloan, Joseph Valvona, and Ross Mullner

Table 2.8. Cont.

11	12	13	14	15	16	17	18	19	20	21	22
1	1	1	1	1	0	0	0	0	0	1	1
0	0	0	0	0	1	1	1	1	1	0	0
0	0	0	0	0	1	1	1	1	1	1	1
1	1	1	1	1	0	0	0	0	0	0	0
1	1	1	1	1	1	1	1	1	1	1	1
0	0	0	0	0	0	0	0	0	0	0	0
0	1	0	0	0	1	1	1	1	1	0	0
0	0	1	1	1	0	0	0	0	0	1	1
1	0	0	0	0	0	0	0	0	0	0	0
0	0	0	0	0	0	0	0	0	0	0	0
0	0	0	0	0	0	0	0	0	0	0	0
0	0	0	0	0	1	1	1	1	1	0	0
0	0	0	0	0	0	0	0	0	0	1	1
0	0	0	1	0	1	0	0	0	0	0	0
0	0	1	0	0	0	1	0	0	0	1	1
1	1	0	0	0	0	0	1	0	1	0	0
0	0	0	0	1	0	0	0	1	0	0	0
0	0	0	0	0	0	0	0	0	0	1	0
0	0	0	0	0	0	0	0	0	1	0	0
1	1	1	0	1	1	1	1	1	0	1	1
0.64	0.48	0.46	0.42	0.33	0.29	0.34	0.51	0.24	0.44	0.34	0.27

Deliveries, both vaginal and cesarean, made up 11 percent of the cases and 7 percent of the total uncompensated care.

With the exception of very expensive care and life support rendered in the neonatal intensive care unit, data from Vanderbilt Hospital suggest that much uncompensated care arises from relatively uncomplex diagnoses and procedures. Such high technology procedures as coronary artery bypass were rarely uncompensated at Vanderbilt Hospital. Less than 1 percent of the patients who received uncompensated care and 2 percent of the total unpaid bill arose from coronary bypass. The uncompensated cases fall roughly into three groups: a large category of patients who incur a moderate expense, a smaller group of catastrophically ill patients, and a large number of patients who appear to have insurance but do not pay their cost-sharing obligation.

Discussion and Conclusions

Aggregate Uncompensated Care Burden

There has been a moderate increase in the aggregate amount of uncompensated care hospitals provide. The trend in the volume of such care, expressed in

Table 2.9. Probability of self-pay or no charge by type of hospital ownership

Patient characteristics	Government	Voluntary, nonchurch	Voluntary, church	Investor-owned
White, female, delivery, South	0.66	0.47	0.43	0.35
Black, female, delivery, South	0.42	0.31	0.28	0.23
White, male, mental disorder, North Central	0.51	0.34	0.29	0.24
White, female, newborn, South	0.65	0.46	0.42	0.33

constant dollars, is highly sensitive to the index one uses to deflate the charity care and bad debt series. The most recent data are for 1982. Hospitals may have provided a substantially higher volume in 1983, a recession year and one sufficiently long after the Medicaid cutbacks which began in full force in 1981 to reflect that change. To the extent that a 1983 increase in uncompensated care was the result of recession, the increase would be largely temporary. If the Medicaid cuts are maintained, however, there may be permanent growth in the real uncompensated care burden.

Distribution of the Uncompensated Care Load among Hospitals

The aggregate volume of uncompensated care is distributed very unevenly among hospitals, and relative shares that major types of hospitals assumed of the total burden were very stable during the period we examined, 1978–82. An unequal distribution is a cause for potential concern for several reasons.

First, persons without the resources to purchase hospital care who are not located near a hospital willing to provide uncompensated care may be placed at an important disadvantage in obtaining needed care. Unfortunately, data are unavailable to permit us to estimate how many people face a combination of

Table 2.10. Percentage distribution of charity care and bad debt at Vanderbilt Hospital, July 1982–June 1983

Service	Unpaid charges	Cases
Nursery	26.9	12.5
Medicine	22.0	22.3
Pediatrics	10.7	12.8
General surgery	9.2	7.8
Neurosurgery	8.8	6.5
Obstetrics/gynecology	9.1	16.6
	86.7	78.5
Other[a]	13.3	21.5
	100.0	100.0

[a] Includes head and neck service, neurology, ophthalmology, oral surgery, orthopedics, pediatric surgery, psychiatry (adult), psychiatry (child), thoracic surgery, and urology.

Frank A. Sloan, Joseph Valvona, and Ross Mullner

geographic and financial barriers to the use of hospital care. Nor is it known how many communities do not have a hospital willing to serve patients on an uncompensated basis.

We have assessed differences in hospital willingness to supply hospital care by metropolitan versus nonmetropolitan location. The willingness of individual nonmetropolitan hospitals to supply uncompensated care has a potentially important effect on the access to hospital care for the poor and uninsured who live in these areas; such persons often have only one nearby source of hospital care. Our finding that nonmetropolitan hospitals have the same or a slightly higher volume of uncompensated care expressed as a percentage of charges is somewhat reassuring, as is the result that these percentages are higher for voluntary and (especially) investor-owned hospitals in nonmetropolitan than in metropolitan areas. Nevertheless, the percentages are not sufficiently high to provide an assurance that all residents of rural areas who may deserve such care actually obtain it.

Second, the unequal distribution raises a concern about the financing of uncompensated care. Do residents of metropolitan areas pay a disproportionate amount, in the form of either explicit or implicit taxes, to finance the uncompensated hospital care? Is a system which taxes the charge-paying patient to pay for the charity care rendered by the hospital equitable? As competition among hospitals becomes more intense and third-party payment more stringent, will hospitals be able to raise funds for indigent care via a tax on the charge-paying patient?

Third, there are important legal differences in the treatment of the three major forms of hospital ownership. A major rationale for differential treatment is that some institutions are expected to engage in nonprofit-maximizing behavior that yields benefits to the community. On the top of nearly everyone's list of community benefits is uncompensated care. Yet hospitals of the same ownership form differ markedly in the amount of such care they provide. One such difference is between voluntary hospitals with and without a major commitment to teaching. Nonteaching voluntaries generally furnish much less uncompensated care than their teaching counterparts. Furthermore, there are substantial differences among hospitals within each of the two categories. In many instances, private hospitals reject poor patients when they judge that the public hospital system in the community has the capacity to care for such patients (see, for example, Sullivan 1984). A hospital may be justified in defending its policy of refusing nonpaying patients when there is access to a public facility. But should not the hospital's refusal have a bearing on its tax exempt status?

If an important rationale for preferential treatment of certain classes of hospitals by government is the provision of a community divdend in the form of uncompensated care, it would appear that it is time to rethink the conditions under which such treatment is granted. Furthermore, it would appear desirable to evaluate the pros and cons of reliance on public and major teaching hospitals as major providers of uncompensated care.

Effect of Uncompensated Care on Hospitals' Financial Health

Provision of uncompensated care has an adverse effect on the financial performance of hospitals, as measured by standard accounting ratios. Profitability and liquidity are adversely affected as more of such care is provided. Moreover, a high charity care and bad debt burden is not viewed favorably by potential investors. Our regression results suggest that a high amount of uncompensated care raises the cost of capital to the hospital; this impression is confirmed by articles in the hospital literature (for example, Kuntz 1983).

An alternative view is that uncompensated care has at most a minor effect on hospital profitability. Rather, not-for-profit hospitals pay a community dividend in the form of uncompensated care. By excluding uncompensated care from reported profits, hospital income statements understate hospital profitability. To be parallel with treatment of dividends to shareholders, the community dividend should be considered part of (pretax) profit. This is an interesting conceptual issue worth pursuing in future research on hospitals.

In any event, it appears doubtful that the survival of more than a very few hospitals is currently being threatened by a high charity care and/or bad debt load. In fact, the community hospitals that closed between 1980 and 1982 had slightly lower uncompensated care burdens prior to closure than hospitals that remained open. The characteristics of hospitals which closed during 1980–82 closely resemble those of hospitals which closed during the 1970s (Mullner, Byre, and Kubal 1983). Although several experts from the hospital industry predict that many hospitals will close during the 1980s (see, for example, Hospitals 1982), the 1980–82 closing rate does not imply a higher rate of hospital closings than experienced heretofore.

Rather than face financial disaster, hospitals will probably take explicit measures to reduce the amount of care they render on an uncompensated basis. Judging from responses to a recent survey, some of the types of hospitals that have historically had high charity care and bad debt burdens are now beginning to adopt explicit limits on the amount of such care they are willing to provide. Since patient ability to pay is particularly poor on certain services (e.g., maternity and outpatient), it is also likely that hospitals will reduce their uncompensated care levels by altering their service mixes.

Characteristics of Patients Who Receive Uncompensated Care

Our data imply that most uncompensated care arises from low- or mid-level technology care rather than from high technology. By "high technology," we mean treatment that was not widely diffused ten or fifteen years ago and is expensive. We have performed a number of consistency checks which confirm our finding.

First, we examined hundreds of ICD-9-CM diagnostic and surgical procedure codes of discharges classified as "self-pay" or "no-charge" in the 1981 Hospital Discharge Survey. We found very few discharges one could define as high technology, either because of the diagnosis or because of the surgical procedure performed.

Second, we examined the source of payment for various high-technology surgical procedures. The percentage of such procedures with a self-pay or no-charge payment source was far lower than for discharges or surgical procedures overall. For example, only 1.6 percent of coronary artery bypasses recorded by the 1981 HDS had a self-pay or no-charge payment source. Corresponding percentages for total hip replacements, permanent cardiac pacing, and peripheral vascular surgery were 1.1, 2.4, and 1.5, respectively. The percentages for some nonelective procedures, such as repair of a detached retina, were higher (5.4%). According to HDS, none of the 10,000 surgical procedures performed for morbid obesity in 1981, a highly controversial elective procedure, were performed on patients with a primary expected payment source of self-pay or no-charge. Unpublished data on surgical utilization from the Commission on Professional and Hospital Activities (CPHA), which are being analyzed for purposes of another study, also show self-pay and no-charge patients to be underrepresented among high-technology surgery patients.

Third, a recent analysis of high-cost illness, based on a special CPHA survey, showed self-pay and no-charge patients to be underrepresented among patients with catastrophic illnesses, which presumably are often, though by no means always, "high-technology" (Kobrinski and Matteson 1981).

To a lesser extent, our conclusion that most uncompensated care is neither high-cost nor high-technology appears to apply to major teaching hospitals as well. Data from Vanderbilt Hospital imply this. Nevertheless, 2 percent of charity care/bad debt patients at this hospital generated over a third of the uncompensated care bill, hardly a trivial share.

The HDS does not link discharges to hospitals by teaching status. Therefore, we constructed three categories for the self-pay/no-charge discharges based on bed size and ownership: "high likelihood of teaching" for public and voluntary hospitals with 500 or more beds; "nonteaching" for investor-owned hospitals and public and voluntary hospitals under 200 beds; and "some likelihood of teaching" for the remaining discharges. The first group provided a substantial, though proportionately smaller, amount of low technology care to self-pay/no-charge patients. For example, three-tenths of the discharges for this group involved deliveries. It is worth considering whether major teaching hospitals should be providing so much of this care on a compensated *or* uncompensated basis. Implications will be developed further in a later chapter.

Barriers to Hospital Care

All the data examined use the hospital as the site for data collection. An unfortunate characteristic of hospital-based data is that they do not describe those persons needing hospital care who are unable to obtain it.

Two important policy questions remain. Are there a large number of persons who, because of a combination of low income, lack of insurance, and an unwillingness of hospitals in the area to supply "free" care, do not have adequate access to hospital care? Are the barriers to certain types of high-technology care particularly severe? That is, is coronary bypass surgery available only to the publicly and privately insured? Or do few uninsured people obtain such care because few of them need it?

The percentage of persons with some form of public or private insurance coverage continued to rise through 1982 and was appreciably higher in 1982 than in 1970. In 1982, almost 90 percent of low-income persons had some health insurance coverage; for others, coverage was almost universal (Robert Wood Johnson Foundation 1983). Likewise, the percentage of payments for personal health services covered by third-party sources was at an all-time high in 1982, but the percentage of payments for hospital care from third-party sources, which has been around the 90 percent mark since the late 1960s, continued a decline that began in 1975 (Gibson, Waldo, and Levit 1983). Uncompensated care, which is nonpayment to hospitals, is not counted in these figures. Yet the slight decline in third-party coverage for hospital care (the portion of total hospital expenditures covered by third parties declined from 92% in 1975 to 88% in 1982) has probably increased both the need and the demand for uncompensated care.

According to the 1977 National Medical Care Expenditure Survey (NMCES), 9 percent of the U.S. population never had insurance during 1977, and another 8 percent were uninsured for part of that year (Davis and Roland 1983; see also Table 8.1, below). The uninsured had substantially lower use rates in 1977—47 patient days per 100 persons for the uninsured versus 90 days per 100 persons for the insured. Unfortunately, NMCES did not obtain a detailed account of the health status of the people it contacted. Therefore, the data do not permit inferences about access to high technology versus other types of hospital care. However, using a measure of self-assessed health status, 15 percent of the uninsured under age sixty-five rated their health as "fair" or "poor" (rather than "excellent" or "good") versus 11 percent of the insured (Davis and Roland 1983).

Widespread Current Interest in the Issue of Uncompensated Care

This chapter contains the first estimates of national expenditures on charity and bad debts for any recent year. The uncompensated care burden nationwide

Frank A. Sloan, Joseph Valvona, and Ross Mullner

in 1982—$6.2 billion—does not seem to be sufficiently high to account for all of the recent interest among both public officials and the public at large in this subject. There are several possible explanations.

First, uncompensated care could be a much greater burden for hospitals than our data suggest. Except for the possibility discussed above—that the load has increased since 1982—we reject this view. The AHA Annual Surveys are the only national data sources on bad debts and charity care. Although hospitals respond to the Annual Surveys voluntarily, they have no incentive to understate the amount of such care they render. This is not to imply that the situation is not much worse in many communities and hospitals than the national statistics suggest. Our results are consistent with data from other sources for particular states and hospital management companies.

Second, hospitals now face increased competition and new pressures from third-party payers. Thus, they are looking for new areas in which to cut costs, and uncompensated care represents one such target of opportunity.

Third, hospitals are now subject to acquisition more than ever before. Especially if the acquiring organization is an investor-owned chain, interested parties in the community are, rightly or wrongly, likely to be concerned about how indigent care is to be handled in the future.

Fourth, the media has publicized the lack of insurance coverage for certain high-technology procedures, such as liver transplants. To date, high-technology procedures have not generally been provided when no third-party coverage is available. Thus, only a small part of the $6.2 billion in uncompensated care can be linked to provision of such procedures.

Fifth, one occasionally hears that a high charity care/bad debt burden is causing some hospitals to go bankrupt. Our data suggest that bankruptcy for this reason must be a rarity. However, a high burden can cause a hospital's financial health to deteriorate, as this and past work with other data bases by others has indicated (Feder et al. 1984).

None of the five explanations for widespread concern about uncompensated hospital care can be said to be "wrong," since there are misperceptions about the current situation. Judging from the empirical evidence, rumors that (1) the volume of uncompensated care has been skyrocketing, (2) the increase is attributable to the fast pace of technological change, and (3) many hospitals are failing because of a high uncompensated burden are more fiction than fact.

Appendix

The following six tables present means, standard deviations, and definitions of variables used in our regressions; bad debt/charity care regressions as well as regressions with financial ratios as the dependent variables; and classification coefficients from the discriminant analysis.

Table 2A.1. Variable definitions, means, and standard deviations

Variable	Definition	Mean	Standard deviation
Dependent variables			
BDCHAR	Bad debt and charity care as a fraction of total gross patient revenue	0.046	0.048
CURRAT1	Current cash and short-term investments + net receivables + other current assets/current liabilities	3.935	42.813
CURRAT2	As above, excluding net receivables from the numerator	1.475	10.599
TM	Total margin: total revenue minus total expense as a fraction of total revenue	0.030	0.078
RFUND	Return on fund balance: total revenue minus total expense as a fraction of fund balance	0.071	2.394
DEBT1	Long-term debt + other liabilities / total unrestricted assets + restricted funds	0.309	0.244
DEBT2	As above, excluding other liabilities from the numerator	0.276	0.228
Explanatory variable			
BED1	Hospital with fewer than 100 beds	0.364	0.481
BED2	Hospital with 100–249 beds	0.338	0.473
BED3	Hospital with 250–399 beds	0.163	0.369
T3	Hospital a member of the Council of Teaching Hospitals	0.068	0.252
T2	Not T3, but hospital associated with a medical school	0.103	0.303
T1	Not T2 or T3, but hospital with an approved residency program	0.023	0.150
PROFIT	Investor-owned hospital	0.057	0.232
GOVT	Hospital operated by state or local government	0.263	0.441
SMSA0	Hospital in a Standard Metropolitan Statistical Area (SMSA) with population less than 1,000,000	0.293	0.455
SMSA1	Hospital is in an SMSA with population of 1,000,000–2,500,000	0.134	0.340
SMSA2	Hospital is in an SMSA with population greater than 2,500,000	0.138	0.345
CHAIN	Takes value of one if hospital is part of a multi-hospital system; zero otherwise	0.244	0.430
PSYAC%	Fraction of beds set up and staffed in psychiatric acute care	0.024	0.056
OB%	Fraction of beds set up and staffed in obstetrics	0.066	0.053

Table 2A.1. (*Continued*)

Variable	Definition	Mean	Standard deviation
PEDIC%	Fraction of beds set up and staffed in pediatric intensive care	0.001	0.003
NEOINT%	Fraction of beds set up and staffed in neonatal intensive care	0.003	0.011
NEOINTM%	Fraction of beds set up and staffed in neonatal intermediate care	0.001	0.005
BURN%	Fraction of beds set up and staffed in burn units	0.001	0.004
EMER%	Estimated emergency charges as fraction of total charges	0.053	0.038
OTHOUT%	Estimated other outpatient charges as a fraction of total charges	0.080	0.054
MCARE%	Fraction of total gross patient revenue which comes from Medicare	0.412	0.111
MCAID%	Fraction of total gross patient revenue which comes from Medicaid	0.088	0.085
BLUE%	Fraction of total gross patient revenue from Blue Cross	0.151	0.093
COM%	Fraction of total gross patient revenue from commercial insurance	0.220	0.124
OTHREV%	Fraction of total gross patient revenue from other sources	0.040	0.081
NE	Takes value of one if hospital is in the Northeast Census Area; zero otherwise	0.179	0.384
NC	Takes value of one if hospital is in the North Central Census Area; zero otherwise	0.346	0.476
W	Takes value of one if hospital is in the Western Census Area; zero otherwise	0.144	0.351
NY	Takes value of one if hospital is in New York State; zero otherwise	0.059	0.236
NJ	Takes value of one if hospital is in New Jersey; zero otherwise	0.022	0.146
MA	Takes value of one if hospital is in Massachusetts; zero otherwise	0.028	0.164
MD	Takes value of one if hospital is in Maryland; zero otherwise	0.014	0.119
CT	Takes value of one if hospital is in Connecticut; zero otherwise	0.008	0.091–
WA	Takes value of one if hospital is in Washington State; zero otherwise	0.017	0.130

Table 2A.2. Regression results: bad debt and charity care

Explanatory variable	Reg. 1	Reg. 2	Reg. 3	Reg. 4	Reg. 5
BED1	−0.0023	0.0028	−0.0001	−0.0007	0.0045
	(0.0038)	(0.0038)	(0.0038)	(0.0036)	(0.0034)
BED2	0.0024	0.0057	0.0039	0.0038	0.0071[b]
	(0.0035)	(0.0035)	(0.0035)	(0.0033)	(0.0031)
BED3	0.0032	0.0040	0.0030	0.0046	0.0059[b]
	(0.0034)	(0.0033)	(0.0033)	(0.0031)	(0.0029)
T1	0.0037	0.0037	0.0041	0.0054	0.0053
	(0.0057)	(0.0056)	(0.0055)	(0.0052)	(0.0049)
T2	0.014[a]	0.0093[a]	0.0099[a]	0.0084[a]	0.0089[a]
	(0.0033)	(0.032)	(0.0032)	(0.0030)	(0.0029)
T3	0.038[a]	0.022[a]	0.023[a]	0.024[a]	0.025[a]
	(0.0042)	(0.0045)	(0.0045)	(0.0043)	(0.0040)
PROFIT	0.0028	0.0047	0.0068	0.0019	−0.0072[b]
	(0.0038)	(0.0037)	(0.0037)	(0.0035)	(0.0034)
GOVT	0.029[a]	0.026[a]	0.026[a]	0.016[a]	0.012[a]
	(0.0020)	(0.0020)	(0.0020)	(0.0020)	(0.0019)
SMSA0	0.0019	0.0012	−0.0004	0.0021	−0.0003
	(0.0023)	(0.0022)	(0.0022)	(0.0021)	(0.0020)
SMSA1	−0.0041	−0.0030	−0.0036	−0.0017	0.0031
	(0.0029)	(0.0028)	(0.0028)	(0.0027)	(0.0025)
SMSA2	−0.0098[a]	−0.0080[a]	−0.0081[a]	−0.0052	−0.0010
	(0.0029)	(0.0028)	(0.0028)	(0.0027)	(0.0026)
CHAIN	0.0014	0.0014	0.0018	−0.0013	−0.0016
	(0.0020)	(0.0020)	(0.0020)	(0.0019)	(0.0018)
PSYAC%		0.027	0.026	0.013	0.023
		(0.015)	(0.015)	(0.014)	(0.014)
OB%		0.085[a]	0.075[a]	0.042[a]	0.079[a]
		(0.016)	(0.016)	(0.015)	(0.014)
PEDIC%		0.47	0.49	0.29	0.40
		(0.32)	(0.32)	(0.30)	(0.28)
NEOINT%		0.40[a]	0.41[a]	0.28[a]	0.27[a]
		(0.091)	(0.090)	(0.086)	(0.080)

Table 2A.2. (*Continued*)

Explanatory variable	Reg. 1	Reg. 2	Reg. 3	Reg. 4	Reg. 5
NEOINTM%		1.13[a]	1.14[a]	0.88[a]	0.79[a]
		(0.16)	(0.16)	(0.15)	(0.14)
BURN%		0.63[a]	0.61[a]	0.45[b]	0.54[a]
		(0.19)	(0.19)	(0.18)	(0.17)
EMER%			0.16[a]	0.14[a]	0.11[a]
			(0.022)	(0.021)	(0.020)
OTHOUT%			0.020	0.016	0.098[a]
			(0.015)	(0.015)	(0.015)
MCARE%				−0.17[a]	−0.14[a]
				(0.011)	(0.010)
MCAID%				−0.13[a]	−0.099[a]
				(0.013)	(0.013)
BLUE%				−0.19[a]	−0.16[a]
				(0.011)	(0.012)
COM%				−0.13[a]	−0.11[a]
				(0.011)	(0.010)
OTHREV%				−0.082[a]	−0.067[a]
				(0.012)	(0.012)
NE					−0.027[a]
					(0.0027)
NC					−0.036[a]
					(0.0019)
W					−0.036[a]
					(0.0025)
CONSTANT	0.035[a]	0.024[a]	0.017[a]	0.16[a]	0.16[a]
	(0.0038)	(0.0039)	(0.0041)	(0.0098)	(0.0092)
	$F_{(12,2979)}$	$F_{(18,2973)}$	$F_{(20,2971)}$	$F_{(25,2966)}$	$F_{(28,2963)}$
	= 30.89	= 30.05	= 30.39	= 42.04	= 57.85
	$R^2 = 0.11$	$R^2 = 0.15$	$R^2 = 0.17$	$R^2 = 0.26$	$R^2 = 0.35$

[a] = Statistically significant at 1% level (two-tail test)
[b] = Statistically significant at 5% level (two-tail test)

Identifying the Issues

Table 2A.3. Current ratio regressions

Explanatory variable	Usual definition			Modified definition		
	Reg. 1	Reg. 2	Reg. 3	Reg. 1	Reg. 2	Reg. 3
BDCHAR	2.031^a	-0.43	-1.93^a	0.58	-1.01	-1.93^a
	(0.62)	(0.67)	(0.72)	(0.52)	(0.57)	(0.61)
BED1		0.15	0.20		0.21	0.25^b
		(0.13)	(0.13)		(0.11)	(0.11)
BED2		0.041	0.10		-0.008	0.037
		(0.12)	(0.12)		(0.10)	(0.10)
BED3		0.014	0.054		-0.037	-0.003
		(0.11)	(0.11)		(0.095)	(0.095)
T1		-0.025	0.020		-0.076	-0.052
		(0.19)	(0.18)		(0.16)	(0.16)
T2		-0.024	0.016		-0.16	-0.132
		(0.11)	(0.11)		(0.92)	(0.092)
T3		-0.095	0.0005		-0.19	-0.13
		(0.15)	(0.15)		(0.12)	(0.12)
PROFIT		0.0085	-0.095		-0.29^b	-0.34^a
		(0.14)	(0.14)		(0.12)	(0.12)
GOVT		0.51^a	0.43^a		0.35^a	0.32^a
		(0.073)	(0.073)		(0.061)	(0.062)
SMSA0		-0.23^a	-0.25^a		-0.17^a	-0.18^a
		(0.75)	(0.075)		(0.064)	(0.064)
SMSA1		-0.57^a	-0.51^a		-0.29^a	-0.26^a
		(0.094)	(0.096)		(0.08)	(0.08)
SMSA2		-0.62^a	-0.48^a		-0.24^a	-0.16
		(0.097)	(0.099)		(0.08)	(0.08)
CHAIN		-0.12^c	-0.17^b		-0.12^b	-0.15^b
		(0.069)	(0.069)		(0.06)	(0.06)
OTHOUT%		-3.49^a	-1.92^a		-2.40^a	-1.42^a
		(0.56)	(0.60)		(0.47)	(0.51)
MCARE%		-1.73^a	-1.68^a		-1.64^a	-1.63^a
		(0.45)	(0.45)		(0.38)	(0.38)
MCAID%		-3.47^a	-3.32^a		-3.56^a	-3.47^a
		(0.53)	(0.53)		(0.45)	(0.45)

46

	(1)	(2)	(3)	(4)	(5)	(6)
BLUE%		−1.76[a] (0.47)	−1.042[b] (0.51)		−1.45[a] (0.40)	−1.17[a] (0.43)
COM%		−0.75[c] (0.44)	−1.17[a] (0.44)		−1.75[a] (0.37)	−1.97[a] (0.37)
OTHREV%		−0.42 (0.49)	−0.55 (0.48)		−0.95[b] (0.41)	−1.00[b] (0.41)
NY			−0.40[a] (0.15)			−0.29[b] (0.13)
NJ			0.15 (0.21)			0.30 (0.18)
MA			−0.29 (0.19)			−0.23 (0.17)
MD			−1.034[a] (0.24)			−0.55[a] (0.21)
CT			−0.23 (0.31)			−0.37 (0.27)
WA			0.11 (0.22)			0.10 (0.19)
NE			−0.59[a] (0.14)			−0.30[a] (0.12)
NC			−0.42[a] (0.080)			−0.22[a] (0.07)
W			−0.42[a] (0.10)			−0.30[a] (0.09)
CONSTANT	2.44[a] (0.040)	4.38[a] (0.40)	4.59[a] (0.40)	1.11[a] (0.034)	3.05[a] (0.36)	3.17[a] (0.34)
	$F_{(1,2692)}$ = 10.81	$F_{(19,2674)}$ = 20.40	$F_{(28,2665)}$ = 16.51	$F_{(1,2752)}$ = 1.23	$F_{(19,2734)}$ = 16.97	$F_{(28,2725)}$ = 12.9
	R^2 = 0.00	R^2 = 0.13	R^2 = 0.15	R^2 = 0.00	R^2 = 0.11	R^2 = 0.12

[a] = Statistically significant at 1% level (two-tail test)
[b] = Statistically significant at 5% level (two-tail test)
[c] = Statistically significant at 10% level (two-tail test)

Table 2A.4. Profit regressions

Explanatory variable	Total margin			Return-on-fund balance		
	Reg. 1	Reg. 2	Reg. 3	Reg. 1	Reg. 2	Reg. 3
BDCHAR	-0.090^a	-0.133^a	-0.176^a	-0.210^a	-0.158^b	-0.298^a
	(0.031)	(0.035)	(0.038)	(0.062)	(0.065)	(0.074)
BED1		-0.040^a	-0.041^a		-0.062^a	-0.056^a
		(0.007)	(0.007)		(0.013)	(0.013)
BED2		-0.020^a	-0.019^a		-0.030^b	-0.017
		(0.006)	(0.006)		(0.012)	(0.012)
BED3		-0.007	-0.007		-0.012	-0.006
		(0.006)	(0.006)		(0.012)	(0.011)
T1		0.0002	0.002		-0.016	0.0004
		(0.010)	(0.010)		(0.020)	(0.019)
T2		-0.007	-0.005		-0.021	-0.012
		(0.006)	(0.006)		(0.011)	(0.011)
T3		-0.008	-0.005		-0.025	-0.0007
		(0.008)	(0.008)		(0.015)	(0.015)
PROFIT		0.015^b	0.012		0.072^a	0.067^a
		(0.007)	(0.007)		(0.016)	(0.015)
GOVT		-0.002	-0.005		-0.013	-0.021^a
		(0.004)	(0.004)		(0.007)	(0.007)
SMSA0		-0.003	-0.003		0.003	0.002
		(0.004)	(0.004)		(0.008)	(0.008)
SMSA1		-0.010^b	-0.009		0.009	0.006
		(0.005)	(0.005)		(0.010)	(0.010)
SMSA2		-0.012^b	-0.008		-0.013	0.008
		(0.005)	(0.005)		(0.010)	(0.010)
CHAIN		-0.002	-0.007		0.014	-0.002
		(0.004)	(0.004)		(0.007)	(0.007)
OTHOUT%		-0.086^a	-0.039		-0.241^a	-0.149^b
		(0.029)	(0.032)		(0.058)	(0.063)
MCARE%		-0.068^a	-0.052^b			-0.080
		(0.023)	(0.023)			(0.047)

	(1)	(2)	(3)	(4)	(5)	(6)
MCAID%		-0.190^{a} (0.028)	-0.177^{a} (0.027)			-0.374^{a} (0.055)
BLUE%		-0.067^{a} (0.025)	-0.005 (0.026)			-0.059 (0.053)
COM%		-0.031 (0.023)	-0.056^{b} (0.023)			-0.107^{b} (0.046)
OTHREV%		-0.002 (0.025)	-0.011 (0.025)			-0.005 (0.050)
NY			-0.036^{a} (0.008)			-0.090^{a} (0.016)
NJ			-0.016 (0.011)			-0.025 (0.022)
MA			-0.012 (0.010)			-0.034 (0.020)
MD			-0.054^{a} (0.013)			-0.076^{a} (0.025)
CT			-0.006 (0.017)			-0.024 (0.032)
WA			-0.019 (0.012)			-0.073^{a} (0.023)
NE			-0.023^{a} (0.007)			-0.030^{b} (0.014)
NC			-0.016^{b} (0.004)			-0.019^{b} (0.008)
W			-0.001 (0.005)			0.029^{a} (0.011)
CONSTANT	0.034^{a} (0.002)	0.133^{a} (0.021)	0.135^{a} (0.021)	0.073^{a} (0.004)	0.125^{a} (0.014)	0.233^{a} (0.042)
	$F_{(1,2771)}$ = 8.145	$F_{(19,2753)}$ = 10.431	$F_{(28,2744)}$ = 10.072	$F_{(1,2712)}$ = 11.364	$F_{(14,2699)}$ = 9.436	$F_{(28,2685)}$ = 12.142
	R^2 = .00	R^2 = .07	R^2 = .09	R^2 = .00	R^2 = .05	R^2 = .11

[a] = Statistically significant at 1% level (two-tail test)
[b] = Statistically significant at 5% level (two-tail test)

Table 2A.5. Long-term indebtedness regressions

Explanatory variable	Usual definition			Modified definition		
	Reg. 1	Reg. 2	Reg. 3	Reg. 1	Reg. 2	Reg. 3
BDCHAR	-0.47[a]	-0.21[b]	-0.27[b]	-0.449[a]	-0.224[b]	-0.333[a]
	(0.091)	(0.10)	(0.11)	(0.096)	(0.107)	(0.116)
BED1		-0.035	-0.029		-0.008	0.002
		(0.019)	(0.019)		(0.020)	(0.020)
BED2		0.034	0.039[b]		0.047[b]	0.055[a]
		(0.018)	(0.018)		(0.019)	(0.019)
BED3		0.040[b]	0.044[a]		0.043[b]	0.050[a]
		(0.017)	(0.017)		(0.018)	(0.018)
T1		-0.037	-0.038		-0.039	-0.036
		(0.028)	(0.028)		(0.030)	(0.030)
T2		-0.015	-0.014		0.026	0.027
		(0.016)	(0.016)		(0.032)	(0.031)
T3		-0.014	-0.002		-0.008	0.008
		(0.022)	(0.022)		(0.023)	(0.023)
PROFIT		0.053[a]	0.050[b]		0.103[a]	0.096[a]
		(0.020)	(0.021)		(0.022)	(0.022)
GOVT		-0.081[a]	-0.080[a]		-0.072[a]	-0.073[a]
		(0.011)	(0.011)		(0.011)	(0.011)
SMSA0		0.041[a]	0.042[a]		0.056[a]	0.057[a]
		(0.011)	(0.011)		(0.012)	(0.012)
SMSA1		0.046[a]	0.041[a]		0.052[a]	0.050[a]
		(0.014)	(0.014)		(0.015)	(0.015)
SMSA2		0.018	0.016		0.045[a]	0.047[a]
		(0.015)	(0.015)		(0.015)	(0.016)
CHAIN		0.003	0.005		0.017	0.017
		(0.010)	(0.010)		(0.011)	(0.011)
OTHOUT%		-0.123	-0.098		-0.193[b]	-0.098
		(0.083)	(0.091)		(0.088)	(0.096)

	(1)	(2)	(3)	(4)	(5)	(6)
MCARE%		0.066 (0.067)	0.061 (0.067)		0.0001 (0.070)	−0.011 (0.071)
MCAID%		0.017 (0.079)	0.009 (0.079)		−0.042 (0.083)	−0.050 (0.083)
BLUE%		−0.018 (0.070)	−0.051 (0.076)		−0.093 (0.074)	−0.112 (0.080)
COM%		0.086 (0.065)	0.108 (0.065)		−0.033 (0.068)	−0.024 (0.069)
OTHREV%		0.029 (0.071)	0.040 (0.071)		−0.051 (0.075)	−0.042 (0.075)
NY			−0.009 (0.023)			0.007 (0.025)
NJ			0.047 (0.032)			0.068[b] (0.034)
MA			−0.038 (0.029)			−0.047 (0.031)
MD			0.077[b] (0.037)			0.037 (0.039)
CT			−0.186[a] (0.048)			−0.187[a] (0.050)
WA			0.018 (0.033)			0.012 (0.035)
NE			0.019 (0.021)			−0.012 (0.022)
NC			−0.008 (0.012)			−0.021 (0.013)
W			−0.009 (0.016)			−0.030 (0.016)
CONSTANT	0.29[a] (0.006)	0.24[a] (0.059)	0.24[a] (0.060)	0.325[a] (0.006)	0.319[a] (0.063)	0.328[a] (0.063)
	$F_{(1,2763)}$ = 26.5	$F_{(19,2745)}$ = 14.6	$F_{(28,2736)}$ = 11.0	$F_{(1,2756)}$ = 22.08	$F_{(19,2738)}$ = 13.06	$F_{(28,2729)}$ = 9.97
	R^2 = 0.01	R^2 = 0.09	R^2 = 0.10	R^2 = .01	R^2 = .08	R^2 = .09

[a] = Statistically significant at 1% level (two-tail test)
[b] = Statistically significant at 5% level (two-tail test)

Table 2A.6. Discriminant analysis classification function coefficients

	1 Self-pay/ no charge	2 Medicaid/ other gov.	3 Private insurance	4 Workmen's compensation
Surgery[a]	2.86	2.97	3.26	3.36
Delivery[a]	6.06	5.89	5.52	5.02
Cesarean	0.34	0.52	0.86	0.75
Accident	2.20	1.36	1.39	5.12
Burn	2.95	2.05	2.01	9.98
Mental Disorder	2.74	2.80	2.12	1.00
Investor-owned	2.47	2.72	3.06	3.24
Church	3.24	3.34	3.41	3.80
Government	4.02	3.64	3.06	2.89
Northeast	4.50	5.28	4.88	4.81
North Central	2.88	3.70	3.51	3.08
West	5.02	5.27	4.91	5.21
Beds 0–99	4.16	4.50	4.31	4.38
Beds 100–299	4.26	4.58	4.50	4.52
Beds 300–499	3.11	3.42	3.42	3.36
Sing F 25[a]	2.35	3.21	1.89	2.09
White	22.80	22.11	24.23	24.29
Black	23.56	24.51	24.74	24.84
Male	1.76	1.49	1.55	3.25
Surlos[a]	0.40	0.39	−0.53	−0.82
Nsurlos[a]	1.12	1.09	1.20	1.27
Against[a]	1.64	1.83	0.75	0.16
Died	1.84	1.47	1.20	0.22
Newborn	−1.06	−1.30	1.45	−2.49
Age 0–14	3.37	4.18	3.27	1.14
Age 45–64	2.15	2.26	2.62	1.96
Surgdadm[a]	0.05	−0.30	−0.19	−0.46
Constant	−18.03	−18.36	−19.31	−21.00

[a] Key: Surgery = surgery performed, other than for delivery or cesarean; Delivery = normal delivery; Sing F 25 = single female age 25 or older; Surlos = surgery, with length of stay greater than 21 days; Nsurlos = No surgery, with length of stay greater than 21 days; Against = discharged against medical advice; Surgdadm = surgery on day of admission.

References

American Hospital Association. 1983. *Hospital Statistics: 1983 Edition.* Chicago: American Hospital Association.

Center for Health Policy Studies. 1984. *Massachusetts Payer Differential Study.* Final Report. Columbia, Md.: The Center, February 19.

Davis, Karen, and Diane Roland. 1983. "Uninsured and Underserved: Inequities in

Frank A. Sloan, Joseph Valvona, and Ross Mullner

Health Care in the United States." *Milbank Memorial Fund Quarterly* 61, no. 2 (Spring): 149–76.

Feder, Judith, Jack Hadley, and Ross Mullner. 1984. "Poor People and Poor Hospitals: Implications for Public Policy." *Journal of Health Politics, Policy, and Law* 9, no. 2 (Summer): 237–50.

Gibson, Robert M., Daniel R. Waldo, and Katherine R. Levit. 1983. "National Health Expenditures, 1982." *Health Care Financing Review* 5, no. 1 (Fall): 1–31.

Ginsburg, Paul B., and Frank A. Sloan. 1984. "Hospital Cost-Shifting." *New England Journal of Medicine* 310, no. 14 (April 5): 893–98.

Hospitals. 1982. "Hospitals Face 1,000 Closures by 1990." *Hospitals* 56, no. 7 (April 1): 23–24.

Kobrinski, Edward J., and Ann L. Matteson. 1981. "Characteristics of High-Cost Treatment in Acute Care Facilities." *Inquiry* 18, no. 2 (Summer): 179–84.

Kuntz, Esther F. 1983. "Indigent Care Hobbles Financings." *Modern Healthcare* 13, no. 3 (March): 97–98.

Mullner, Ross, Calvin S. Byre, and Joseph D. Kubal. 1983. "Hospital Closure in the United States, 1976–80: A Descriptive Overview." *Health Services Research* 18, no. 3 (Fall): 437–50.

Robert Wood Johnson Foundation. 1983. *Special Report: Updated Report on Access to Health Care for the American People.* Princeton, N.J.: The Foundation.

Sullivan, Ronald. 1984. "New York Hospitals Now Bill Poor According to What They Can Pay." *New York Times*, February 22, p. 1.

U.S. Department of Commerce. 1984. *Statistical Abstract of the United States.* Washington, D.C.: U.S. Government Printing Office.

THREE

High Technology and Uncompensated Hospital Care

James M. Perrin

9130
6211
US

54·71

Do high-technology services account for a sizeable proportion of uncompensated hospital care? If so, should uncompensated patients be treated in specific centers for their care? That is, where high technology and lack of compensation interact, should special facilities be developed? What benefits, especially in cost or efficiency, would arise? Can efficiency and effectiveness in providing high-technology medical care be maximized in this manner? Should high-technology services be provided to patients who are unable to pay and for whom no third-party insurance carrier has responsibility (i.e., "uncompensated patients")?

Several classes of uncompensated patients may be distinguished, including (1) those who do not pay deductibles or co-insurance, leaving relatively small unpaid balances after hospitalization; (2) patients without third-party coverage hospitalized for relatively routine illnesses or procedures (pregnancy, fractures, overdose); and (3) patients without coverage hospitalized for certain highly specialized, technological services (burn care, intracardiac surgery, neonatal intensive care). The first group tends to be fairly evenly distributed across all hospitals. Public hospitals provide the bulk of care to the second group, and the third group is concentrated in academic health centers.

High technology, high cost, and high uncompensated cost define distinct but overlapping groups. *High technology* refers to the application of sophisticated techniques to diagnosis, monitoring, or treatment. Such techniques are usually fairly expensive and available mainly in specialty (tertiary care) centers. *High cost* (of hospitalization) refers to episodes of hospital care that generate large expenses, whether through the use of high technology, long stays, or greater than usual use of "normal" technologies. If high costs are generated without reimbursement, they become *high uncompensated costs.* High technology and high uncompensated care interact mainly in academic health centers, with the third group of uncompensated patients identified above.

Chapter 2 documents main sources of uncompensated hospital care and whether lack of compensation arises mainly from high-technology services or from uninsured populations. The focus here is, first, on those circumstances where high technology is a major source of uncompensated care, and second, on an assessment of organizational and policy options for providing those high-technology services. Some empirical evidence is presented concerning the options. However, such evidence is very limited, and therefore this chapter includes recommendations for needed research to guide policy.

The Interface between High Technology and Uncompensated Hospital Care

Schroeder and colleagues (1979), studying high-cost illnesses in San Francisco area hospitals, found that relatively few conditions (compensated or not) are high-technology problems. Four diagnostic categories accounted for almost two-thirds of the high-cost patients in their studies: circulatory diseases, neoplasms, accidents and violence, and digestive disorders. The patients incurring the highest costs (among patients with sizeable frequency in the sample) were infants with problems of prematurity (especially with respiratory distress syndrome) and congenital illnesses. High-cost patients tended to be concentrated within referral (or tertiary) hospitals. Percentages of hospital costs due to patients with charges greater than $4,000 (1976 dollars) varied from 20 to 59 percent in nontertiary hospitals and from 59 to 68 percent in tertiary hospitals. Between 1 and 2 percent of nontertiary hospital patients had charges greater than $10,000, whereas 6 percent of all tertiary hospital patients had charges greater than that level. The two county hospitals in the sample were both about mid-range between the nontertiary and tertiary hospitals in percentage of patients with charges greater than $10,000, and particularly received a large percentage of trauma and substance abuse patients. Assault, motor vehicle accident, fall or burn victims, and alcohol and drug abuse cases accounted for 61 percent of the high-cost patients at these two hospitals. Schroeder and coauthors concluded that the typical high-cost adult patient had a chronic condition, mainly heart disease or cancer, and had been receiving treatment for some time. Adult conditions were basically long-term rather than acute. High-cost medical technologies were used by a small proportion of this sample of adult high-cost patients (less than 1% received a coronary artery bypass, less than 2% total hip replacement, and about 2% had end-stage renal disease). With more widespread diffusion of these procedures in recent years, they may now account for a somewhat larger proportion of high-cost care. For children, high-technology services played a greater role, in the treatment of premature infants and congenital anomalies. Information on source of payment and which patients were uncompensated is unavailable from Schroeder et al.

The uncompensated care experience of a large academic referral hospital in the Southeast, Vanderbilt University Hospital, is presented in Tables 3.1

Table 3.1. Distribution of unpaid bills by amount unpaid, Vanderbilt University Hospital, fiscal year 1982–83

Amount unpaid	Number of cases		Amount of uncompensated care	
$1–$999	1,656	(59%)	$ 450,743	(5%)
$1,000–$9,999	961	(34%)	3,007,146	(35%)
$10,000–$24,999	144	(5%)	2,130,305	(25%)
$25,000+	59	(2%)	3,030,499	(35%)
	2,820	(100%)	$8,618,691	(100%)

through 3.3. These tables are based on data from accounts opened and closed during 1982–83, and they therefore reflect only part of the uncompensated care for the year. Two percent of the cases had unpaid bills over $25,000 and accounted for 35 percent of uncompensated care (Tables 3.1 and 3.2). Another 5 percent of patients had unpaid bills between $10,000 and $24,999; these patients accounted for another 25 percent of the total amount of uncompensated care at Vanderbilt University Hospital (Table 3.1). At the other end of the spectrum were patients with unpaid bills of less than $1,000, who represented almost 60 percent of those patients with at least some part of the bill unpaid. These are the patients who in the main evidently did not pay their cost-sharing obligation. Such patients, while numerous, accounted for only about 5 percent of total uncompensated care at the hospital. Services to newborns accounted for about 1 percent of cases and 18 percent of uncompensated costs (Table 3.2). Review of diagnostic categories responsible for at least $50,000 of uncompensated care again highlights perinatal services to mothers and children (Table 3.3). Only four of these categories had average costs per case greater than $10,000: burns, orthopedic surgery, prematurity, and lym-

Table 3.2. Cases admitted and financially completed generating $25,000 or more in uncompensated care, Vanderbilt University Hospital, fiscal year 1982–83

Main diagnostic group for high cost case	No. of cases $25,000–$49,999	No. of cases $50,000 and above	Total cases	Total uncompensated cost
Conditions affecting the newborn				
Prematurity	13	10	23	$1,280,849
Other	2	3	5	279,771
Neoplasms (esp. lymphoma)	3	6	9	573,708
Central nervous system conditions	8	1	9	297,772
Cardiovascular diseases	5	1	6	210,568
Other	4	3	7	387,831
	35	24	59	$3,030,499

James M. Perrin

Table 3.3. Diagnostic groups admitted and financially completed generating $50,000 or more in uncompensated care, Vanderbilt University Hospital, fiscal year 1982–83

Diagnostic group	Number of cases	Total uncompensated cost	Average cost per case
Neurosurgery			
Craniotomy	48	$ 355,480	$ 7,406
Neurosurgical infection	43	155,869	3,625
Cardiopulmonary			
Chronic lung disease, pneumonia, pleurisy	49	138,665	2,830
Cardiovascular surgery	74	481,334	6,505
Gastrointestinal			
GI procedures and diseases	108	386,802	3,581
Nutritional and misc. metabolic	29	80,526	2,777
Genitourinary			
Kidney, ureter, bladder procedures	18	62,749	3,486
Renal failure, without dialysis	30	67,278	2,243
Orthopedic: hip-femur surgery	7	100,584	14,369
Skin and injuries			
Skin grafts	17	71,645	4,214
Burns	4	121,185	30,296
Other injuries	21	91,445	4,355
Lymphoma-leukemia	40	479,148	11,979
Obstetrics-gynecology			
Nonradical hysterectomy	22	61,726	2,806
Cesarean section	89	259,057	2,911
Vaginal delivery	224	343,945	1,535
Neonatal			
Prematurity	126	1,671,723	13,268
Other neonatal problems	75	712,374	9,498
Normal newborn care	174	112,916	649
Total, high-uncompensated diagnostic groups	1,198	5,754,451	4,803
Total uncompensated care	2,820	8,618,691	3,056

phoma-leukemia. The first two groups, however, include only eleven cases, accounting for only a small amount of uncompensated care. Neurosurgical conditions (especially related to trauma), cardiothoracic surgery, and gastrointestinal disease and procedures (predominantly among children) account for other large sources of uncompensated services. Some conditions, especially sick newborn care, demand sophisticated technology. The services required for other conditions are available in several area hospitals. Roughly, $4 million of uncompensated care (46%) reflected high-technology categories. Of the high-technology figure, about 60% came from sick newborns.

Data from the 1981 National Hospital Discharge Survey also highlight the problem of uncompensated newborn care. High-cost categories include mainly perinatal events, trauma, chronic illnesses (especially neoplastic), accidental injuries, psychiatric conditions, and problems of alcohol and drug abuse.

High Technology and Uncompensated Hospital Care

Hospitalizations of sick newborns, however, are twice as likely to fall into a self-pay category (18%) as are hospitalizations in general (9% excluding Medicare) (Table 3.4). Though self-pay is not equivalent to uncompensated care, these patients without coverage are most likely to generate uncompensated services.

High technology appears to account for an important proportion of the problem of uncompensated hospital care. Data from the study by Schroeder and associates emphasize both adult chronic illnesses and perinatal events as main sources of high-cost care. Data both from Vanderbilt Hospital and from the National Hospital Discharge Survey indicate even greater skewing to perinatal events and trauma as major sources of uncompensated high-cost care, after reimbursed illnesses are removed from the analysis.

The data reviewed above reflect only the hospital side of the uncompensated care problem and probably underestimate need from the perspective of consumers. Presumably many people needing services but lacking a source of private or public payment avoid hospitalization. Uncompensated hospital care accounts for only an unknown fraction of total needs for hospital services among populations with limited or no financial resources.

In sum, it appears that high technology and uncompensated care intersect mainly in neonatal intensive care. Certain malignancies, especially of blood elements, also account for sizeable amounts of uncompensated high-technology care. Victims of motor vehicle accidents may consume large amounts of medical and surgical resources, especially if they require significant blood replacement, multiple operations (especially neurosurgical), and careful and complex monitoring to maintain cardiovascular or pulmonary stability. Yet, with certain exceptions, such as severe burn injuries, many accident victims do not require access to major new technologies. Major advances here have come less from breakthroughs in medical and surgical technology than from improvements in the organization of services, especially emergency medical transport programs (Fielding and Walsh 1976).

Why should these groups contribute substantially to uncompensated hospital care? The affected age groups are least likely to have adequate third-party coverage. Injuries from motor vehicle accidents are most common among late teenage and young adult males (McFarland et al. 1968; Fielding and Walsh 1976), the age group most likely to lack public or private health insurance coverage (Kasper et al. 1980). Malignancies of blood elements, unlike many other forms of cancer, are skewed to children and young adults. Similarly, young families beginning child bearing are least likely to have adequate third-party coverage. Young adults who do have employment-related health insurance often have individual coverage only and lack family coverage for major perinatal events (Weeks 1985). Furthermore, low-birth-weight infants are much more common among younger women and in lower socioeconomic

Table 3.4. Major payment sources: sick newborn care

Health problems	No. of cases (percentage of total)			
	Blue Cross / private insurance	Medicaid	Self-pay	Total
Extreme immaturity	2,042 (54%)	693 (19%)	1,020 (27%)	3,755
Other preterm	77,126 (58%)	30,337 (23%)	24,739 (19%)	132,202
Severe asphyxia	354 (22%)	154 (10%)	1,090 (68%)	1,598
Respiratory distress syndrome	37,176 (64%)	8,957 (16%)	11,631 (20%)	57,764
Other respiratory ailments	90,064 (68%)	24,347 (18%)	18,852 (14%)	133,263
Ventricular hemorrhage	2,557 (57%)	741 (16%)	1,226 (27%)	4,524
All hospitalizations[a]	22,259,448 (77%)	4,087,329 (14%)	2,560,189 (9%)	28,906,966

Source: Unpublished data from National Hospital Discharge Survey, 1981.
[a] Excludes hospitalizations supported by Medicare.

classes, thereby increasing the high correlation between lack of adequate third-party coverage and greater risk of low birth weight.

In distinction from the policy problem of high-technology surgery, sick newborns, severe accidents, and certain cancers affect a clientele less likely to have adequate third-party coverage for services. Renal transplants, cardiovascular or coronary artery surgery, and total hip replacement, for example, are well-reimbursed procedures, for which most recipients have third-party coverage, much of it from Medicare (Table 3.5). Few of these services are provided to self-pay patients. Again, there is the likelihood that sizeable numbers of people who might benefit from these procedures have inadequate coverage and may avoid hospital care. The question of how to limit investment in high-technology services, especially where the benefit may be low (Schroeder et al. 1979; Office of Health Economics 1979) or is limited to brief prolongation of life, is a major policy problem. It takes on a new character when compounded by a high proportion of uninsured patients, such as high-risk newborns.

Newborn Care: A Model for High-Technology Uncompensated Care

With neonatal intensive care, complex and sophisticated new technologies have markedly improved the survival of very small babies, mainly through improved cardiovascular and pulmonary monitoring and treatment (Hein 1980; Budetti et al. 1981; Budetti and McManus 1982). Immature lungs can be made to function more effectively, malfunctions in cardiovascular systems can be repaired, and other physiologic homeostasis can be improved. Along with new technologies have come transportation systems to transfer high-risk infants from smaller hospitals to infant intensive care units where such new

Table 3.5. Main source of payment (percentages), selected procedures

	Medicare	Medicaid	Blue Cross	Private insurance	Self-pay
Cardiac bypass	1.8%	6.1%	34.7%	57.3%	0.0%
Simple mastectomy	41.4	3.6	23.2	26.6	3.3
Cataract surgery	72.6	4.0	9.1	10.3	1.4
Lens implant	80.4	1.0	7.5	9.3	1.0
Hip replacement	74.2	3.6	8.8	11.0	1.1
Cesarean section	0.3	13.6	30.4	42.2	9.0
Other deliveries	0.2	12.9	28.1	41.9	10.9
Coronary artery surgery	36.2	2.2	21.4	36.5	1.6
Peptic ulcer treatment	44.5	5.5	19.1	23.5	4.2
Prostatectomy	75.0	1.4	9.6	12.1	0.9
Cholecystectomy	29.5	7.1	26.0	31.6	3.4

Source: Unpublished data from National Hospital Discharge Survey, 1981.

James M. Perrin

technologies are available. As newborn intensive care is a major source of uncompensated high technology care, I here describe some elements of high-risk newborn case in greater detail.

Neonatal Intensive Care: Costs

Prematurity accounts for a large proportion of uncompensated care in a hospital like Vanderbilt; among uncompensated cases, the mean bill was $13,268 in 1982–83 (Table 3.3). Do most sick infants generate high costs, or are the high-cost ones a small proportion of total infants seen in intensive care units? Phibbs and colleagues (1981) reviewed the experience of the University of California in San Francisco during a thirty-month period in the late 1970s. Mean total cost was $8,059, with a median, however, of only $3,610. Infants with very low birth weights accounted for 18 percent of cases but more than 37 percent of costs. Only five of 1,185 children generated bills greater than $100,000, and only 10 percent of the children had bills greater than $20,000. Three factors were associated with especially high bills in this study: whether any surgical procedures were carried out, whether the birth weight was low, and whether the infant required assisted ventilation for twenty-four hours or more. Other nurseries may have a smaller percentage of their clientele hospitalized for surgical problems and thus a higher percentage of low-birth-weight infants. During the year in which 23 infants generated uncompensated bills of $25,000 or more at Vanderbilt, approximately 750 infants were admitted to the neonatal intensive care unit. In neonatal intensive care units, the very high-priced infant care case (greater than $100,000) is a relatively rare but costly phenomenon.

Neonatal Reimbursement and Coverage

Who pays the bill for these infants? For 150 infants transported to the neonatal intensive care unit at Denver Children's Hospital in early 1976, total charges generated were approximately $1.5 million. Of this amount, 85 percent was paid by third parties and approximately 11 percent of charges were written off by the hospital. An additional twenty-four accounts, however, were still pending two years after discharge, and the authors expected that the written-off amount would ultimately exceed 15 percent of total charges. The largest single category of write-offs was attributable to contractual adjustments obtained by Medicaid. That is, the 15 percent of infants on Medicaid generated charges of about $250,000, of which Medicaid reimbursed only about $150,000 (McCarthy et al. 1979).

National Hospital Discharge Survey data (1981) suggest problems of uncompensated care somewhat greater than implied by the Denver study (Table 3.4). Among infants with diagnoses of extreme immaturity or preterm birth, approximately 23 percent were covered by Medicaid, in comparison with approximately 14 percent covered by Medicaid for all hospitalizations. Furthermore, an additional approximately 19 percent of these infants were categorized as self-pay, in comparison to approximately 9 percent self-pay for all hospital discharges (excluding Medicare discharges).

Efficacy and Efficiency

What is known about the outcome of using the expensive technology of infant intensive care? Do available data support sizeable public investment in the care of sick infants? Many therapies within intensive care units have been carefully evaluated, with documentation of the benefit of numerous specific techniques (Ferrara 1977; Sinclair et al. 1981). Yet most studies enroll only children who have found their way to intensive care nurseries. The low-birth-weight infants remaining (or dying) in smaller nurseries have been less well studied. Infants not transferred to the referral center represent a different population from those who are. It may be inappropriate to generalize from the higher-risk and sicker patients in the academic health centers to all patients with a given condition receiving the same procedure (Starfield 1985). A procedure effective in a complex, high-technology center may be ineffectively and inefficiently applied throughout a larger geographic area. Documentation of the effectiveness of many interventions requires evaluation both of infants seen in referral centers and of infant mortality and morbidity across an entire region.

Most research evidence in newborn intensive care concerns physiologic improvement in lung or cardiovascular mechanisms from special support efforts. Much less is known about the relative costs of different means of implementing services. And only recently have the implications for early parent-child interaction and bonding, arising from complex modern technologies that separate infants and parents at the time of birth, been examined (Klaus and Kennell 1982). The importance of this early interaction and bonding in preventing later disorders of parenting, including child abuse, is increasingly clear. Most programs are now committed to increasing parent interactions, even with very small infants, yet some separation will be unavoidable with centralized, highly-specialized treatment units. An infant flown from Grand Junction, Colorado, to Denver will have access to the highest quality of specialized services, but it is likely that his mother will be unable to come with him or to interact with him for any considerable amount of time if he spends three months in that nursery.

Surviving infants appear to have little (and in recent years decreasing) long-term disability, although again the emphasis on intensive-care-unit survivors may skew the data. Hospital-based studies of low-birth-weight infants born in the 1960s and 1970s indicated that only about 10 percent of survivors had handicaps on follow-up (Stewart and Reynolds 1974; Sabel et al. 1976). A study with a stronger epidemiologic base and looking at eight regions of the

James M. Perrin

country indicated that closer to 40 percent of children whose birth weights were less than 1,500 grams had minimal, moderate, or severe developmental delay at one year of age (Shapiro et al. 1980). The efficiency of newborn intensive care programs has received little attention: could resources presently applied to newborn programs be better applied elsewhere, or could they be more wisely applied within newborn services? Though several studies have described costs of care, little has been done to compare different options or to examine costs under different organizational schemes. Does intensive newborn care diminish the likelihood of long-term morbidity or handicap? What are the impacts on family productivity? Claims vary from the statement that the most cost-effective policy would be to close all newborn intensive care units, thus allowing many very small infants to die rather than to survive in an impaired state, to the statement that investment at this early point in life represents one of the most effective health-care investments available. Regrettably, neither of these positions is well-supported by data at present.

Organizational and Policy Options in High-Technology Uncompensated Hospital Care

High-technology services or care for uncompensated groups could be centralized or decentralized. Services could be provided by special treatment facilities or distributed more broadly among all hospitals. Is there efficiency in concentrating no-pay patients? There has been little analysis of cost effectiveness, despite the sizeable variations in the management of no-pay patients in different sections of the country. Current social policy concentrates no-pay patients mainly in academic and public hospitals. Are there benefits to increasing or decreasing the concentration?

Specialized Treatment Centers

Some examples of specialized treatment centers now exist: the Shriners' hospitals for crippled children and for burn patients, and the highly specialized units for certain complex surgical procedures. In England, sophisticated neurosurgical procedures are performed in only one hospital in the country. "Quaternary" centers for similar highly specialized care exist in this country: the only heart-liver transplant performed so far was in Pittsburgh; certainly not all procedures will be carried out even in the many specialty or tertiary care centers of America.

The question at present lies less with these very special services (such as experimental transplants) than with more commonly performed high-technology or high-cost services (such as cardiothoracic surgery, newborn intensive care, or treatment of multiple trauma from accidents). The development of specialized treatment facilities for high-cost uncompensated care groups might call for uncompensated patients suffering from accidental injuries to be stabilized in whatever emergency room they come to, and then to be transferred to a specialized treatment center for further care. Or those (very few) patients without third-party coverage undergoing coronary bypass would have such services provided in such a center. Sick newborns lacking adequate third-party coverage would be referred to centers specializing in uncompensated high-risk newborn care. Specialized treatment centers for high-technology services would be justified on the assumption that concentrating the relatively few patients requiring such services will produce economies of scale, diminishing cost per patient and (optimally) improving quality as well. Developing treatment facilities for patients without compensation would reflect the assumption that greater efficiencies similarly can be obtained by concentrating patients based on their third-party coverage, or that greater public or political support would be available for these patients if they are concentrated within visible institutions. If there are medical or technological benefits of concentrating no-pay patients, presumably those benefits would be based on evidence that no-pay patients have needs for access to specialized technology different from the needs of patients who do have reimbursement.

There is efficiency in concentrating high-technology procedures (Bunker et al. 1982). Providers with extensive experience with a complex surgical procedure are likely to do it more quickly, with fewer side effects, and at lower per-case cost than are providers with less experience. Whether similar savings may occur through concentrating medical services, as distinguished from surgical services, is unclear. Experience with the problem of childhood chronic illness suggests that children receive better care if they have access to specialists with the most recent information about a disease and an awareness of unusual complications which a physician with less experience with the disease may not know.

Are specialized treatment centers or regionalized service programs anticompetitive? Should development of competing systems be encouraged in regions? Would separate facilities emphasizing specific health problems or attracting patients who are presently uncompensated encourage providers to enter the market? Are there incentives for capitated programs such as health maintenance organizations to provide services to high-cost patients, compensated or not?

Policies that encourage the development of a single high-technology service in a region (e.g., a burn unit) and then regulate access so that all patients meeting certain criteria make their way to the unit, appear anticompetitive. One solution for this problem might be the use of time-limited agreements supporting each treatment center, requiring them to come up for review every three to five years and thus allowing other suppliers to enter the market. This approach might increase the competitive nature of centers, but new suppliers might be unlikely to enter the field, both because of the high costs of initial investment and equipping and because of the difficulty of amortizing construction or initial investment costs with short-term contracts.

The experience of competing high-technology surgery units might be instructive. Where two or more thoracic surgery units compete for patients, as in many larger cities, are there increased efficiencies associated with the competition? Thoracic surgery, unlike newborn care, involves few uncompensated patients, whereas high percentages of no-pay patients are likely to make newborn services less attractive to providers (unless some public support is available). Should a state like Arizona support one or two or three major centers for high-technology infant intensive care? Should a smaller city in Arizona with two level II or mid-range-technology nurseries be encouraged to maintain those two with incentives built in to encourage greater efficiency in the use of resources, or would lower costs in general arise from encouraging the closing of one of those two nurseries?

In addition to specialized treatment centers there are several other options for the distribution of high-technology services to uncompensated patients. In general, they follow three forms: a public hospital model, a tertiary care model, and a random distribution model. All assume some form of public support, either through direct subsidy or through special treatment under reimbursement plans.

Public Hospital Care

In the public hospital care option, all uncompensated patients requiring high-technology services would be transferred to public facilities, except patients too unstable to move. High-risk newborns without compensation would be transported to intensive care nurseries in public facilities. Public hospitals would increase their capacities in other areas of care likely to be uncompensated, such as accidental injuries, as well as continue the large number of low-technology services presently provided for patients without compensation, such as routine deliveries and general surgery.

This option would support the traditional mission of public hospitals and increase their capacity to provide technological services. Concentration of uncompensated patients might increase public awareness of the needs of these patients and would diminish the problem of uncompensated hospital care for other hospitals. Insofar as public hospitals generally offer fewer amenities than do hospitals in the private or not-for-profit sectors, the costs of services might be lower than in other hospitals. (On the other hand, increased unionization in public hospitals might diminish the cost savings. Nevertheless, a recent study by Becker and Sloan [forthcoming] that compared hospital costs by ownership type found that public hospitals may be less costly than other community hospitals and certainly no more costly.)

The disadvantages of this model might include a lack of sufficient political support to allow adequate funding of public facilities. Public hospitals have been chronically underfunded; adding complex and expensive new technologies to their current responsibilities might only exacerbate the problem without improving political support. Furthermore, there remains the question of whether expensive, capital-intensive high-technology services should be duplicated in a given region. Should a community have two high-technology newborn intensive care services, one for compensated patients and one for uncompensated patients? Or will greater efficiency be achieved by integrating the two services and providing some public support for uncompensated patients in the unified service?

Academic Tertiary Care

The second option calls for the concentration of uncompensated high-technology patients within tertiary care centers, especially teaching hospitals. Arguments for this option include the recognition that academic health centers are already major repositories of high-technology care and the development of new technologies. Furthermore, they serve a main role in teaching new professionals. If high-cost uncompensated patients aid the teaching function, their concentration in that sector would fit well with the teaching mission of the academic health centers.

Arguments against this option include the incentives for shifting unpaid charges to patients with insurance (and their insurers) to support uncompensated high-cost patients. This shift would lead to increased rates for compensated patients, whether or not they are high-technology patients. The routine gallbladder surgery becomes more expensive in this site than in other hospitals providing less high-technology uncompensated care. The consolidation of obstetric and newborn services in many communities over the past decade has followed this trend. Those hospitals which have retained these services are predominantly in the academic and public sectors.

Insofar as lack of compensation seems to select out only certain forms of high-technology care (especially care for newborns and accident victims), policies to concentrate uncompensated high-cost patients in academic centers may leave these centers without important high technologies (for example, those for cardiovascular or major orthopedic procedures) also necessary for the teaching mission. Teaching hospitals specializing in high-technology patients face the further problem of disjunction between educational goals and research agendas. Research faculty may be nurtured by the exotic, but trainees need less emphasis on rare high-technology patients and more on the common problems of medicine and surgery. If the institution of high-technology, specialized-treatment programs in academic centers makes it more likely that patients will go elsewhere for gallbladder surgery, trainees will lack important areas of experience.

Random Distribution of Patients

The third option presumes that there are no clear benefits of concentrating high-technology uncompensated patients. They would be absorbed in the operating costs of all participants in the hospital sector. Regulatory or financial disincentives would be imposed to discourage transfer of patients solely on the basis of their source of third-party coverage (or its absence). Transfer decisions would be based entirely on availability and need of specific technologies. This option would allow uncompensated high-technology care to be carried out in either public or private sectors.

Arguments for this option include the lack of evidence that concentrating uncompensated high-cost patients provides any medical or other health outcome benefit to patients. Where technology exists, access to it should be based more on clinical need than on some measure of ability to pay. Arguments against this option include its unenforceability and its strong incentives for hospitals to withdraw from providing technologies having a high likelihood of uncompensated patients.

Future Directions

Choices among the options outlined above will be better made when information about a number of important research questions is available. Policy choices should be made with the recognition that the overlap between uncompensated hospital care and high technology occurs mainly in a few select areas, and that most recipients of high-technology services apparently have adequate third-party coverage. Research in several areas will improve the basis on which decisions are made.

Efficiency

Is investment in high technology an efficient use of limited resources? Would resources be better spent in developing preventive programs, to limit the need for coronary artery bypass or to diminish prematurity and the need for newborn intensive care units? Greater investment in preventive technologies rather than halfway technologies which palliate may bring much greater benefit. What other efficiencies could decrease the cost of high-technology services, for example, by replacing services in high-cost centers with others from less expensive providers? Policy could direct that the high costs faced by newborn intensive care units be allocated back to hospitals where the children were born. Yet this allocation would only redistribute the uncompensated costs without introducing real efficiencies into the system. A more fundamental question is whether infants themselves can be returned to smaller hospitals with lower costs but no loss in quality of care.

Is there a difference in the efficient use of public and private funds? A traditional view of public health argues that public funds be applied mainly to preventive rather than to curative or treatment services. In other words, whether high-technology services should be available to uncompensated patients remains a political question. Although some may question public responsibility for certain services to adults, it seems difficult to deny sick newborns access to needed treatment services because they lack third-party coverage.

Programs for high-risk newborns have achieved a moderate amount of specific public support (both federal and state) in the past decade. Such support reflects a public commitment to provide for infants who need these technological services, regardless of ability to pay. Are there similar ethical or public mandates for other uncompensated groups? Are accident victims less deserving, perhaps because a large number of accidents reflect self-injurious behavior, either directly or through substance abuse? Resolution of such issues of public responsibility and the efficient use of public resources remains a problem for social policy. Their resolution would aid in defining the responsibilities of various components of the hospital sector for uncompensated care.

Quality of Care

Evidence provided above supports the conclusion that resource-intensive surgical and medical procedures have better outcomes in specialized treatment centers. Three main areas in quality need further research attention as they affect high-technology care. First, at what point can new technologies be safely and appropriately disseminated outside the major specialized centers? How does a new intracardiac surgical procedure develop? When is it understood adequately enough to be used by thoracic surgeons in smaller community hospitals, and when should it remain limited to specialized centers? The dissemination of liver transplants in the next few years will probably raise these questions.

Second, what new technologies are likely to have greater or less benefit? Which technologies, despite demonstration of clinical efficacy, have little real benefit for patients, especially in the context of their very high cost? Recent controversies about coronary artery bypass, not an area where lack of compensation has been a serious issue, reflect this question. Further understanding of the clinical applicability of bypass surgery has suggested that the procedure is effective for far fewer people than originally projected. Much study of new technology is with small population samples, and there is great potential of distributing new technologies long before identifying the people who will most benefit from them.

Third, partly because of narrow definitions of outcomes in most studies of new technologies, more is known about the physiologic improvement engendered by a new procedure than about the financial, social, and family impact of the procedure. Efficacy studies need broader outcome measures.

Competition

Will the introduction of competitive forces diminish costs in the area of high-technology uncompensated care? Direct competition could come from the development of two similar, but competing high-technology units in the same community, both bidding for the opportunity to provide care to patients who are presently uncompensated (assuming public support is provided for these patients). Or would duplication of resources, many of which are very capital-intensive, increase total costs within the community? Less direct competition could be obtained through a franchise mechanism, by which providers bid for the opportunity to provide services to uncompensated clients for a set period of time in a given community.

Future Technologies and Compensation

Newer technologies may bring policy problems different from current issues of whether and how uncompensated patients should obtain access to high-technology services. Some new technologies are highly capital-intensive—for example, the implant of artificial organs. Until recently, the initial experimentation with these technologies was supported almost entirely with public funds, mainly through the National Institutes of Health. Corporate investment began once the initial testing and development were completed. Private funds to support further refinement and production were spurred on when the related technological procedures achieved third-party coverage. Recently, private investment, having more access to capital than does the federal research establishment, has begun support of such high-cost technologies as the development of the artificial heart. This investment, although involving a certain amount of risk, assures that sufficient external funding (private or public) will support the use of the artificial heart after the initial experimentation phase.

This changing pattern of investment raises certain policy questions. What are public and private responsibilities for the support of expensive new technologies, both in their development and in payment for direct services to patients? How should decisions be made on which technologies to support? Should there be technology-moderating bureaucracies, or can it be assumed that the trend away from fee-for-service payment to varied forms of prepaid care will moderate technology in satisfactory ways? The National Center for Health Care Technology, instituted mainly to make judgments about which technologies to support through public third-party funds, had a very brief history in the late 1970s. The Congressional Office of Technology Assessment carries out a few limited studies of health care technologies.

What rationing of high-cost technologies should occur? In reviewing the British experience, Aaron and Schwartz (1984) note that capital-intensive technologies are much more likely to be rationed than are other high-cost procedures. For example, there has been great restraint on the dissemination of

CT scanning and renal transplant technology, both mainly dependent on the investment decisions of program administrators. Renal dialysis, however, is widely distributed, with the prescription of the multiple devices and treatments mainly dependent on the recommendations of the patient's physician. Aaron and Schwartz contend that most rationing will focus on capital-intensive technologies, and they predict that the capital costs involved in some new technologies will be of far greater magnitude than most current technologies.

Summary

Much uncompensated hospital care does not involve high-technology services. Nevertheless, a sizeable proportion does arise from the intensive care of sick and premature newborns, accident victims, and people suffering from certain malignancies. In one private academic teaching hospital, newborn care accounts for almost 25 percent of uncompensated care. Without development of a reliable source of compensation, these patients will continue to generate large amounts of high-technology uncompensated care. Furthermore, there are increasing numbers of high-technology procedures (liver transplants, artificial organ implants) which, at least initially, will be uncompensated. Payment for these high-technology services could come from several sources, including direct public subsidy (through grants or public insurance), public transfer of funds through taxation of premiums for hospital insurance, direct charitable donations, or investment from the private sector (with the expectation of eventual third-party coverage or other economic benefit).

Given the amount of uncompensated hospital care arising from high-technology services, policy questions include the definition of responsibilities to support current care and to restrict or assure access to current technologies. How to support the development of capital-intensive new technologies and whether and how to ration very expensive new procedures are additional policy problems.

References

Aaron, Henry J., and William B. Schwartz. 1984. *The Painful Prescription: Rationing Hospital Care,* Washington, D.C.: The Brookings Institution.

Becker, Edmund R., and Frank A. Sloan. Forthcoming. "Hospital Organization and Performance." *Economic Inquiry.*

Budetti, Peter B., and P. McManus. 1982. "Assessing the Effectiveness of Neonatal Intensive Care." *Medical Care* 20, no. 10 (October): 1027–39.

Budetti, Peter B., N. Barrand, P. McManus, and L. A. Heinen. 1981. *The Costs and Effectiveness of Neonatal Intensive Care.* Office of Technology Assessment, Background Paper no. 2, Case Study no. 10. Washington, D.C.: U.S. Government Printing Office, August.

Bunker, John P., H. S. Luft, and A. Enthoven. 1982. "Should Surgery be Regionalized?" *Surgical Clinics of North America* 62, no. 4 (August): 657–68.

Ferrara, Angelo. 1977. "Evaluation of Efficacy of Regional Perinatal Programs." *Seminars in Perinatology* 1, no. 3 (July): 303–8.

Fielding, Jonathan E., and Diane C. Walsh. 1976. "Comprehensive Health Care and Motor Vehicle Safety." *New England Journal of Medicine* 294, no. 15 (April): 841–43.

Hein, Herman A. 1980. "Evaluation of a Rural Perinatal Care System." *Pediatrics* 66, no. 3 (September): 540–46.

Kasper, Judith A., Daniel C. Walden, and Gail R. Wilensky. 1980. *Who Are the Uninsured?* National Health Care Expenditures Study, Data Preview 1. Hyattsville, Md.: U.S. Department of Health and Human Services.

Klaus, Marshall, and J. Kennell. 1982. "Interventions in the Premature Nursery: Impact on Development." *Pediatric Clinics of North America* 29, no. 5 (October): 1263–73.

McCarthy, John T., B. L. Koops, P. R. Honeyfield, and L. J. Butterfield. 1979. "Who Pays the Bill for Neonatal Intensive Care?" *Journal of Pediatrics* 95, no. 3 (September): 755–61.

McFarland, Ross A., G. A. Ryan, and R. Dingham. 1968. "Etiology of Motor-Vehicle Accidents, with Special Reference to the Mechanisms of Injury." *New England Journal of Medicine* 278, no. 25 (June): 1383–88.

Office of Health Economics. 1979. "Scarce Resources in Health Care." *Milbank Memorial Fund Quarterly* 57, no. 2 (Spring): 265–87.

Phibbs, Charles S., R. L. Williams, and R. H. Phibbs. 1981. "Newborn Risk Factors and Costs of Neonatal Intensive Care." *Pediatrics* 68, no. 3 (September): 313–21.

Sabel, K.-G., R. Olegard, and L. Victorin. 1976. "Remaining Sequelae with Modern Perinatal Care." *Pediatrics* 57, no. 5 (May): 652–58.

Schroeder, Steven A., J. A. Showstack, and M. E. Roberts. 1979. "Frequency and Clinical Description of High-Cost Patients in Seventeen Acute Care Hospitals." *New England Journal of Medicine* 300, no. 23 (June): 1306–9.

Shapiro, Samuel, M. C. McCormick, B. H. Starfield, J. P. Krischer, and D. Bross. 1980. "Relevance of Correlates of Infant Deaths for Significant Morbidity at One Year of Age." *American Journal of Obstetrics and Gynecology* 136, no. 3 (February): 363–73.

Sinclair, John C., G. W. Torrance, M. H. Boyle, S. P. Horwood, S. Saigal, and D. L. Sackett. 1981. "Evaluation of Neonatal Intensive-Care Programs." *New England Journal of Medicine* 305, no. 9 (August): 489–94.

Starfield, Barbara. 1985. "The State of Research on Chronically Ill Children." In *Issues in Childhood Chronic Illness*. Ed. N. Hobbs and J. Perrin. San Francisco, Calif.: Jossey-Bass.

Stewart, Ann L., and E.O.R. Reynolds. 1974. "Improved Prognosis for Infants of Very Low Birthweight." *Pediatrics* 54, no. 6 (December): 724–35.

Weeks, Karen. 1985. "Private Health Insurance and the Chronically Ill Child." In *Issues in Childhood Chronic Illness*. Ed. N. Hobbs and J. Perrin. San Francisco, Calif.: Jossey-Bass.

FOUR

Designing Hospital Care Subsidies for the Poor

Peter H. Schuck

A merican society decided some time ago that it believed that health care was a special kind of good, one that should be allocated according to "need" rather than ability to pay. That distributional principle, of course, has never been fully implemented, even in the realm of basic hospital care, as Myers points out in Chapter 7. Nevertheless, the idea that access to a minimum level of health care, like the right to attend public elementary and secondary school, is an irreducible entitlement of all individuals remains a fundamental, durable commitment of the modern welfare state. Although the more general policy of transfers to the poor has recently come under serious attack (Murray 1984), even the Reagan Administration, while often disputing which individuals are actually in need, has publicly endorsed this goal. The uncompensated care requirement under the Hill-Burton Act is one important manifestation of it, as Blumstein points out in Chapter 5.

The commitment to a basic level of publicly financed health care for the poor, especially in acute care hospitals where life and physical well-being are often directly at stake, rests upon a number of grounds; some justifications, avowedly moral in nature, include belief in the value of promoting individual dignity, nourishing feelings of self-worth, strengthening the human linkages between society's members, and encouraging equal participation in community life. These equitable notions, although abstract (and difficult to put into operation), probably explain most of the widespread public support for treating hospital care for the poor as a nonmarket good.

However, most public discussion of health care subsidies currently revolves around concerns about cost and inefficiency. The persistent questions are, How much equity in hospital care can society afford? How can more equity for a given level of public subsidy be achieved? In short, how can one design subsidies to accomplish society's distributional goals most efficiently? In attempting to address these questions, this chapter will draw to some extent upon the language and conceptual apparatus of economics. In the end, however, considerations of efficiency must serve society's equitable intuitions and purposes concerning health care. Efficiency can never be a complete justification for health policy.

To the economic mind, there are several reasons for subsidizing hospital care for the poor, most of which also apply to health care generally. First, our society clearly regards hospital care as a merit good in the economic sense—that is, one whose consumption increases the welfare not only of the consumer but of other individuals as well. Most of us believe that we benefit when those who cannot afford adequate hospital care can nonetheless receive it.

Second, hospital care has certain spillover effects upon persons other than the immediate providers and consumers. Many of the costs of illness are externalized to society in the form of increased insurance premiums, lost productivity, emotional effects upon family and friends, and the like. Thus, we subsidize hospital care for the poor at least in part because we anticipate that it will reduce the accompanying social costs of illness. This externality rationale, of course, does not necessarily imply that increased hospital care is the best way to reduce these social costs. It might suggest quite different policies, such as taxing or regulating conduct associated with ill health.

Third, some forms of hospital and nonhospital care are also public goods. A public good is one whose consumption by one person does not make it less available to others. A rational individual, especially a poor one, would not voluntarily pay for or endure quarantine, immunization, or pollution control, for example; he or she would prefer to "ride free" on the contributions of others while enjoying all the benefits. The market will systematically underprice such goods, and they therefore must be publicly provided or mandated if they are to be adequately supplied. In any case, coercing or subsidizing consumption may be necessary to serve both individual and social goals (Zeckhauser and Schaefer 1968).

Fourth, certain local hospitals and other providers may possess locational, staffing, or regulatory advantages enabling them to charge monopolistic prices. Such pricing is especially disadvantageous to the poor. If government allows that market power to resist or flourish—for example, through weak antitrust enforcement or regulatory constraints on competition—subsidies to the poor may be the only way to assure that they can afford adequate levels of care.

Fifth, the poor, being more prone to illness and occupational accidents, are unusually vulnerable to adverse selection and moral hazard problems. They may also have greater incentives to conceal their true preferences and need for hospital care and insurance because they fear that revealing them might reduce their employment opportunities. For these reasons, they may find it difficult to purchase insurance at reasonable cost (or at all) even if their precarious financial positions were not an independent obstacle to adequate insurance.

If the economic efficiency reasons for subsidizing hospital care for the poor are generally rather clear, the design specifications for such subsidies remain quite controversial. Even before turning to these more difficult design questions, however, it is important to note that the basic notion of a subsidy involves some basic conceptual and definitional problems. Two issues are particularly difficult to resolve.

The first relates to the background assumptions concerning the conditions and constraints under which individual consumers exercise choice. If subsidized hospital care is defined as a public expenditure designed to encourage consumers to purchase more hospital care than they would otherwise purchase, a difficult question is immediately raised: What do we mean by "otherwise"? The baseline might be defined in terms of quality and other attributes of hospital care that the consumer would purchase if certain "true" preference-revealing conditions—for example, optimal information, competition among suppliers, and low transaction costs—prevailed. Alternatively, it might be defined in terms of what consumers would purchase, absent the subsidy, under the conditions of choice that presently exist in the real world. Other baseline criteria falling somewhere in between these two, such as those that assume improved (but suboptimal) consumer information or altered incentives, can readily be imagined. The problem, of course, is that each of these baseline concepts is both plausible and in some sense arbitrary. It is not obvious which of them—and thus, which definition of subsidy—should be preferred.

In thinking about the idea of subsidy, a second set of problematic background assumptions—those involving the tax system—are also crucial. In addition to direct public expenditures, the tax system can be used to confer subsidies upon providers and consumers of health care. The deductibility of employer-paid health insurance premiums, of course, is a striking example.[1] Yet to speak of tax subsidies is to beg some rather fundamental questions about the boundaries of private property rights. Construed broadly enough, the notions of "tax expenditure" and "tax loophole" imply that private property is at the disposal of the government and that the government's failure to tax therefore constitutes a subsidy of the untaxed activity. This implication may make perfectly good sense as applied to certain tax provisions (including the example just mentioned), but it has alarming implications for the concept of private property if extended too far. The difficulty, of course, is to identify the point at which the failure to tax an activity can usefully be called a subsidy of that activity. Neither economic nor political theory provides a clear answer to this question.

Even if one sets these nettlesome definitional problems to one side, the question of how hospital care subsidies for the poor should be designed involves a complex set of choices that must be resolved within a difficult set of political, economic, administrative, and moral constraints. The following five sections will clarify some of these choices and constraints. The first is an analysis of the various forms that subsidies of hospital care might take. Second is a discussion of the appropriate level of government for financing and administering such subsidies. The third is an examination of the advantages and disadvantages of explicitness in the creation of subsidies. The fourth is an analysis of some of the considerations relevant to the choice between subsidization of hospital care through entitlements or through closed-ended programs. The fifth section is a discussion of the question of the appropriate scope and level of hospital care subsidies. The chapter concludes by raising a number of issues relevant to the rational design of a hospital care subsidy program that can meet not only society's redistributional goals but cost control objectives as well.

Different Forms of Hospital Care Subsidy

The linkage between the hospital and nonhospital sectors of organized health care is especially important in analyzing the role of subsidy. If, for example, inpatient hospital care and nonhospital ambulatory care are (or might be made) close substitutes, a subsidy policy directed at one is likely to affect the other significantly. Many reform efforts, including the redesign of insurance benefit packages and alteration of provider reimbursement schemes, have sought to exploit precisely this substitution effect. Efficiency gains to the health care system as a whole may be possible from changes that may seem undesirable when viewed from the narrower perspectives of the hospital or of the hospital patient. This possibility, of course, lies at the heart of the so-called competition and health maintenance organization (HMO) enhancement policies.

A subsidy of hospital care can, of course, assume many different forms, of which uncompensated care is only one. An important variable relates to the purposes for which the consumer may properly use the subsidy.

Cash Payments

First, consumers could be given cash payments that they are free to spend on hospital care or other goods, as they see fit. A cash benefit under an income support program like Aid to Families with Dependent Children, for example, maximizes consumer choice, increasing the likelihood that consumption patterns will accurately reflect "true" consumer preferences for hospital care versus other goods, and thus increase economic efficiency.

Tax Deductions

Allowing consumers to deduct the cost of their hospital care expenditures from income for tax purposes is a second form of subsidy. This type possesses several politically attractive features: It need only be voted upon once. It will not appear as a discrete spending item on the government's annual budget. And although it affects the politically unorganized poor (unlike a tax credit), it is actually worth more to those in higher tax brackets. But because the deduction can be taken only for certain health-related expenditures, it somewhat distorts consumer preferences—a source of some inefficiency. Moreover, because it is enjoyed most by those who need it least, this form of subsidy is decidedly "target-inefficient."

Vouchers

Society, however, may believe that consumers are poorly informed or that even subsidized consumers, if left to their own preferences, would not spend "enough" on hospital care relative to other, less "deserving" activities. Society may choose, then, a third form of subsidy in which consumers are given cash equivalents, such as vouchers, that may be spent only upon hospital care (or hospital insurance). Because such near-cash forms somewhat restrict consumer choice, however, this approach risks serious inefficiencies at the individual consumer level and perhaps at the social level as well.

Each of these forms of subsidy—the direct cash grants, tax deductibility, and the near-cash voucher—may seem unsatisfactory in some respects. First, each relies upon consumer purchases in a relatively unconstrained market for hospital care. As applied to groups such as the poor and the elderly that are at relatively high risk of costly illness, however, these arrangements may encounter problems of adverse selection; HMOs, preferred provider organizations (PPOs), and insurance carriers may refuse to accept those risks except at rates that will tend to drive out lower-risk groups, thereby causing rates to rise still further. This could defeat society's distributional objectives or lead to unacceptable self-insurance, which in turn could lead to new externality effects and other inefficiencies. Second, government may wish not merely to expand the market for hospital care but to constrain choice in the hope of influencing provider and consumer behavior in the interests of higher quality, cost control, and other social goals.

In-Kind Benefits

For these reasons and others (some, of a more political nature), society may prefer a fourth form of hospital care subsidy: packages of legally defined in-kind programmatic benefits to which consumers are either entitled or which they enjoy with more limited access. Since the 1960s, this has been the preferred form for subsidizing the poor (Medicaid, community health centers), the elderly (Medicare), and certain other favored groups such as veterans and Indians. The major criticism of this approach has been its growing cost, which reflects a combination of factors: general inflation in price levels, an increased number of eligibles (due to changing economic conditions, new eligibility standards, or both), increased intensity of services per patient, increased cost per unit of service, and increased administrative costs. Presumably most of these cost increases are independent of the particular form that the subsidy takes; it is unclear, therefore, what portion of them is attributable solely to programmatic inefficiencies and administrative burdens. In addition to these cost concerns, a subsidy in the form of an in-kind benefit package usually restricts consumers' freedom of choice by limiting them to participating providers and facilities, to services covered by the program, and to the particular government-prescribed terms and conditions under which benefits are made available. It can also restrict providers and distort their incentives in undesirable ways, as well as impose significant costs in the form of paperwork, administrative burdens, and delay in obtaining reimbursements and dealing with government auditing, inspection, and other activities.

Mandated Provision: Uncompensated Care Requirement

An uncompensated care requirement for hospitals is a fifth form of subsidy. In addition to the uncompensated care mandated by the 1979 U.S. Department of Health, Education, and Welfare regulations for Hill-Burton described by Blumstein in Chapter 5, uncompensated hospital care may also be required under common law theories of charitable obligation on the part of hospitals that enjoy tax-exempt status or that publicize their emergency room service, or *de facto* by hospitals that receive inadequate reimbursement for services to the poor provided under Medicaid. An uncompensated care requirement entails a distinctive set of advantages and disadvantages. As with direct grants, tax deductibility, and vouchers, the relationship between provider and patient is a direct one essentially unmediated by the government; thus, the value of autonomy is protected.

This kind of subsidy is inefficient and inequitable in important respects, however. If free hospital care is available but free ambulatory care is not, for example, the patient will tend to use the former even if the latter would be superior and less costly. Moreover, a patient's freedom of choice of providers— indeed, his or her very access to free hospital care—is far more random and unpredictable than with most of the other forms of subsidy; both choice and access depend upon whether, to what extent, and when particular providers offer uncompensated care. Not all hospitals are required to provide it, and those that are required to do so offer only a limited volume. If a particular patient is fortunate enough to qualify and to claim service before that limit is reached, the patient will receive the care he or she seeks. If the hospital does not offer such care or if its limit has already been reached, however, the patient must look elsewhere for care.

The efficiency of this kind of subsidy may also be reduced by the way in which the provider administers it. If the hospital is obligated to render a certain volume of uncompensated care, it may (apart from consideration of potential malpractice liability) be largely indifferent to whether that care is truly needed by and rendered efficiently to eligible low-income consumers, at least until it has provided enough uncompensated care to have fulfilled its fixed obligation. Indeed, it may be tempted to discharge its uncompensated care obligation as quickly as it can, even if done wastefully. Similarly, a hospital has no economic incentive to concern itself about whether uncompensated care is being rendered to the poorest or medically neediest of the eligibles, so long as the care that it does render reduces its obligation. Under those circumstances, patterns of subsidized services are likely to be determined less by need than by such fortuitous factors as the insurance coverage of those who happen to seek care, the cost-sharing for particular services, and the hospital's debt collection practices.

Like the tax deductibility of hospital expenditures, an uncompensated care obligation imposed on private hospitals possesses a powerful attraction for the government that mandates it: its cost does not appear on the government's budget. Indeed, the budgetary advantage is even greater in the case of an uncompensated care obligation; whereas tax deductibility diminishes government revenues, an uncompensated care obligation leaves both the revenue side *and* the expenditure side unaffected. This singular political virtue, however, encourages an important social inefficiency. Because the government bears none of the costs of providing uncompensated care but externalizes them all to private-sector providers, it may have an incentive to mandate more uncompensated care than is socially optimal. Relieved of the necessity to balance expenditures on uncompensated care against the costs and benefits of other social goods, government may require too much of it relative to the alternative uses to which the same resources could be put. Especially in times of budgetary stringency, the temptation to achieve important social objectives such as subsidization of hospital care for the poor through mandated private expenditures rather than by raising taxes may prove nearly irresistible.

A rational health care system that wished to maximize economic efficiency, freedom of choice, and horizontal equity in the allocation of hospital resources would not seek to subsidize low-income consumers through the system of uncompensated care that current law requires or through hospitals' random absorption of bad debts by poor patients. But given the reality of provider domination of most health care markets, even the more desirable methods of subsidy would still have to be augmented by a combination of decentralized incentives and central controls capable of achieving adequate levels of quality assurance, consumer information, and provider competition.

The Level of Government

The optimal design of a program to subsidize hospital care for the poor must be concerned not only with the particular form that the subsidy takes, but also with the level of government responsible for financing and administering the subsidy. At present, all levels of government subsidize hospital care to some degree. Many local governments, for example, support public hospitals that provide free care to indigents. States operate Medicaid programs for the poor and, in some cases, for the medically needy as well. The federal government finances hospital care under Medicaid and Medicare and directly provides care to certain categories of the poor, such as veterans and Indians. Public health programs are also operated at all three levels.

There are several strong arguments in favor of organizing the subsidization of hospital care for the poor primarily at the federal level. First, some scale economies are likely to be realized by a single federal administration as compared to fifty separate state subsidy programs. The relatively low administrative costs of the Social Security Administration, for example, suggest that enormous public bureaucracies are not inevitably inefficient, at least with respect to certain kinds of administrative tasks.[2] Second, the federal government is a superior mechanism for collecting and redistributing income to the poor. For a variety of historical, constitutional, political, and economic reasons, its powers to tax and borrow are far broader than those of the states and localities. Its power to spend also vastly exceeds that of the other levels, which are often legally prohibited from operating at a deficit.

Third, interstate mobility of individuals and firms and the zero-sum competition between states (and also between localities) for low tax rates with which to attract business create certain perverse effects upon state-level efforts to subsidize the poor. States face powerful incentives to keep their subsidies and tax rates low, thereby exporting their poor to high-subsidy states and attracting business away from those states. In a dynamic process similar to adverse selection in insurance, the ensuing interstate migration would compel high-subsidy states to raise taxes still further in order to fund the subsidies for the newly arrived poor; this pattern reinforces the dynamic. The high-subsidy states would eventually be obliged to reduce their subsidies in order to recover their tax bases. Subsidies to the poor would be pawns in this inherently unstable interstate competition. The point is not that interstate variations in tax levels or governmental benefits are necessarily undesirable, but that state-level subsidies are likely to be ineffective ways to subsidize hospital care for the poor.

It is arguable, moreover, that whatever the status or acceptability of interstate variations with respect to other goods, significant differences in the minimum levels of hospital care available to poor people, depending upon the states in which they happen to live, would not merely undercut the effectiveness of state-level subsidies but would be socially or morally objectionable. That principle of uniformity, or something very much like it, seems to underlie Medicare, the Occupational Safety and Health Act, and many environmental programs in which national standards not subject to local variation are mandated. Even Medicaid, in which numerous state-by-state variations are permitted and in which coverage does not extend to all poor, prescribes some mandatory minimum benefits for those who are covered. These examples suggest that, at least within certain limits, American society demands nationally uniform minima with respect to health care for the poor, a goal that can be achieved and sustained only through federal-level subsidies.

If one focuses on the externality justification for subsidy, the argument in favor of financing it at the federal level still applies, though somewhat more narrowly. Some public health programs, such as the regulation of air pollution and the prevention of communicable diseases, are directed at risks that transcend local or state boundaries. If such spillover effects are to be effectively controlled, federal intervention is required. But most health care programs, notably those that subsidize hospital care, neither impose costs nor confer benefits across state lines to any significant degree (except when the facility is located near the border). For such programs, a pure externality justification for federal subsidy is relatively weak.

Finally, there are important advantages in administering a hospital-care subsidy program at the same level of government that finances and operates other health programs. The different financing, benefits, eligibility standards, and service patterns of certain programs that may serve the same population (for example, Medicare, Medicaid, community health centers, Veterans Administration, uncompensated care, and Social Security disability) draw upon the resources of all levels of government. The difficult coordination problems that often result may be best addressed at the federal level. Moreover, because these programs are financed in whole or in large part by the federal government, it can, at least in principle, use its enormous purchasing and regulatory power to exert leverage over providers, imposing a discipline upon program costs that has been notably lacking in the past. In a society as complex and geographically far-flung as ours, of course, state or local administration may have some advantages. For example, it may encourage greater responsiveness to diverse local values and conditions, facilitate more effective implementation of services, reduce administrative burdens, and increase public participation and program flexibility. That at least is part of the promise of federalism. But centralized financing presents the alluring possibility of countervailing market power on behalf of taxpayers and consumers, a prospect that probably outweighs these inefficiencies. Thus, an efficient and equitable program to subsidize hospital care for the poor probably requires federal financing. If so, it probably requires some considerable degree of federal administration as well.

Explicit versus Concealed Subsidies

Once a decision has been made to subsidize hospital care, a choice must be made as to how explicit the subsidy ought to be. This choice may have profound economic, moral, and political implications. To the economist, the case for explicit subsidies is straightforward and compelling. At the most basic

Peter H. Schuck

level, rational social choice (if there be such a thing) requires that society decide how it wishes to allocate socially controlled resources in light of its collective purposes. Rationality, after all, demands constant attention to both means and ends and to the relationship between them. To the extent that a society conceals from itself both what it wishes to do and what in fact it does, it relinquishes policy control and increases the risk of botching the job.

Implicit subsidies, almost by definition, elude careful scrutiny of the policy choices underlying them. Indeed, they are often kept implicit for precisely that reason. When subsidies are concealed in other forms, such as regulations mandating that lower levels of government or private individuals or entities take certain actions, they are likely to be poorly targeted; often, they will end up conferring advantages on some persons or activities that the designer of the subsidy did not intend to benefit. The uncompensated care requirement under Hill-Burton is an example. Who, for example, will bear the costs of complying with regulations requiring certain federally assisted hospitals to provide un-compensated care to the poor? The hospital's donors? Its employees? Its uninsured patients? Blue Cross subscribers in the community? Those ill persons turned away as a result? Overcrowded municipal hospitals? (Schuck 1981.) One can ask the same questions, of course, about the distribution of the subsidy's benefits. Thus, although Hill-Burton's uncompensated care require-ment was designed to benefit the poor, and although it seems safe to assume that most beneficiaries of uncompensated care are poor people, it is not clear whether they are the poorest or medically neediest of the poor.

Explicit lump sum transfers, although not eliminating the ubiquitous prob-lem of unanticipated consequences, are likely to be more target-efficient. To the extent that the Bell System's telephone rate structure was designed and maintained in order to subsidize local service, for example, that subsidy was enjoyed by many relatively well-off individuals and households who did not, under prevailing notions of equity, deserve it. From an efficiency point of view, it would have been better to design the rate structure so that all classes of service covered their costs; a refined, explicit subsidy targeted upon only those low-income users who could not afford essential local service—analogous to so-called lifeline residential utility subsidies—would then be an appropriate way to achieve whatever equity goals society wishes to pursue.

Concealed subsidies are likewise objectionable from a moralist's point of view. They represent a kind of dishonesty, an effort to disguise society's values and moral choices. Those whose resources are being taken and used to finance the subsidy—long distance users, in the Bell System example—have special cause to complain. In essence, they are being taxed without the legal and institutional forms of explicit taxation having been observed. The benefici-aries of a concealed subsidy may also be unfairly treated if, by reason of its low visibility, they do not know of its availability and how it may be claimed.

To the politician bent upon conferring a subsidy, however, the appropriate degree of explicitness is a far more complex question. The answer will depend upon the particular situation. On the one hand, the politician wishes a subsidy to be explicit enough that those who will benefit from it will be able both to recognize that a benefit has been conferred and to identify the politician as their benefactor. At the same time, the politician wishes to avoid making the subsidy so explicit that those who will bear the costs will be alerted to its existence and therefore oppose it. The desired level of explicitness, then, will reflect some balance between the politician's desire to take credit and his or her desire to build a successful coalition so that there will be credit to be taken. Such a strategic approach to creating and designing subsidies is part of the political art and may take many forms. Elaborate signalling may be used to identify and reassure allies and to mislead or disarm opponents. A subsidy may be designed so that, although it seems small and perhaps even temporary at the time of adoption, it has "grow power." The authority to create the subsidy may be delegated by the legislature to an administrative agency, where the supporters of the subsidy are thought to enjoy greater influence. These and other subsidy-concealing techniques are especially important when the subsidies are intended to benefit politically weak groups, such as the poor.

It is plausible to suppose that the explosion of regulatory activity during the 1970s and the resulting dramatic shift of policy initiative from Congress to the agencies represented in part an effort by politicians and interest groups to devise subsidies that would not have been adopted legislatively in explicit form. It seems most unlikely, for example, that the uncompensated hospital care regulations issued in 1979 for Hill-Burton would have been enacted into law either by the Congress that adopted the original Hill-Burton Act or by the Congress that sat in 1979 if the choice had been presented in that explicit form. Congress can, of course, control administrative policy when it can muster the institutional will to do so. But mobilizing that institutional will and building a legislative majority in any particular case is often very difficult. As a result, agencies do enjoy some latitude to make policies, including developing subsidy programs that Congress would neither adopt in the first instance nor manage to overrule after the fact. As the infrequent use of legislative vetoes attests, it is difficult to unscramble an egg, especially when it has been cooked in someone else's kitchen.

There is another perspective on the question of how explicit subsidies should be, one that may divide the pragmatic politician from both the efficiency-mongering economist and from the principled moralist. The economist, as already noted, prefers an approach to subsidies that clearly distinguishes between efficiency and equity objectives. This preference betrays not so much the economist's hostility to equity through public subsidies as a belief that such subsidies are often designed crudely and inefficiently; that is, they are not carefully tailored to achieve the redistributive goal at the lowest cost. By charging all consumers the marginal cost of producing what they consume, and

Peter H. Schuck

effecting the desired equitable redistribution through explicit, lump-sum transfers, society would be better off than if it attempted to accomplish the redistribution by pricing the service below marginal cost for the target group. Some would go so far as to embrace the Kaldor-Hicks criterion of efficiency, under which a policy change is deemed efficient if the gainers *could* compensate the losers through a separate, explicit subsidy or side payment, even if they do not *in fact* do so (Zeckhauser and Schaefer 1968).

To the politician, however, the economist's advice is at best irrelevant and at worst nonsense. Unless the subsidy actually occurs, the recognition that the gainers *could* hypothetically subsidize the losers and still be better off than they are under the status quo is, politically speaking, meaningless. Indeed, from a political perspective, the failure to compensate the losers makes matters worse. In that event, the losers will seek to block the change altogether, which is relatively easy to accomplish under our fragmented political system. If they are so insular and weak a minority that they fail and the change is implemented without a compensating subsidy to them, they and the politicians who represent them will not be solaced by the knowledge that Kaldor-Hicks efficiency has triumphed and society in the aggregate may therefore be said to have been made better off.

A politician who favors a subsidy for a particular group is likely to value equity for that group more highly than he or she values efficiency for the society as a whole. The benefits of equity (and the costs of inequity) to that group are highly concentrated on those to whom he or she owes a political representation, while the costs of inefficiency, being diffused throughout the entire society, are scarcely visible. The politician will favor a subsidy that conceals its true redistributive implications (e.g., by embedding it in some regulatory program) even if it could be achieved far more efficiently (from society's point of view) in a more perfect, rational world. In the real world of the 1970s and 1980s, the fate of welfare reform and legislative resistance to protecting welfare benefit levels against inflation suggest that it may be politically futile to propose explicit subsidies for the poor. If so, concealed subsidies, with all of the inefficiencies and artifice that they imply, may be the only way in which our political system is prepared to redistribute income to the poor. The uncompensated care regulations under Hill-Burton respond to this reality. As I have indicated, however, they are likely to be extremely inefficient and inequitable, both with respect to assuring care to the neediest among the poor and with respect to allocating the burden of caring for the poor among different hospitals. By transferring costs from governmental budgets to private ones, these regulations evade difficult trade-offs between competing social goals.

Entitlement versus Closed-Ended Subsidies

Some public subsidies are created as legal entitlements. Any individual who meets the prescribed standards for the subsidy enjoys a legal right, enforceable in a court, to receive it. Other subsidies are "closed-ended"; all individuals who meet the prescribed standards for the subsidy may claim it, but none possesses any legal right to receive it. When a statute establishes a closed-ended subsidy, each claimant ordinarily enjoys a constitutional right not to be discriminated against on certain invidious grounds in the allocation of the subsidy among competing claimants, but Congress and the agencies enjoy very broad discretion to classify claimants in reasonable ways. There is no straight-forward answer to the questions of whether and to what extent a subsidy ought to be distributed in the form of an entitlement rather than under a closed-ended program. Indeed, these are extremely controversial issues in law, economics, and philosophy. It may be useful, however, to review some of the relevant considerations.

The cost of providing a subsidy as an entitlement is ordinarily greater than providing it in closed-ended form. This is not inevitable, of course, for the cost of each ultimately depends not upon its character as an entitlement or closed-ended subsidy but upon the level of the benefit and the number of individuals who receive it. If the eligibility standards and benefit levels of an entitlement are defined narrowly, while those of a closed-ended subsidy are defined relatively generously, the latter may be more costly than the former. As a legal matter, closed-ended subsidies are subject to a cost constraint—the level of appropriated funds—that does not bind entitlements. Congress need not appropriate any funds for the former, but it is legally obligated (although that obligation is probably not judicially enforceable against Congress) to appropriate whatever sums are necessary to fund benefits at the statutory level for all individuals who meet the legally prescribed eligibility standards for entitlements. In principle, therefore, closed-ended programs are more easily controllable in budgetary terms.

In practice, of course, the value of entitlements can be controlled. Obviously, the legislature can act to reduce benefit levels, restrict eligibility, or indeed eliminate an entitlement entirely. The Reagan Administration's successful efforts to reduce the costs of what were previously described as "uncontrollable" entitlement programs demonstrated that clearly enough. And even if the legislature simply does nothing, the value of an entitlement will steadily diminish in the face of inflation or changed conditions that have the effect of limiting the number of eligibles. By the same token, the level of closed-ended subsidies may increase steadily and dramatically, as was true of programs serving the elderly during the 1970s. For all that, however, subsidies in the form of entitlements enjoy an enormous political advantage—the ability to persist without regard to the annual appropriations process.

Many other differences between entitlements and closed-ended subsidies flow from this fundamental one. These differences help to explain why some subsidies were designed as one or the other in the first place, and why they tend to retain their character as entitlements or closed-ended programs over time.

First, entitlements seem most obviously justified when, as with Social Security retirement benefits, the beneficiaries have contributed directly into the fund from which the subsidies are paid. This is true even if (as in the case of Social Security) most beneficiaries receive considerably more than they paid in. Apart from this rather special category, however, entitlements also seem desirable when one wishes to subsidize basic services for groups whose levels of political organization and skill are, and are likely to remain, relatively weak. If Aid to Families with Dependent Children (AFDC) recipients, the blind, and the disabled had to organize to influence the budgetary and appropriations processes each year in order to be assured of the most basic income support and medical care, especially at a time of great fiscal stringency and political conservatism, life for them would be even more precarious and fearful than it is. Some of these groups simply cannot count upon being able always to muster the kind of political support from the more privileged in our society that would protect their interests. In a sense, entitlements protect them against the fickleness of political elites.

There is, of course, a paradox here. In order to succeed in establishing an entitlement, a group must possess considerable political support to begin with, yet such a group would seem not to need the special protection of an entitlement. But it is one matter to win a political struggle to create an entitlement, and quite another to be able to sustain that fragile victory over the long haul. The major entitlement subsidies—AFDC, Medicaid, Medicare, Social Security, food stamps, unemployment insurance—were created during two distinctive eras in American political history that are unlikely to recur: the New Deal and the Great Society. (The veterans programs, which were first established in the post–Civil War period and enjoy continued, powerful political support, are notable and revealing exceptions.) Once they were established, the considerable inertia of our political system protected these entitlements. That same inertia, however, makes it doubtful whether some of these entitlements, especially those for the poor, would be adopted for the first time today.

These considerations suggest the conditions under which entitlement subsidies are most justified, at least *prima facie*. The first condition relates to the importance of a benefit to the individual's fundamental well-being. If the inability of an individual to obtain the benefit would substantially reduce that person's physical, psychological, or moral well-being below the level that society regards as minimally tolerable, there is a strong argument that it should be provided as an entitlement. That argument is further strengthened if individuals who lack the benefit are not generally perceived as being morally responsible for their inability to procure it, as is the case with income support for retirees, small children, and (to a lesser extent) mothers of preschoolers. The same is true if the rest of the society is adversely affected by the inability of some individuals to afford it, as in the case of merit goods such as education and immunization against communicable diseases. If, in addition to the conditions just mentioned, society is concerned about obliging the individual to rely for the benefit upon the charity, goodwill, or bureaucratic discretion of others with respect to such a benefit, an entitlement may be further warranted. Society may believe that tolerating such vulnerability would undermine the individual's sense of dignity and self-worth, or would encourage corruption or overreaching by those with control over the benefit.

In addition, political, administrative, and constitutional considerations may militate in favor of creating an entitlement rather than a closed-ended subsidy. Politicians who wish to favor certain groups, especially those who cannot be certain of always prevailing, may seek to consolidate their victories by entrenching a subsidy in the form of a permanent entitlement. (On the other hand, politicians may prefer an arrangement under which they can take credit for creating benefits *over and over again*—for example, through annual appropriations—rather than only once and for all. This was traditionally true of Social Security benefits.)

There may also be administrative advantages to entitlements. When the eligibility criteria are relatively clear and straightforward, as in the Social Security retirement program or in categorical eligibility for Medicaid, the program can be far simpler to administer than a closed-ended subsidy program in which eligibility does not automatically entitle one to the benefit but is simply one precondition for receiving it. But not all entitlement programs are like Social Security retirement in this respect. In some, like AFDC or the Social Security disability program, eligibility depends not upon a determinate, immutable condition, such as reaching age sixty-five, but upon attributes, such as income, employability, and medical need, that are difficult to measure and may change rapidly. This is also true of an uncompensated hospital care subsidy in which eligibility is based upon income level or medical need. Such programs require officials to resolve difficult factual questions under ambiguous legal standards and after individualized hearings. They inevitably generate high administrative costs, especially if one includes the costs of error.

Finally, the Constitution itself may require that certain benefits be provided to the poor as entitlements. Indigent defendants, for example, are entitled to free trial transcripts for purposes of appeal. Moreover, all persons are entitled to certain procedural protections before they can be deprived of life, liberty, or property, interests that are themselves defined in terms of legal expectations or entitlements. These procedural protections may, as a practical matter, sometimes amount to access to a substantive right. And although the courts have rejected the argument that individuals enjoy a substantive constitutional right to receive welfare benefits or free health care, it is fundamental that governments may not provide such benefits to one group of individuals and withhold them from another on the basis of arbitrary, irrational distinctions.[3] In designing and limiting entitlements, then, government may draw lines, but those lines must have some reasoned basis.

Peter H. Schuck

In general, however, individuals' access to uncompensated hospital care enjoys only the most limited legal protection. Thus, the Supreme Court has held that would-be patients lack standing to challenge the charitable, tax-exempt status of hospitals that refuse to render uncompensated care to indigents.[4] Moreover, the lower courts have held that a claim to uncompensated care by a Hill-Burton hospital is not an entitlement and therefore can be denied by the hospital without affording the claimant due process of law.[5] And although some state courts have required hospitals that advertise their emergency rooms to render care to indigents who rely upon those representations, these rulings seem to have rested not upon a notion of entitlement but upon a "holding out" theory—that is, the idea that by encouraging the public to rely on its services, the hospital incurs an affirmative legal obligation to serve.[6]

That free hospital care for the poor is not yet recognized as a constitutional entitlement probably reflects several factors. First, since Medicaid created a statutory entitlement to such care, one that is extensive and quite costly, the courts may be reluctant to intrude constitutional principles into an area in which legislatures have been reasonably responsive to perceived needs. Second, to recognize a constitutional entitlement to hospital care, the courts would be obliged to specify its precise dimensions, a technical allocative task that is peculiarly legislative and administrative in character. Third, the need for hospital care is sometimes, and to some unknown degree, a condition for which individuals may be morally responsible. A study of high-cost users of hospital care, for example, found that over 60 percent of long- and short-stay hospital costs during a given year were accounted for by only 2 percent of the population, and that the high-cost users were often repeat admissions suffering disproportionately from life-style-related maladies, such as cirrhosis of the liver, obesity, and untreated diabetes (Zook and Moore 1980). Even for illnesses like these, of course, the issue of moral responsibility is not a simple one; for example, much alcoholism appears to be transmitted genetically and through nongenetic family patterns (e.g., Wolin et al. 1980). Still, it is doubtful that according a constitutional right to free hospital care for them would comport with the moral intuitions of our courts or our people.

The enactment of Medicaid in 1965 and its subsequent adoption by every state demonstrates that a social consensus does exist in favor of establishing hospital care for the poor as a *statutory* entitlement. In several respects, however, it is a weak entitlement. Millions of poor people are not covered by Medicaid.[7] Moreover, as the post-1980 program cuts remind us, whether hospital care for the poor is treated as an entitlement or not is a less important question than the benefit levels and eligibility criteria that society is prepared to fund. In that crucial sense, the differences between entitlement and closed-ended subsidies for hospital care seem less significant than they were before the diminution of entitlements in the early 1980s.

Appropriate Scope of Subsidy

Although the scope or size of a public subsidy is obviously a matter for political judgment, it is possible to examine some of the considerations that ought to inform such a judgment. A subsidy's scope should be influenced by how deserving or needy society believes the beneficiaries are, how numerous they are, what we feel we can afford, how well we can target the subsidy upon the intended beneficiaries, the alternative uses to which the resources might otherwise be put, the anticipated incentive effects of a subsidy, and our expectations about the need for future changes in the subsidy level. Only a few of these considerations are susceptible to systematic analysis.

In designing a subsidy for hospital care, a crucial question is whether it ought to be available on a universal or on a narrower, categorical basis, such as for those who are of low income. Where the principal objective of a subsidy is to increase consumption of a good by the poor, our moral values, cost constraints, and efficiency may strongly dictate means testing. Most people probably subscribe to the norm that when government intervenes to redistribute income, it should redistribute from the relatively advantaged to the relatively disadvantaged, not the other way around.[8] Moreover, means testing is an economically efficient way to design such a subsidy, for it promises to assist the target group at the lowest cost.

Notwithstanding these powerful arguments for means testing, at least three important considerations may militate in favor of a universal subsidy in certain circumstances. First, the administrative costs (including error costs) of means testing may be substantial, depending upon the difficulty of applying the standards of eligibility. At some point, these administrative costs may be so high that, taking both direct subsidy and administrative costs into account, most of the efficiency advantages of means testing will be lost. In such a situation, universalizing the subsidy may, all things considered, be preferable.

Second, means tests may demean individuals by requiring that they justify their claims to the subsidy. This requirement, so the objection goes, places claimants in the inferior position of supplicants rather than affirming their unconditional entitlements to the subsidy. This difference alone may create a two-class system of care, one subject to means testing and the other not, that undercuts to some degree the equality and dignity-enhancing purposes of the subsidy. It is difficult to evaluate this objection. As broadly formulated, it seems too sweeping. Rather, its force would seem to depend upon the spirit in which the means test is applied and the details of the administrative and service settings in which the program is carried out. Neither of these objections to means testing seems very significant in the case of uncompensated hospital care, at least as that program is now organized. As noted above, the hospital's incentive to discharge its fixed obligation under the regulations as soon as possible may induce it to administer the means test very loosely and to provide first-class care to beneficiaries (even if their number may thereby be reduced). However, if the subsidy were organized in a way that gave hospitals an incentive to underserve the indigent (for example, due to inadequate reimbursement levels), this objection to means testing might be considerably stronger. Whether it would then outweigh the efficiency and fiscal advantages of means testing cannot be answered in the abstract.[9]

A third objection is more political and strategic. By imposing a means test, the subsidy is, by definition, limited to poor people. Even if a means-tested program would in fact be a more target-efficient way to assist the poor, it may not be politically viable. As discussed earlier, the predominantly middle-class electorate may either reject or inadequately fund programs that seek to benefit only poor people. They may be willing to subsidize poor people only as part of a broader subsidy program that benefits the middle class as well.

The increasing universalization of subsidies for hospital care seems to support this political intuition. At first, the favored consumers were narrowly defined groups. At the federal level, for example, public hospitals were created to care for veterans and Indians. State and local hospitals were established to serve poor people, victims of tuberculosis, and the mentally ill. The Hill-Burton Act of 1946, however, both nationalized and universalized this subsidy policy. By authorizing federal grants and loans for hospital construction, the Hill-Burton program subsidized patients throughout the country and without regard to their financial need, diagnosis, or status. The uncompensated care provision of the Hill-Burton Act, of course, was intended to focus more narrowly upon the poor. Today, many other forms of public subsidy for hospital care, such as the deductibility of hospital expenses and tax-exempt bond financing, reinforce this more universal dimension of the hospital care subsidy. An analogous movement toward universalization has occurred in many other large subsidy programs outside the health area, such as farm subsidies, the deductibility of child care expenses, and federal student assistance.[10] This movement stands in rather stark contrast to society's unwillingness in recent years to expand programs that serve only the poor, such as AFDC and Medicaid.

One way to meet this political need for universality without abandoning the goal of target efficiency would be to create a universal subsidy but to tax the benefits progressively. Obviously the same considerations that make universalization of subsidies politically necessary also make progressive taxation of benefits politically problematic. The decision in 1983 to tax Social Security benefits above moderate income levels, as well as an earlier, similar change with respect to the taxation of unemployment compensation benefits, demonstrates that such a reform, while difficult, is not impossible.

Several other problems concerning the scope of a subsidy should be briefly mentioned. First, the incentive effects of subsidies that terminate too abruptly when a particular level of income is reached may be perverse. Where eligibility standards for different subsidy programs are closely related, additional earnings may cause the beneficiary to lose eligibility for several subsidies, resulting in an effective marginal tax rate exceeding 100 percent. The so-called Medicaid notch problem suggests that this disincentive is especially severe in the case of hospital subsidies, whose possible value to a beneficiary, especially in the event of extended hospitalization, may be very great.

Second, a subsidy program may create incentives on the part of providers to relax eligibility standards *de facto* rather than *de jure*. This possibility is especially great in the hospital setting. There, diagnostic and utilization decisions are made by physicians who have few if any incentives to think in economizing, marginal, cost-benefit terms; indeed, they have powerful ethical, professional, and other incentives *not* to do so. Under such conditions, we should not be surprised to learn, for example, not only that the cost of the end-stage renal disease program under Medicare has escalated rapidly but that an increasing number of the patients who participate in it are marginal in terms of the expected benefits from dialysis. Similar findings have been made in connection with hospital services such as intensive care units (Russell 1979). More generally, as noted above, hospitals subject to the current uncompensated care requirement have an incentive to relax eligibility standards *de facto* in order to discharge their fixed obligation quickly.

Conclusion

The earlier discussion suggests that from various policy perspectives, the existing uncompensated care requirement under Hill-Burton seems inferior to a number of possible alternative arrangements for subsidizing the consumption of hospital care by the indigent. Lump-sum cash (or near-cash) transfers to the neediest individuals, especially to the many who are not covered by Medicaid or other programs, would probably serve consumer autonomy, provider efficiency, administrative simplicity, political accountability, instrumental rationality, and most notions of equity far better than the current scheme.

Unfortunately a lump-sum cash transfer to poor individuals does not look quite so attractive when viewed from certain other perspectives. The subsidies need not be spent on hospital care, which constitutes a virtue to advocates for the poor and to economists, who defer to revealed consumer preferences, but is a distinct liability to politicians and others, who wish to redistribute not income in general but access to hospital care in particular. Even if the latter concern were satisfied through a system of near-cash or voucher transfers or a refundable tax credit for hospital expenditures, other objections would remain. Federal budget constraints, for example, would lead politicians and bureaucrats to search for an off-budget subsidy whose costs would be borne, at least in the first instance, by private hospitals. But such a solution, of which the Hill-Burton uncompensated care regulations are a requirement, produces inefficiency and inequity. Moreover, *none* of these solutions—cash transfers, voucher transfers, tax credits, uncompensated care regulations, or Medicaid-type entitlement programs—adequately responds to what is an increasingly crucial criterion of subsidy policy in the health care realm: cost control. Indeed, it seems clear that the structures of the Medicaid entitlement and the uncompensated care program actually undermine cost control.

Each of the contending approaches to cost control—for example, peer and utilization review, consumer cost-sharing, prospective reimbursement, expansion of HMOs, the so-called competition strategy, state hospital rate-setting, primary care networks, certificate of need, preferred provider organizations, centralized rationing of hospital care, and others—could in principle be combined with some form of subsidized hospital care for the poor. The effectiveness of many of these cost control techniques, however, appears to be quite disappointing, while for others, the results are not yet in.[11] In order to predict which approach (or, more likely, which combination of approaches) will best integrate subsidy and cost control objectives, we will probably need to know a great deal more about the micro features of uncompensated care and other forms of hospital subsidies for the poor. The documentation provided by Sloan and co-authors in Chapter 2 and by Perrin in Chapter 3 are only first steps in this direction.

Answers to the following types of questions are needed: Which poor people with what kinds of conditions seek uncompensated hospital care? What portion of them are high-cost, chronic users of hospitals? How much of their care could be rendered more efficiently on an outpatient basis? What kind of care is now being provided on a charity basis to those poor people who do not qualify either for uncompensated care or for Medicaid? To what extent would types of market incentives, such as patient cost-sharing and increased taxation of toxic products such as cigarettes and alcohol, be effective and to what extent would their regressive effects defeat the redistributive purposes of subsidized care? What is the effect of the Hill-Burton uncompensated care requirement upon hospital debt collection practices? Is there any system of hospital cost control short of centralized budgetary rationing[12] that physicians who provide subsidized care cannot manage to "game" and confound through their individualized diagnostic and treatment decisions? Our woeful ignorance on these and other relevant questions suggests an important policy research agenda.

Notes

The author wishes to acknowledge the helpful comments of Richard Nelson and Frank Sloan on an earlier version of this chapter.

1. According to Congressional Budget Office estimates, this subsidy will reduce 1985 income tax revenues by about $23.5 billion, and will reduce Social Security trust fund revenues by $8.2 billion (U.S. Congressional Budget Office 1984).

2. It is also widely believed that most federal employees are of higher competence

than their state and local counterparts. Whether this is true or not and whether, if true, that difference is fully explained by salary differentials, I do not venture to say.

3. E.g., Memorial Hospital v. Maricopa County, 415 U.S. 250 (1974).

4. Simon v. Eastern Kentucky Welfare Rights Org., 426 U.S. 26 (1976).

5. Newsom v. Vanderbilt Univ. Hosp., 653 F.2d 1100 (6th Cir. 1981).

6. E.g., Guerrero v. Copper Queen Hosp., 537 P.2d 1329 (Ariz., 1975).

7. See Myers, Chapter 7 below. Davis and Schoen (1983) conservatively estimated that only two-thirds of the poor were covered by Medicaid in 1976, leaving more than 9 million poor ineligible. And program benefits have been severely reduced in many states since then, even as the number of poor people has increased.

8. This norm is much honored in the breach. See, generally, Page (1983). For an argument that the most important costs of transfer programs are borne by the "deserving poor," see Murray (1984).

9. See, for example, the exchange between Professors James F. Blumstein and Rand Rosenblatt in *Texas Law Review* (Blumstein 1981; Rosenblatt 1981).

10. I refer to the Middle Income Student Assistance Act of 1978, not the subsequently narrowed interpretation.

11. See, e.g., Barker et al. (1979); Luft (1981); Moore, Martin, and Richardson (1983); Sloan and Steinwald (1980); and "Jersey Studies Rise in Hospital Costs," *New York Times*, March 13, 1984, p. B2, col. 1.

12. For a discussion of how such a system might operate in the United States, see Aaron and Schwartz (1984).

References

Aaron, Henry J., and William B. Schwartz. 1984. *The Painful Prescription: Rationing Health Care.* Washington, D.C.: The Brookings Institution.

Barker, W. Daniel, et al. 1979. *Controlling Health Care Costs by Direct Charges to . Patients: Snare or Delusion?* Toronto: Ontario Economic Council.

Blumstein, James F. 1981. "Rationing Medical Resources: A Constitutional, Legal, and Policy Analysis." *Texas Law Review* 59, no. 6 (November): 1345–1400.

Davis, Karen, and Cathy Schoen. 1983. *Health and the War on Poverty: A Ten-Year Appraisal.* Washington, D.C.: The Brookings Institution.

Luft, Harold S. 1981. *Health Maintenance Organizations: Dimensions of Performance.* New York: Wiley.

Moore, Stephen H., Diane P. Martin, and William C. Richardson. 1983. "Special Report: Does the Primary-Care Gatekeeper Control the Costs of Health Care? Lessons from the SAFECO Experience." *New England Journal of Medicine* 309, no. 22 (December 1): 1400–1404.

Murray, Charles. 1984. *Losing Ground: American Social Policy, 1950–1980.* New York: Basic Books.

Page, Benjamin. 1983. *Who Gets What From Government?* Berkeley and Los Angeles: University of California Press.

Rosenblatt, Rand. 1981. "Rationing 'Normal' Health Care: The Hidden Legal Issues." *Texas Law Review* 59, no. 6 (November): 1401–27.

Russell, Louise B. 1979. *Technology in Hospitals: Medical Advances and Their Diffusion.* Washington, D.C.: The Brookings Institution.

Schuck, Peter H. 1981. "The Politics of Regulation." *Yale Law Journal* 90, no. 3 (January): 702–25.

Sloan, Frank A., and Bruce Steinwald. 1980. "Effects of Regulation on Hospital Costs and Input Use." *Journal of Law and Economics* 23 (April): 81–109.

U.S. Congressional Budget Office. 1984. *Reducing the Federal Deficit: Report of the Senate and House Committees on the Budget*. Washington, D.C.: Congressional Budget Office.

Wolin, Steven, L. A. Bennett, D. L. Noonan, and M. A. Teitelbaum. 1980. "Disrupted Family Rituals: A Factor in Intergenerational Transmission of Alcoholism." *Journal of Studies on Alcohol* 41:199–214.

Zeckhauser, Richard J., and Robert Schaefer. 1968. "Public Policy and Normative Economic Theory." In *The Study of Policy Formation*, ed. R. Bauer and K. Gergen, pp. 58–60. New York: Free Press.

Zook, Christopher J., and Francis D. Moore. 1980. "High-Cost Users of Medical Care." *New England Journal of Medicine* 302, no. 18 (May 1): 996–1002.

FIVE

Providing Hospital Care to Indigent Patients: Hill-Burton as a Case Study and a Paradigm

James F. Blumstein

9130, 9110, 3230
US

94-107

Setting the Analytical Framework

For a long while, the health policy arena has suffered from an overdose of symbolic, rhetorical posturing about an amorphous "right" to medical (or health) care. Oftentimes, the "right" has been articulated as "equity" of access, in which the term "equity" has been equated with equality. And in determining the meaning of "equality," advocates for access egalitarianism have focused, at varying times, on equality of access, equality of actual utilization of inputs across income groups, need-adjusted equality of inputs, or equality of outcomes (President's Commission 1983, pp. 11–35).

Clearly, there is a consensus in American society that indigent patients should have an opportunity to obtain some types of medical care that, without a subsidy of some kind, they might not otherwise be able to afford. Traditionally, that consensus has been verbalized in the form of an indigent patient's right to some forms of medical care. Yet, there is no constitutional foundation for the development of any such right. If a right to medical care does exist, it stems from an ethical and, ultimately, a political judgment about the legitimate claims of indigent patients to some form of subsidy (Blumstein 1981).

In the political arena, formulating and then implementing rights on behalf of indigent patients necessitates analysis of the character and scope of the rights being established. It also necessitates focusing on the other side of the equation: To whom will responsibility be assigned for the financing of the rights being established? (President's Commission 1983, pp. 30–35.) These are important but, though interrelated, clearly distinct analytical questions. As public budgets have become increasingly tight, pressures of two kinds have emerged: to redefine the breadth of the underlying right and to shift responsibility off-budget for financing this subsidy.

The recent report of the President's Commission for the Study of Ethical

Problems in Medicine and Biomedical and Behavioral Research has contributed substantially to the rationalization of discourse about providing care to those who cannot afford to pay. Instead of focusing on the question whether there is a right to medical care, and if so what its contours are, the commission concluded that "[s]ociety has a moral obligation to ensure that everyone has access to adequate care without being subject to excessive burdens" (President's Commission 1983, p. 22). The commission quite properly noted that "[a]s long as the debate over . . . access to health care is carried on simply by the assertion and refutation of a 'right to health care,' the debate will be incapable of guiding policy" (ibid., p. 34).

The emphasis on society's "obligation" rather than on a particular individual's right frames the proper question more pragmatically. It targets attention on the entity ultimately responsible for fulfilling the societal obligation—namely, government. And it then asks what the appropriate level of responsibility is (Blumstein 1982). In what can only be labeled a breakthrough in the rhetorical muddle all too typically surrounding health policy debates, the President's Commission (p. 18) boldly rejected the concept of equity as equality—whether equal access to care, the expenditure of equal health dollars, or equal health outcomes. Since, as the commission recognized, vast income and wealth differentials exist, assurance of equality might require prohibiting private expenditures for medical services—that is, coercively leveling down. Yet that process of "leveling down would promote gross inefficiency, lower quality, achieve a dubious sort of equity in which waiting time would be the main resource allocator, and threaten fundamental precepts of freedom by barring individual expenditures for health above some arbitrary limit set by government" (Blumstein and Sloan 1981). Such coercion is a staggering and possibly unconstitutional intrusion on individual liberty. Pragmatically, the commission noted, such an effort "would probably result in a black market for health care" (p. 19).

While leveling down is ethically and constitutionally questionable, and politically and administratively impractical, leveling up might be excessively expensive (Blumstein and Zubkoff 1979). Providing care according to "need" does not account for other societal priorities. Since health is one of a number of competing objectives, "it would be irrational for a society . . . to make a commitment to provide whatever health care might be beneficial regardless of cost" (President's Commission 1983, p. 19). Thus, health is an instrumental, not an ultimate, value (Zubkoff and Blumstein 1978), and society must consider trade-offs between health care objectives and other similarly important needs (Havighurst and Blumstein 1975).

Having rejected equity as equality and equity as access solely according to benefit or need, the commission embraced the concept of equity as an "adequate" level of health care (pp. 35–43). The term "adequacy" suggests a debate concerning its precise contours—a rather familiar "more versus less debate [that] can proceed along customary political lines" (Blumstein and Sloan 1981).

The thrust of the President's Commission, in adopting an approach that a number of us have advocated over the years, is important because of its implications for formulating policy. In the past, the impetus of access egalitarians had been to promote an individual entitlement or right to equality of medical care resources. The Medicaid and Medicare programs were responsive to this objective, providing public financing for access to "mainstream" medicine for poor and elderly patients.

The entitlement approach in medical care has emphasized the importance of equality and the notion that targeted patients who fulfill specified eligibility criteria should receive medical care at public expense. By limiting the range of decisionmakers' discretion to deny treatment, the entitlement approach promotes human dignity and reduces the opportunity for bureaucratic arbitrariness or unfairness. At the same time, the entitlement approach permits judicial oversight of program administration, facilitating patient redress of perceived inequities (further discussed in Chap. 4 by Schuck).

The disadvantages of the entitlement approach stem from the lack of budgetary control. Since "rights" are legally established independent of cost, and their definition is set by providers who determine "medical necessity," public payers have very few control levers on overall levels of consumption of services. Costs are projected and budgets formulated, but no sense of trade-offs enters into decisionmaking. Funds are committed to a program in accordance with criteria of need, which in turn are not linked to costs or influenced by other competing public priorities. In essence, public expenditures are driven by private decisions of patients and providers, who face very few budgetary constraints.

An approach that focuses on overall societal or institutional obligations— while at the same time deemphasizing individual patient entitlements—would allow for the allocation, in advance, of a fixed budget. The amount of this budget would be determined at the outset of a fiscal year and would reflect the level of the societal commitment to a particular program or institution. Such an approach has the advantage of allowing a budgetary control on program outlays.

In addition, the societal or institutional obligation approach allows debates about the allocation of resources to take place at the "statistical" level, where delicate matters such as the value of human life and health are viewed more abstractly (Havighurst et al. 1976). Rational discussion of priorities, risk factors, competing needs, and so forth can be factored into the debate. Symbolic blackmail, caused by the potential breach of the comforting myth that "life is beyond price," is more easily invoked when "identifiable" lives are involved (Blumstein 1976). It is very difficult to say no to an applicant in an entitlement

James F. Blumstein

program when the only tangible benefit observed by a decisionmaker derives from a decision to say yes. To the contrary, in a fixed budget context, decisions are framed as "either/or." If X receives services, then some other person (Y) does not. In that context, saying no to X is easier because the decisionmaker views the choice as one between X and Y. If he or she says no to X, then that allows a yes decision for Y (Blumstein and Sloan 1981).

To the extent that general allocations are made to programs or institutions, those programs or institutions become responsible for making resource allocation choices. That, in turn, allows government to dissociate itself from "micro" allocation choices, leaving those responsibilities to the programs or institutions. That type of dissociation avoids the societal demoralization that stems from the public perception that government is somehow responsible for the deprivation of life or health.

Probably the most graphic illustration of this type of societal demoralization concerns the issue of capital punishment. Vicious killers face execution; yet, since government is directly involved in snuffing out a human life, we feel very squeamish about our collective responsibility for that type of public death-causing conduct. The public anguish over capital punishment illustrates the demoralization problem associated with public identification of the government with the infliction of harm. The farther government distances itself from these decisions, the less likelihood there is that this type of demoralization effect will emerge (Blumstein 1981).

The disadvantage to reliance on a program-based or institutional obligation is the very flexibility it offers. Inherent in a system that allows greater flexibility is the potential for standardless arbitrariness. Governmental distance and passively permissive oversight may be perceived as public abdication of responsibility. The lack of a legally enforceable right or entitlement makes judicial or administrative oversight more difficult. And, when decisionmaking standards for resource allocation become blurred, dramatizing particularized human suffering becomes more difficult. Use of the munificent feeling we have for identified individuals in peril (symbolic blackmail) to effectuate enhanced allocations of funds to specific individuals, programs, or institutions also becomes more difficult.

The Hill-Burton Act: From Obligation toward Entitlement

The distinction between a rights approach and an obligation approach to the problem of indigent hospital care is reflected in the evolution of the Hill-Burton Act.[1] As originally administered, the program focused entirely on the obligation of hospitals receiving Hill-Burton funds to provide assurances that indigent patients as a group would have access to a reasonable volume of uncompensated services (Rose 1975). As currently administered, after numerous rounds of litigation, the Hill-Burton program has moved in the direction of an entitlements approach (Vand. L. Rev. 1979). The remainder of this chapter will focus on the evolution of the administration of Hill-Burton and the policy implications for designing a program of indigent patient hospital care.

The Early Years

Enacted in 1946, the Hospital Survey and Construction Act (the Hill-Burton Act) provided funds for the development and improvement of hospital facilities. The overriding objectives were to develop a rationalized system of health planning that would identify long-range needs for hospital facilities and to provide resources to fulfill those needs through the construction and modernization of hospitals. Evidence before Congress, in the immediate postwar context, indicated that there was a substantial need for more hospital beds.[2]

President Truman sought comprehensive health legislation to provide access to medical care to all citizens. His plan encompassed a number of features. The construction of hospitals was one component, responding to the perceived shortage of such facilities. Other elements included improved maternal and child health services, sponsorship of medical research, income security to guard against the loss of income stemming from illness or disability, and a system of financing to guarantee access to medical care to those unable to pay for it.

Enactment of the Hill-Burton Act responded only to a portion of the comprehensive program proposed by President Truman—the need for the construction and modernization of hospital facilities (Rosenblatt 1978). Although President Truman had identified a national problem of access to medical services, the Hill-Burton legislation was not primarily designed as a program to pay for indigent care (Md. L. Rev. 1970). Rather, it was a program designed to develop facilities to which all would have access on a nondiscriminatory basis. The problem of financing medical care for indigents was left to a later day— until the enactment of Medicaid and Medicare nearly twenty years later, in 1965.

Nevertheless, Congress was aware of the problem of access to hospital care for indigent patients and, in the Hill-Burton legislation, authorized the surgeon general to require, as a condition of approval of a project, that the applicant furnish assurances that a "reasonable volume of services" would be provided to "persons unable to pay therefor" as well as assurances that the facilities financed under the act would be "made available to all persons residing in the territorial area of the applicant." These are known as the uncompensated care and the community service assurances, respectively. Their meaning has been a focal point of modern Hill-Burton litigation and regulatory change.

Yet, for nearly twenty-five years, these assurances played only a minor role in the administration of Hill-Burton. No quantifiable obligation was imposed.

No requirement for an allocation plan was imposed. No method of oversight was established. No separate budgetary accounting procedure was mandated, and hospitals were expressly permitted to take Hill-Burton credit for indigent patients' care when other sources of reimbursement were available and used. Thus, hospitals were not required to absorb the cost of care rendered under Hill-Burton. The essential inquiry was whether indigent patients were securing access to a reasonable volume of services (Blumstein 1984).

In the postwar context Hill-Burton can be understood as requiring express affirmation of the common expectation that nonprofit hospitals would continue to provide charity care consistent with their historic mission of community service. In that view, hospitals had a self-perceived obligation to provide uncompensated services to needy patients as resources permitted. The Hill-Burton assurances prevented a diversion of those efforts elsewhere.

As administered for twenty-five years, Hill-Burton did not require a hospital to develop a "program" of indigent patient care. The uncompensated care assurance merely contemplated continuation of the status quo. From an administrative perspective, the uncompensated care assurance was precatory—exhortative, not coercively enforced through regulatory oversight. The Hill-Burton Act was seen as "distributive" (i.e., providing facilities for all citizens) not "redistributive" (i.e., targeting resources for an identifiable segment of the population, the poor).[3] To the extent that it had a redistributive component, Hill-Burton imposed an unenforced general duty on hospitals to provide an undefined amount of services to a class of beneficiaries, poor patients.

The Period of Transition

Beginning in 1972, in response to litigation by advocates for indigent patients, the federal government began to enforce the uncompensated care assurance. A quantifiable level of services was established as the administrative definition of "reasonable volume." Since it could be obliged to show its compliance, a hospital would have had to establish a Hill-Burton program as a separate accounting matter. Only care rendered to income-eligible patients could be counted, and hospitals therefore had to determine which patients were eligible. Smaller hospitals, however, were able to satisfy their obligations by agreeing to treat all patients irrespective of income—the "open-door" policy. In a fundamental change in approach, hospitals that were reimbursed by Medicare, Medicaid, or by some other source were barred from counting such care as eligible for Hill-Burton. The availability of a reasonable volume of services to "persons unable to pay therefor" under Hill-Burton was construed to require separate hospital funding for indigent patient care beyond the care made available under other programs.

One thrust of the regulatory change in the period of transition was to enhance accountability and enforceability. That shift established Hill-Burton, at least in part, as a redistributive program of indigent patient hospital care, potentially subject to serious administrative oversight and enforcement. It required grantee hospitals to set up their Hill-Burton programs as independent entities in an accounting sense so that, if audited, they could demonstrate compliance in the aggregate with their quantitatively defined "reasonable volume" of uncompensated services.

Leaving to one side the question whether Hill-Burton should have been reconstrued as a redistributive program for providing hospital care to indigent patients, one can see that the regulatory features of the transition period established a way of enforcing and overseeing a definite obligation of the grantee hospitals to the class of indigent patient beneficiaries. The duty was imposed as a responsibility of hospitals, which were administratively account-able to governmental auditors to demonstrate compliance in the aggregate with their duty to provide uncompensated services to indigent patients as a class.

In terms of this chapter's introductory analytical framework, government was establishing an institutional obligation to a group, without creating any counterpart rights on the part of individual eligible beneficiaries. Decisions concerning allocation of scarce resources were essential because Hill-Burton hospitals were not expected, in general, to provide sufficient uncompensated services under Hill-Burton to satisfy the need for uncompensated hospital services in a geographical area. Yet, those nitty-gritty micro decisions were not to be made by government but by the recipient hospitals themselves. They were at liberty to allocate their Hill-Burton care in accordance with a plan or on an *ad hoc* basis. They could provide the same quality of care and the same amenities as they provided to paying patients, or they could use different standards for the two groups. They could focus on patients' needs or on institu-tional priorities (such as "teaching material" for an instructional program). They could emphasize emergency care or ambulatory care. Or, if they wished, hospitals could limit Hill-Burton care to particular inpatient services, such as obstetrics or infant care. Formulation of procedures for decisionmaking was left to the grantee hospitals' discretion.

In sum, this aspect of the regulatory change during the period of transition was compatible with the obligation approach to the delivery of uncompensated hospital care to indigent patients. Grantee hospitals had a fixed obligation—specified in dollars—to provide uncompensated services to a class of eligible potential beneficiaries. Compliance with that obligation could be reviewed and enforced administratively, but the overall level of commitment was fixed, based on the size of the Hill-Burton grant received by the institution.

A second thrust of the transition-period regulations was more ominous for hospitals. By disallowing Hill-Burton credit for Medicare and Medicaid care, the Hill-Burton regulations diverted the focus from the availability of hospital services to poor patients to a focus on the source of funding for care provided to those patients. This facet of the regulations suggested that Hill-Burton was to be an independent source of supplemental funding for hospital care for poor patients not otherwise covered by Medicare, Medicaid, or some other program. The result of that requirement was an inevitable search for someone to absorb the additional cost—the beginning of the hospital version of the shell game now known as cost- or charge-shifting (see also Chaps. 6 and 7, below).

The "free lunch" approach of this component of the Hill-Burton regulations was undoubtedly generated by a conviction among advocates for poor patients that requiring Hill-Burton services to be "add-on" or incremental would squeeze out additional funds for indigent care. The assumption was that if credit toward satisfying the Hill-Burton obligation was applied only where hospitals provided otherwise unreimbursed care to poor patients, then hospitals would increase overall levels of care furnished to indigent persons.

Aggregate support for poor patients may have increased by hospitals' use of cost-shifting, but the imposition of this type of independent financial obligation after the fact is a very risky and questionable approach. The distributive consequences are unknown, and the financial consequences may be severe for hospitals that cannot shift costs or whose margin of profit does not leave much room for fiscal flexibility. Moreover, because cost-shifting imposes costs on private, not public, budgets, there is a definite and pernicious attraction for public officials that, like addictive drugs, should be shunned at the outset. The lure of this type of "solution" to societal obligations to pay for indigent care is, like the songs of the sirens, so beckoning and so potentially unconstrained and irresponsible that public officials should be discouraged from pursuing this path even in a gingerly, exploratory manner.

A third thrust of the transition period regulations, imposed on the government by a federal district judge, began the evolution of Hill-Burton from an obligation approach toward an entitlement approach. In *Corum v. Beth Israel Medical Center*,[4] the court held invalid a regulation that allowed hospitals to credit toward their Hill-Burton obligations care provided to persons whose Hill-Burton eligibility was not determined until after bills were rendered. Under *Corum*, for care to qualify under Hill-Burton, a written determination of a patient's eligibility was required "prior to any collection effort other than the rendition of bills."

The Court noted the disadvantage to indigent patients of a system that permitted determination of eligibility after the fact: "[M]any truly indigent persons may incur liabilities . . . in the hope of qualifying for free . . . services, which they will later be hard pressed to pay for if the hospital declines to treat them as beneficiaries of its Hill-Burton assurances. . . . [M]any such persons will be discouraged by the uncertainty of their status from seeking any medical assistance at all."[5]

The view of the *Corum* court was that the proper focus for enforcement of the Hill-Burton program should be on the needs of individual eligible patients within the class of primary beneficiaries of the act—indigent patients. Quite clearly, the *Corum* court directed attention away from the obligation of a hospital to provide uncompensated services in the aggregate to a class of indigent patients. Instead, *Corum* compelled the government to require an inquiry by a hospital into the merits of particular cases. The essential conceptual transformation wrought by *Corum* was to shift the unit of inquiry away from the hospitals' duty to a class of persons and toward an individual class member's particularized claim for uncompensated hospital care.

Although *Corum* did not go so far as to establish a right to care under Hill-Burton for individual indigent patients, it did bar hospitals from taking credit under Hill-Burton in the normal course if patient eligibility was not determined prior to the delivery of services. That helped shape perceptions of Hill-Burton as a program in which individual eligible patients had a cognizable interest in knowing in advance whether their care would be covered under Hill-Burton. The *Corum* decision, and HEW's acquiescent response, helped crystallize an emerging view that Hill-Burton was, at least in part, a redistributive entitlement program—a source of private financing for hospital access for individual indigent patients. The enactment of new legislation in 1975[6] reinforced and gave impetus to that direction.

The Current Regulations

The current Hill-Burton regulations were put into effect by the U.S. Department of Health, Education, and Welfare (HEW) in May 1979.[7] They were adopted under order of the district court in *Newsom v. Vanderbilt University*,[8] a decision extremely influential in shaping a transformed vision of the way in which the Hill-Burton program should be administered. Parenthetically, and ironically, the relevant portions of the district court decision in *Newsom* were reversed on appeal by the Sixth Circuit Court of Appeals in 1981,[9] but by then the HEW regulations had already been promulgated. Any modification of the regulations at that time would have required an affirmative political mobilization, which no group in the Hill-Burton arena had been able to effectuate in the history of the program. Stalemate and inaction had been the political facts of life, and the same was true once HEW, under court order, issued the 1979 regulations.

The tone of the 1979 regulations was clearly set by the district judge in *Newsom*. He recognized a "constitutionally protected right" on the part of each indigent patient "to needed uncompensated services under the Hill-Burton Act."[10] The finding of such an entitlement (that is, a "property" interest) was a prerequisite to the court's ultimate holding that procedural due process standards were violated by the defendant hospital. The district court held that, to satisfy due process standards, hospitals were required to provide individual notice of the availability of Hill-Burton uncompensated care to potentially eligible patients and to establish and apply written eligibility criteria for the allocation of such care. If an individual was denied Hill-Burton care, each such person must be given "timely and adequate written notice detailing the reasons for the proposed denial of benefits, review by a decisionmaker who has not participated in making the initial finding of ineligibility, and a written statement of the reasons for the decision and the evidence relied on."[11]

The vision of the Hill-Burton program embodied in the district court's decision in Newsom placed virtually exclusive emphasis on the particularized interests of each potential beneficiary of uncompensated hospital care. The concern with individual notice, stemming from individual entitlements to care, reflected a fundamental transformation of Hill-Burton into a privately financed "mini-Medicaid" program. No longer was a hospital's obligation satisfied by the provision of a gross volume of uncompensated care to a class of persons. No longer did the Hill-Burton program represent a macro allocation of government dollars to be used with minimal constraints by decentralized decisionmakers, in a way analogous to the structure of the legal services program. Instead, there was an obligation to inform and explain to each patient the details of the Hill-Burton program and why he or she did not qualify for uncompensated care. Under Newsom the program imposed a duty on those private providers expressly to make the kind of interpersonal comparisons that can be so very demoralizing. Indeed, the philosophy of the district court was that government had an affirmative responsibility to become involved and identified with micro allocation choices. Failure to become so involved was viewed as an abdicaton of responsibility.

In response to Newsom, HEW issued the current regulations the very next year. With respect to the quantified definition of a "reasonable" volume of services, the 1979 regulations introduced an annual upward adjustment according to the consumer price index for medical care. Also, any annual shortfall must be added to future years' obligation and adjusted upward for inflation. Finally, the open-door option was eliminated. Therefore, hospitals that do not attract indigent patients in sufficient numbers now have to adopt a program of affirmative action, advertising the availability of uncompensated care for eligible beneficiaries. Actual delivery rather than mere availability of uncompensated services is now required.

As significant as those changes are for hospitals, they do not in themselves undermine the obligation approach by which institutions take responsibility for allocating a fixed—albeit annually adjusted—amount of care to a class of beneficiaries. However, in responding to the district court decision in Newsom, HEW also required hospitals to furnish individual written notice "of the availability of uncompensated services to each person who seeks services in the facility on behalf of himself or another."[12] The individual written notice must "[s]et forth the criteria the facility uses for determining eligibility for uncompensated services," and it must "[s]tate that the facility will make a written determination of whether the person will receive uncompensated services, within two working days of a request for uncompensated services." If a request for uncompensated services is denied, the hospital must supply a "written and dated statement of the reasons for the denial."[13] And a hospital must adopt a plan by which its Hill-Burton services will be allocated. Thus, a facility must state the types of services that are to be made available and guarantee that it will provide uncompensated services "to all persons eligible under the plan who request uncompensated services."[14] If a hospital does not adopt a plan, then it must allocate delivery of its uncompensated services on a first-come, first-served basis.[15]

Clearly, the 1979 regulations direct attention to the decision to treat or not to treat individual members of the beneficiary class. The regulations do not necessarily establish a right to care for all indigent patients because each hospital has some flexibility in developing its allocation plan. Moreover, a hospital presumably can establish subjective, discretionary criteria that would deprive patients of any enforceable entitlement to treatment. But the obligation to provide services "to all persons eligible under the plan who request uncompensated services" seems to contemplate that, as a general principle, hospital plans will confer rights on at least some individuals within the beneficiary class.

The individual written notice requirement, the duty to respond in writing within two days to a request for uncompensated services, the duty to give reasons for the denial of care, and the requirement that facilities put the provisions of an allocation plan in writing are all aimed, so it would seem, at emphasizing the rights of individual claimants under Hill-Burton and deemphasizing the group character of the obligation imposed on grantee hospitals.

In sum, the thrust of the *Newsom* litigation and its impact on the 1979 regulations is to transform Hill-Burton in a fundamental way—from a program imposing a flexible obligation on an institution to make available a "reasonable volume" of uncompensated services to a class of beneficiaries, to a program of entitlements to certain individual members of a beneficiary class, modeled after Medicaid and Medicare but with a limited overall budget.

Conclusion: Hill-Burton in Policy Perspective

In its early years, Hill-Burton was not administered as a redistributive program of indigent patient hospital care. It was viewed as a distributive program of providing facilities for general community use, with a proviso that nonprofit grantee hospitals continue to provide a reasonable volume of care, as affordable, to members of the community who were unable to pay for hospital services.

In the period of transition, evolving Hill-Burton regulations established a quantitative measure of what constituted a "reasonable volume" of uncompensated services for each Hill-Burton hospital—10 percent of the total Hill-Burton grant per year for twenty years. That facilitated oversight and enforcement yet retained the macro allocation character of Hill-Burton. The hospital had an established obligation to provide a fixed amount of uncompensated services to a class of beneficiaries. Government's involvement in and supervision of micro allocation choices were minimal or nonexistent, so that the risk of demoralization from public participation in "tragic choice" situations was attenuated. Decentralized units—Hill-Burton hospitals—made allocation choices without having to articulate standards or give reasons for particular decisions. That insulated government from the symbolic blackmail that exists when the public views government as responsible for inflicting harm on identified individuals. Political pressure for public financial intervention becomes nearly insurmountable in the face of such symbolic blackmail, potentially distorting resource allocation decisions made at the more abstract, statistical level.

In the current period, the Hill-Burton regulations, precipitated by judicial intervention on the part of lower courts, have pushed the program in the direction of an emphasis on the rights or entitlements of individual indigent patients to care. The provisions for individual written notice, written determinations of ineligibility, written formulation and application of an allocation plan, and delivery of uncompensated services to all eligible persons who request such services—all suggest an approach more consistent with an individual entitlement program than with an institutional obligation program.

It is ironic that Hill-Burton, at least before 1979, was an example of an obligation program approach implicitly endorsed in principle by the 1983 Report of the President's Commission for the Study of Ethical Problems in Medicine and Biomedical and Behavioral Research. Yet, spurred by litigation, HEW has adopted and retained regulations that place greater emphasis on a rights approach. Still, Hill-Burton, even as currently administered, is not an open-ended, blank-check fiscal commitment. A fixed—albeit inflation-adjusted—level of resources amounting to 10 percent of the Hill-Burton grant must be allocated by each institution annually. Despite the changed administrative emphasis since 1979, Hill-Burton continues to reflect an approach toward the delivery of services to indigent patients that differs in important ways from such programs as Medicare and Medicaid.

Budgets are fixed in advance, and obligations exist only up to the point at which the aggregate level of care for a given year is satisfied. Allocation criteria are not entirely based on need. Institutional allocation plans allow grantees to control, within constraints, the basis for allocation decisions. Determinations of allocative priorities, therefore, rest in nongovernmental hands, allowing government to be distanced from micro allocation decisions. Government enforcement and oversight are largely confined to macro issues, such as whether a facility delivered, in the aggregate, a sufficient volume of services to eligible patients. Policing of and responsibility for individual determinations of eligibility and allocations of resources are left in the hands of non-federal-government grantee hospitals, at least in the first instance.

Thus, Hill-Burton provides an interesting alternative model to Medicare and Medicaid for financing indigent patient care. However, because the administration of the act was so dramatically altered after most grantees received their funding, the practical effect of Hill-Burton has been to shift some responsibility for indigent patient care from government to hospitals, which in turn have sought to shift the burden to self-pay patients and willing third-party carriers. Any suggestion that Hill-Burton be used as a viable alternative model for the public financing of indigent care includes a stipulation that the precise financial obligations of grantee institutions be specified in advance, not after the fact, as has been the case in the real-world implementation of Hill-Burton.

Notes

1. The full title is the Hospital Survey and Construction Act. Public Law no. 79-725, 60 Stat. 1040 (1946), codified at 42 U.S.C. 291–291o (1976).
2. See American Hospital Assoc. v. Schweiker, 721 F.2d 170, 172 (7th Cir. 1983).
3. This terminology was developed by Theodore Lowi (1964, pp. 691–715).
4. 373 F. Supp. 550 (S.D.N.Y. 1974).
5. Ibid., p. 557.
6. Title XVI of the National Health Planning and Resources Act of 1974, Public Law No. 93-641, 80 Stat. 2258, codified at 42 U.S.C. 3005 (1976).
7. 44 Fed Reg. 29,372 (1979), codified at 42 C.F.R. 124.501–.607 (1979).
8. 453 F.Supp. 401 (M.D.Tenn. 1978).
9. 653 F.2d 1100 (6th Cir. 1981).
10. 453 F.Supp. 423.
11. Ibid., p. 424.
12. 42 C.F.R. 124.505(b).
13. Ibid., 124.508(c).
14. Ibid., 124.507(a)(5).
15. Ibid., 124.507(b).

References

Blumstein, James F. 1976. "Constitutional Perspectives on Governmental Decisions Affecting Human Life and Health." *Law And Contemporary Problems* 40, no. 4 (Autumn): 231–305.
———. 1981. "Rationing Medical Resources: A Constitutional, Legal, and Policy Analysis." *Texas Law Review* 59, no. 8 (November): 1345–1400.
———. 1982. "Distinguishing Government's Responsibility in Rationing Public and Private Medical Resources." *Texas Law Review* 60, no. 5 (May): 899–918.
———. 1984. "Court Action, Agency Reaction: The Hill-Burton Act as a Case Study." *Iowa Law Review* 69, no. 5 (July): 1227–61.
Blumstein, James F., and Frank A. Sloan. 1981. "Redefining Government's Role in

Health Care: Is a Dose of Competition What the Doctor Should Order?" *Vanderbilt Law Review* 34, no. 4 (May): 849–926.

Blumstein, James F., and Michael Zubkoff. 1979. "Public Choice in Health: Problems, Politics and Perspectives on Formulating National Health Policy." *Journal of Health Politics, Policy, and Law* 4, no. 3 (Fall): 382, 389.

Havighurst, Clark, and James F. Blumstein. 1975. "Coping with Quality/Cost Trade-Offs in Medical Care: The Role of PSROs." *Northwestern University Law Review* 70, no. 1 (March–April): 6–68.

Havighurst, Clark, James F. Blumstein, and Randall Bovbjerg. 1976. "Strategies in Underwriting the Costs of Catastrophic Disease." *Law and Contemporary Problems* 40, no. 4 (Autumn): 122–95.

Lowi, Theodore. 1964. "American Business, Public Policy, Case Studies, and Political Theory." *World Politics* 16:677–715.

Md. L. Rev. 1970. Note, "The Hill-Burton Act, 1946–1980: Asynchrony in the Delivery of Health Care to the Poor." *Maryland Law Review* 39:316–75.

President's Commission for the Study of Ethical Problems in Medicine and Biomedical and Behavioral Research. 1983. *Securing Access to Health Care: The Ethical Implications of Differences in the Availability of Health Services.* Washington, D.C.: U.S. Government Printing Office.

Rose, Marilyn. 1975. "Federal Regulation of Services to the Poor under the Hill-Burton Act: Realities and Pitfalls." *Northwestern University Law Review* 70, no. 1 (March–April): 168–201.

Rosenblatt, Rand. 1978. "Health Care Reform and Administrative Law: A Structural Approach." *Yale Law Journal* 88, no. 2 (December): 243–336.

Vand. L. Rev. 1979. Note, "Due Process for Hill-Burton–Assisted Facilities." *Vanderbilt Law Review* 32:1469–1510.

Zubkoff, Michael, and James F. Blumstein. 1978. "The Medical Marketplace: Health Policy Formulation in Consideration of Economic Structure." In *National Commission on the Cost of Medical Care, 1976–77,* 2:73–116. Chicago: American Medical Association.

SIX

Cross-Subsidies and Charge-Shifting in American Hospitals

Charles E. Phelps

A few patients pay for their hospital care directly, and a few receive either reduced rates or free care, as a charitable activity of the hospital. Yet, even ignoring this small group of charity patients, substantial differences may exist between the costs of resources used by any given patient (or class of patients) and the payments made on their behalf.

Historically, many health insurers in the United States have paid all charges billed by the hospital to the insurer. Without any audit of particular costs, nothing prevented a hospital from increasing its normal charge for room and board (the basic charge for a day's stay in the hospital) in an attempt to raise revenues.[1] This would not occur in a classic competitive market, where a rise in price would ordinarily result in a loss of customers to competitors. In the view of many analysts of the hospital industry, however, widespread comprehensive hospital insurance has made consumers of hospital care quite insensitive to price (Newhouse 1978), thus allowing the hospital some pricing discretion. This pricing discretion has been used in the past, in part, to recover costs from care that was otherwise uncompensated, including charity care, bad debts, and medical research conducted in the hospital. In general, hospitals have displayed considerable pricing latitude and considerable variation in price but have been subject to incomplete comparison shopping among consumers.[2]

As competition among hospitals increases, any pricing latitude previously held could diminish or vanish. This raises directly the central concern of this volume: if hospitals have used pricing latitude in the past to cover the costs of uncompensated care, what will happen if competition eliminates that pricing latitude?

The following are some ways a hospital might make use of pricing latitude. A hospital might choose deliberately to raise its prices to one set of patients, while reducing it for another for a variety of reasons:

1. Deliberate subsidy for a class of patients (e.g., the poor) or for a type of medical care (obstetrics, research, pediatric orthopedics) at the choice of the hospital managers or trustees;
2. Deliberate price favoritism to match the desires of the medical staff, e.g., to increase the profits made by the medical staff;
3. Strategic pricing by the hospital to enhance its market position.

Each of these types of hospital behavior has been explored in the past by various researchers. Newhouse (1970) has modeled how the choices of a hospital board of trustees or manager might shift its output choices in one direction or another. The model of a hospital shifting its pricing and output decisions to the economic benefit of the medical staff was first offered by Pauly and Redisch (1973) and forms a common basis of analysis for assessing behavior of the not-for-profit hospital. Finally, even with any of these or other models of pricing behavior, the hospital may wish to alter its prices for strategic purposes, to enhance its long-run market position (Baumol, Panzar, and Willig 1982). For example, the hospital may wish to construct excess capacity in a market to deter entry by a potential new entrant. Another such strategy might be to install some unusual and desirable diagnostic capability to attract a class of business (e.g., cardiac care) from one set of doctors (e.g., cardiologists) and their patients.

Other events may force the hospital to price in other ways than might emerge in a truly competitive market. In particular, if one third-party insurer pays less than billed charges from the hospital, the hospital must then either charge those patients directly for any difference between payments and cost, increase charges to other patients whose insurance continues to pay billed charges, and/or alter its cost structure. The first approach is common in hospital plans with deductibles, copayments, internal limits (e.g., on dollars per day in the hospital), and other limits on payment, and produces no consequences for other patients. But if the third-party payer has somehow reached an agreement with the hospital that the patient will *not* be charged any underpaid amount, then the hospital must either alter its cost structure or turn to other sources to maintain its revenues. (Whether the hospital can succeed in this is a separate question, to be considered in more detail later.) This latter strategy—"cost-shifting" or, better, "charge-shifting," since the behavior is more related to charges and prices—gives rise to the following types of policy questions.

Should these practices continue or cease? If our society holds as a goal that hospitals should provide care for all—even those who cannot or do not pay for care—how does society best accomplish this social goal? What would be the consequences to the providers and the consumers of any change in public policy that alters the flexibility in pricing that hospitals may now enjoy? Most particularly, if one enhances the competitive nature of hospital and health care markets through changes in tax law, hospital planning and certificate-of-need activity, antitrust enforcement, and changes in HMO law, one should carefully consider the consequences for those now receiving care without paying.

Causes of Charge-Shifting

Just as a hospital (or any other seller) can affect its market in some circumstances, so too can a buyer sometimes affect its market. Neither of these types of behavior is possible in a purely competitive market, where both buyers and sellers accept prices as given. When the seller possesses the power to set prices (monopoly power), the price can be raised above competitive level. When the buyer possesses similar power (monopsony power), the price can fall below the usual competitive price, at least in some circumstances. This combination—by common allegation—is the source of much charge-shifting in the hospital industry: one or more buyers drive down the price paid for hospital care (exercising monopsony power against the hospital), and the hospital responds by exercising monopoly power against other buyers to recoup costs. The hospital—according to the usual model—could have used this monopoly power previously, but chose not to do so, in part because of its not-for-profit legal status. But when "forced" to do so in the face of monopsony buying, the hospital is said to exercise this power.

The most direct allegation about charge-shifting arises (as might be expected) from the parties who feel they are paying the long share. According to the trade association for commercial (for-profit) health insurers:

> Current federal and state regulations permit the government to pay less than its fair share of expenses incurred by hospitals and physicians for treating patients covered by Medicare and Medicaid. Providers then find that they must charge private sector patients more to compensate for this shortfall in government reimbursement. . . .
>
> In a number of states, Blue Cross plans also avoid paying certain elements of hospital costs. This adds to the reimbursement shortfall which must be made up by other patients.[3]

Expenses paid by Medicare have always included bad debts by non-Medicare patients. Now, new financial arrangements used by Medicare—diagnosis-related-group (DRG) payments—will unlink Medicare payments from any hospital-specific cost measure. Similarly, a recent survey of Blue Cross plans showed that, of ninety-five respondent plans, only a third recognized bad-debt costs as allowable regardless of source, and less than a third of the plans recognized free-care costs as reimbursable (Hoover and Mullen 1979).

Hospitals and insurers can also enter into voluntary agreements that have the same effect. The current movement toward preferred provider organizations (PPOs) results in circumstances greatly similar, at least externally, to charge-shifting. In these arrangements, a hospital and an insurer agree to a lower price for the PPO insurer's patients in exchange for a higher potential volume sent to that hospital. There may be actual cost saving associated with a PPO, including a saving on bad debts, selling costs, and claims-processing costs, which allow the hospital to lower its price in response to true cost differentials rather than to engage in charge-shifting. But the hospital may also attempt to shift charges to other insurers as a part of the arrangement, and it possesses as much power to do so as when faced with a unilateral price reduction from some other third-party payer.

In any discussion of charge-shifting, one can find apparently well-reasoned and logical explanations of the viewpoints of both parties, the hospital and the third party buyer. The following provides some stereotypical versions of these viewpoints, and shows how they are in fact logically compatible one with another.

Two Views of Hospital Costs

The Buyer's View

Large buyers of hospital care, particularly some Blue Cross plans and Medicare, commonly justify payments lower than the hospital's billed charges on grounds that the costs of caring for their particular patient group differ from the "average" patient's costs. They also assert that they should not be made to pay for certain activities of the hospital (for example, medical or paramedical education), since their patients are not receiving the benefit of those activities.

Blue Cross has commonly argued for and often received a "discount" for its patients, often several percentage points or more in those states where discounting is practiced (Sloan and Becker 1984). This discount, according to Blue Cross, reflects both the lower costs of the hospital because of its not having to face bad debts and because of reduced collection costs, as well as a refusal by the Blue Cross plans to pay for certain educational expenses of the hospital (Center for Health Policy Studies 1984). And of course, some Blue Cross plans do not use a discount formula, but rather, pay billed charges as commercial insurers have also commonly done (Hoover and Mullen 1979).

The history of Medicare payments to hospitals has been more varied. Initially, and for most of its history, Medicare paid for elderly patients on a complicated cost-reimbursement formula, based in part on an accounting system required by law for hospitals participating in the Medicare program. The formula—ratio of costs to charges, applied to charges (RCCAC)—has been analyzed extensively by Danzon (1982).

Subsequent changes in the Medicare law have reduced Medicare's payments to hospitals. Under provisions of the tax reform act (TEFRA) in 1982, Medicare pays hospitals on the basis of an average cost per day in the hospital for a specific geographic area. Until then, Medicare had imposed limits only on room and board charges. Furthermore, Medicare has also limited its payments towards medical malpractice insurance (on the grounds that elderly patients receive smaller-than-average malpractice awards) and has eliminated previously paid extra differentials for nursing services. Each of these payment changes has been made—or at least justified—on the basis of how the costs of caring for Medicare patients might differ from those of the remainder of the population. And in each case, Medicare has sought to show how proper accounting for differences in costs of treating Medicare patients leads to lower-than-average costs. But even this cost-based justification for payments is now changed.

New regulations—the DRG system—place even more stringent limits on Medicare payments. Each hospital admission will be paid on the basis of the average cost of an admission in the DRG. One can think of this as paying the average price per day for the average length of stay for the DRG. While the DRG payment categories are adjusted by region and hospital category, the DRG payment plan clearly poses considerable new financial uncertainty to the hospital, particularly since Medicare accounts for three-eighths of all hospital revenues. For the first time, Medicare payments will be essentially independent of the actual costs of any given hospital. Medicare will pay a single offer-price, and hospitals which do not succeed in that environment will either change or perish. Rather than seeking to justify lower payments on the basis of lower costs, the single most important payer for care will now ignore costs entirely. This represents a very marked—if not radical—change in the methods of payment for hospital care.

The Seller's View

From the point of view of the seller—the typical private hospital in the United States—what does this "typical" hospital wish to achieve, and how does it finance that activity? To answer this question, one needs a general model of hospital behavior. The model developed here draws primarily on the theory of regulation, rather than on theories of institutional or business behavior.[4] The analogy explores the central task of regulatory bodies and authorities: the need to define effective property rights and set rules of behavior for those areas of society where contracts and property rights either cannot or have not been established. This approach pertains to modeling a not-for-profit hospital precisely because the regulatory body and the hospital directors face the same problem: each must allocate scarce resources among competing groups, all of whom can claim some laudable purpose for using the resources, but whose collective claims add up to more than the available resources.

To develop but a single example, consider how regulators would manage a public forest. The Sierra Club, miners, synthetic fuel developers, cattlemen, sheepherders, river rafters, and farmers all see preferred ways of managing our forest resources. These interests inevitably come into conflict. Regulators choose among their claims, balancing off the pressures each of these groups poses, to reach some compromise management plan for the forest. How large a voice each has in the final outcome depends upon their separate strengths and adeptness in the political and regulatory process. Logically, each such party would invest in efforts (educational campaigns, lobbying, perhaps even outright bribery) to sway the regulatory process in its favor. Each should be ready to quit further investment only when a dollar's worth of investment adds just a dollar's worth of benefits. Each interest group in such a setting should eventually hold equal power to further modify the political process. Like giant sumo wrestlers, they will push and shove the regulatory process until an equilibrium has been reached, and then come to an apparent standstill. All will have equal power to move the events further, even though one may have captured the lion's share of the available resources.

In the for-profit firm, the owners of the firm hold the legal power to direct its operations and to receive any economic benefit from the activity of the firm. Whether or not the owners can effectively gain the full cooperation of managers and workers in achieving the owner's goals is a difficult question, described generally as the question of whether a "principal" can get his "agent" to act appropriately (Jensen and Meckling 1976; Walking and Long 1984). But at least on paper, the firm acts to satisfy the desires of the owners.

In the not-for-profit hospital setting, absent a formally designated "owner," various groups similarly compete for control of the resources of the hospital: the medical staff seeks to guide the hospital for its own purposes (e.g., curing people and making income for themselves); the patients seek lower cost and better care; the administrative staff may seek a larger organization to manage; the staff may seek better wages and shorter hours; the board of trustees (in whom official control rests) may often be the least interested party, but it eventually must mediate the interests of the others. Each of these various interest groups has been the subject of various theories of the not-for-profit hospital, each considering how the hospital would behave if any one of these parties "captured" the hospital for its own gains. [5]

There is no reason at all, however, to believe that any single one of these contesting parties must always be dominant. Depending upon the constitution of the hospital, the strength of personalities involved, and interaction with external market forces, we could find any of the special theories of hospital behavior appearing to represent the matter adequately. [6] In some hospitals, the doctors may dominate; elsewhere, a board of trustees may dominate. In other settings, the employees may gain the upper hand and receive higher than normal wages.

The hospital may generate revenues above its operating costs from a variety of sources. Even in a competitive market, the hospital may enjoy the economic fruits of population or income growth in an area, superior efficiency, increased insurance coverage of its potential patients, as well as "normal" returns on capital investment. Further, if the hospital holds economic power in the market, it may be able to price as a monopolist, charging prices systematically higher than its costs. The greater the monopoly power of the hospital, the greater its ability to generate extra revenues to further the many interests of the parties affiliated with the hospital.

As the hospital generates revenues in excess of its costs ("profits" in another setting), choices must be made about the purposes to which these excess revenues will be put. Presumably, the medical staff will seek additional staff and equipment to augment its own goals. It would be terribly naive, however, to consider the medical staff as uniform in purpose. Rather, many small groups of physicians (and other professionals) will hold divergent views about the appropriate expenditure pattern. Other groups will push toward their own goals, as their authority and effectiveness in the politics of hospital control permit.

An external change such as an increase in the stringency of Medicare payments has significant effects on the economics of such a hospital. If the hospital was in "political equilibrium" before the event, it will tend to move to a comparable equilibrium after the event. If the external event generates added wealth for the hospital, we should expect all to share in the windfall. If a loss arises, we should expect each actor to bear part of the brunt. In a comment on Peltzman's (1976) model of the regulatory process, Becker (1976) dubbed this a "share-the-gain and share-the-pain" model of regulation, and this applies similarly to the not-for-profit hospital.

The other broad generalization of this model suggests that only if the ability of one party to "manufacture" political strength is altered will its relative position be improved or reduced. For example, unless changes in Medicare payments to hospitals also alter the bargaining position of doctors, administrators, patients, employees, or trustees, one should find the consequences of the fiscal change shared proportionately by all affected parties. But if, for example, certificate-of-need laws eliminate the ability of the hospital to provide new equipment for physicians' use, then their bargaining power will fall, relative to, say, workers' power for wage bargaining.

This approach to hospital decisionmaking establishes a simple framework to explore the hospital's view of price-setting and charge-shifting. Consider first how the hospital would choose its mix of services and capabilities for each, the prices it would charge for those services, and the payments it would make to its employees, keeping in mind that the hospital (typically) operates under a just-break-even constraint because of its not-for-profit legal form. One would expect the hospital to price some services above their incremental cost, and possibly to subsidize others below incremental cost, in order to satisfy the various purposes of the hospital. The prices marked up the most would probably match those activities for which the demand was least sensitive to price changes, because such a pattern of markups would generate more revenue for the hospital to accomplish its various purposes. Subsidies would benefit various parties, according to their relative strengths. For example, a hospital with a relatively strong physician staff might use resources to subsidize an ambulatory care center available to the private staff for treating their patients. In a hospital where other parties were more dominant, such an ambulatory clinic might well hire its own doctors, in competition with the community's physicians.

Consider the issue of payment for uncompensated care from this point of view: the decision to grant free or reduced-rate care to some patients, or (comparably) the decision not to pursue bill collection as avidly as possible, represents a compromise of views about the proper uses of the hospital revenues. The trustees may seek some uncompensated care in their role as representatives of the surrounding community. The doctors may also attempt to have the hospital grant some such relief to the patient, for such relief from the hospital bill might enhance the patient's ability to pay the physicians' bills. In more sophisticated terms, the reduced price of hospital care should increase demand for physician services, since the two goods are consumed in tandem rather than as substitutes for one another (Newhouse et al. 1981).

Each decision to subsidize uncompensated care represents a choice to give up alternative uses of those funds within the hospital. With more uncompensated care, there is less available to satisfy other demands on the hospital. For example, the choice of scope of services offered represents a major area of contest between the various forces in the hospital. Internal medicine specialists will seek new diagnostic devices or improved and esoteric laboratory capabilities. Surgeons may wish a laminar air-flow surgical suite, better radiologic facilities in the operating room suite, or more specialized surgical recovery/intensive care units. Oncologists might opt for newer, stronger radiation therapy devices and the specialized staff needed for their operation. Each of these alternatives may find support from another sector; all increase the prestige of the hospital to some degree, to the board's satisfaction; all add staff and—under some circumstances—revenues, to the administrator's gain. The important point here, of course, is that any delivery of uncompensated care within the hospital also competes with each of these potential uses of hospital funds. Subsidies to the poor, whether deliberate or inadvertent (through inactive bill collection), reduce funds available to expand the scope of various services, to augment the equipment of some particular medical service, or to enhance any other activity of the hospital. Sloan and co-authors in Chapter 2 support this analysis and find higher amounts of uncompensated care reduce the profitability of the hospital.

When viewed from this perspective, we should anticipate that virtually every kind of charge-shifting imaginable might be found in any particular hospital. And if confronted with a reduced payment from a large third-party payer, the hospital would be expected to reorganize and reshuffle its costs and charges in an attempt to preserve the same set of activities (to the extent still possible) that were previously being conducted. Depending upon the economic conditions facing each hospital-buyer combination, the buyer may or may not be successful in forcing the hospital to accept such pricing.

In addition to in-hospital adjustments, the hospital may attempt to increase its price to other buyers to offset partly or in whole the revenue loss brought about by the change in government payment policy. If one observes a hospital increasing its charges to some parties in the face of payment reductions by others, one can immediately infer that the hospital is able to increase these charges because it holds some previously unexercised monopoly power. If it had held monopoly power that it exercised fully, then no further increase in price would be profitable, in the broad sense of the word. Furthermore, if the hospital were in a purely competitive market, raising prices would cause revenue losses from other consumers.

Why might a hospital have chosen to leave possible extra profits lying on the table? In part, because the various classes of consumers form one of the interest groups competing for the resources of the hospital, along with the doctors, the staff, and the administrators, and in part, because the not-for-profit structure of the hospital does not legally permit continual accumulation of profits. There is nothing at all inconsistent about the notion that the typical American hospital holds unexercised monopoly power. But we should recognize explicitly that it is a necessary ingredient of the usual charge-shifting story portrayed in recent years.

A recent study by Hadley and Feder (1984) sheds some light on the success of patient groups in reducing overall charges. They found that hospital charges generally are set to maximize "profits" of the hospital, even though the hospitals in their sample were wholly nonprofit institutions. While they did not directly compare pricing patterns of for-profit and not-for-profit hospitals, their study suggests that there has been little unexercised monopoly power. If so, then decreases in payment (for example, under Medicare DRGs) would result in actual reductions in hospital costs, rather than in charge-shifting.

The central point is that cross-subsidies and apparent charge-shifting within the typical hospital might arise either from the hospital's own actions and market position or from the actions of buyers. The extent to which these occur will increase with the power each party has to affect market prices, either as a seller or a buyer. In general, it seems that meaningful cross-subsidization and charge-shifting cannot occur without some market power by the hospital. Whether the cross-subsidies arise owing to hospital action alone or are due also to buyer action depends upon whether some buyers can affect prices through exercise of monopsony power.

Measurement of Charge-Shifting and Cross-Subsidies

In order to discuss charge-shifting accurately, one needs a standard of measurement representing the pricing patterns that might emerge without any cross-subsidies or charge-shifting. This first requires some standard definitions of costs.

Incremental Costs. If the hospital expands a particular service slightly, the incremental costs are those arising because of the expansion. True incremental costs are notoriously difficult to measure in any business, particularly one conducting multiple activities, but the concept is a useful benchmark for considering other alternatives. When a hospital bills each patient for particular services rendered (one hour of therapy, two bedpans, one catheterization packet, eight hours of special nursing care, etc.), this itemized billing reflects an attempt by the hospital to charge each patient the incremental cost of delivering care to that patient rather than some average cost for all patients. In a competitive market, to the extent that incremental costs can be identified by a reasonable measurement effort, a competitive market will tend towards full incremental costs as the basis of prices.

Common (Joint) Costs. In any organization delivering multiple products (the hospital offers hundreds, if not thousands, of products), some costs cannot be attributed specifically to any single activity. Rather, they are costs that arise jointly with a cluster of activities. Administration, property taxes, and the like are obvious examples of fixed costs that contribute to many activities; these are commonly included in a hospital's "overhead rate." But the hospital contains many examples of more refined common costs. The floor nurse provides a prime example: her activities include patient care in the usual sense, administration, medical record-keeping, pharmaceutical services, assistance to physicians in medical procedures, and a whole host of other activities. How can one account for the nurse's time in a meaningful sense? Even if the nurse maintained an infinitely detailed record of her minute-by-minute activities, some activities would be truly "joint production" of two or more services. Talking to the patient while changing a bed, for example, may represent both housekeeping and clinical psychological care, and observing the patient's vital signs and general demeanor at the same time represents the practice of medical diagnosis. There is no meaningful way to separate such common costs into distinguishable categories of "marginal costs" of each activity.

Average Costs. In a factory producing pencils (and nothing else), the average cost of pencils can be easily established: divide total costs by the number of pencils produced. But if both pencils and pens are made, no simple average can be calculated. Two alternatives appear available to summarize the average cost structure of such a business. One approach would calculate how many pencil equivalents each pen represented, and then convert every activity into the common denominator of "pseudo-pencils." The conversion would require assigning weights (for example, retail prices) to each product before the total could be added up. An alternative (proposed by Baumol et al. 1982) asks how average costs of a given mix of services change the total scope as the enterprise expands. For example, one can consider the average costs of bundles of pencils and pens representing two pencils and one pen (two-thirds and one-third mix) at 100 bundles (200 pencils, 100 pens), 200 bundles, 500 bundles, and so on. One could readily calculate the average cost of each of these bundles. Of course, the average cost changes differently as one focuses on different bundles, but for many purposes, such as in a hospital setting, the concept of average cost per bundle of product appears more useful than other alternatives. In the hospital, if every patient received the same bundle of services, then this simple average cost per bundle would provide an appropriate measure of resources used and would reflect the price one would charge to avoid cross-subsidies. [7]

Unfortunately, patient days or "bundles" differ considerably. The only meaningful way to address this issue would be to use a sophisticated case-mix adjusted average cost measure. If the case mix adjustment is correct, then it should bring the average cost measure back to the most useful method—the concept of a cost of a given bundle of services.

Several studies have attempted to assess just how costs do differ among patient classes. Most are limited either in geographic scope or because they studied only a part of all relevant costs (e.g., nursing costs).

In a recent empirical study, Sloan and Becker (1984) examined how the costs of hospital care varied with the proportion of patients from a set of payment groups. They found that costs per patient day were higher on average for Medicare patients, but equal for other groups. They also showed that only a very small part of the variation in hospital costs arises from the mix of patients across the payment group. They concluded that there are no systematic differences in cost that can be attributed to the source of patient payment. While important cost differences arise owing to case mix and severity of patient illnesses, those severity differences do not correlate with the source of payment. These results are strikingly important, for they imply that differences in payment observed from different buyers do not correspond to cost differences that would arise in a competitive market. Rather, they appear to be attempts of each buyer to exercise monopsony power, possibly to offset previously exercised monopoly power by the hospitals. The Sloan-Becker study provides added support for this notion by showing that discounts forced upon hospitals by third-party buyers markedly affect profits, but (as noted) not costs of hospitals.

Sloan and Becker, of course, analyzed average costs of a hospital day. This raises the question of whether the hospitals might have patients of different severity. If so, then hospitals would not necessarily be delivering the same "bundle of services" that we want to measure. But Sloan and Becker also assessed average cost per day while holding constant the severity-of-patient mix. To the extent that they successfully adjust for complexity, they have

Charles E. Phelps

portrayed, in effect, the average costs per bundle of service as-discussed above. With this adjustment, they found that no patient class (Medicare, Medicaid, Blue Cross, or commercial insurance) showed higher or lower costs than others. In a setting with considerable common costs among services, this is the most reliable measure available of the "subsidy-free" cost structure of a hospital. And if Sloan and Becker's results stand up under further scrutiny, those results provide strong evidence that current charge-shifting by third-party buyers is not cost-justified.

Is Charge-Shifting Necessarily Bad?

Whenever it is economically feasible, the hospital may be expected to generate some profits and use them for the various purposes of groups in and around the hospital. These uses alone will generate a complex set of cross-subsidies. Interwoven among these may be differences in payments (vis-à-vis costs) imposed from outside, that is, by government or insurer monopsony behavior. In considering the overall desirability of such behavior, one must ask what society expects from its hospitals, especially in exchange for the customary not-for-profit legal status and accompanying tax exemption.

In the broadest sense, one could argue that a social contract has been formed between hospitals and society. Certainly part of the contract specifies that hospitals will treat patients whose health would be impaired by turning them away (even if those patients are later transferred to another hospital). But the general care of low-income patients has usually been treated as a broad social responsibility, not merely a task for the hospitals.

The poor still receive much of their care from the county hospitals, as they have historically, but other hospitals still contribute resources to a myriad of causes, including care of the poor, the mentally ill, the handicapped, patients of their most important surgeons, children, and mothers. One cannot treat these activities as undesirable in general; they support at least broadly the social contract with hospitals, and they provide important transfers of income-in-kind to many disadvantaged groups, even if imperfectly targeted from society's point of view.

The major issue with cross-subsidies is not how they are spent, but how they are financed. Major cross-subsidization implies exercising of monopoly pricing power, which of course could cause undesirable economic consequences. Higher prices, even for hospital care, deter persons from using that care. Thus, if the hospital finances its desired activities by raising the prices of certain other activities above costs, there may arise distortions in the pattern of use. The pricing patterns transfer income, of course, from those using the "unfavored" types of care to those using the "favored" services. Aside from whether the transfer is viewed as undesirable or desirable, one should also assess whether the distortions in prices reduce hospital use in an undesired fashion. The issue is empirical: if people's consumption of the unfavored care is relatively insensitive to prices (e.g., if nearly fully insured), then there will only be income transfers, but little if any distortion of the use of care. But if the use of unfavored care appears highly sensitive to price, then substantial distortions could arise. Conversely, if the use of favored goods is highly price-sensitive, then even small subsidies could lead to large changes in behavior.

Harris (1979) studied hospital pricing patterns and concludes that the distortions in pricing are probably desirable, given the overall constraint that some people will not be made to pay for care. He concluded that the pattern of prices observed in his study hospital reasonably matched those that a well-informed regulator would choose if he were attempting to maximize the total well-being of our society, given the overall constraint that the hospital revenue cover its costs. If true (even if not exactly), then the not-for-profit hospital, while obviously susceptible to manipulation by special-interest groups, may perform about as well as any institution one can currently envision for the complicated social functions we ask the hospital to perform. The alternative would have the costs of meeting these social goals paid directly by our entire society, and would have the hospital charging prices as close as possible to costs. Under this alternative, all of society, rather than the part of society buying the "unfavored" hospital care, would support the social goals we ask of hospitals.

A more difficult question is how to view the externally imposed charge-shifting, where one set of payers reduces its payments below the hospital charges (or even below documentable costs of the hospital). If the payment differentials relate to cost differences, then the outcome certainly matches what a competitive market would produce. But if there are no cost differences, as found by Sloan and Becker, then the monopsonistic purchasing by large buyers merely adds to the burden shouldered by others in the hospital to finance the "favored" activities of the hospital.

Alternatives to Cross-Subsidies

Three distinct groups seek to alter the way hospitals acquire and distribute resources. The first group—a set of external buyers of care, the private and public insurers—may wish to impose upon the hospital payments less than what the hospital seeks to charge for care. Its primary mechanism for action is pure market power. A second group—physicians, managers, trustees, patients, and employees—is represented directly in the hospital governance.[8] It acts primarily through hospital bylaws and rules. The third group includes other members of society not represented in the hospital governance structure. It acts primarily through local, state, or federal laws or regulatory processes to attempt to affect the resource uses in the hospital. Regardless of which of these groups should or should not have its interests realized, it is apparent that any attempt to change the current status must rely on different actions to affect

Charles E. Phelps

each. Market, legal, or bargaining choices are available to change the power of monopsonistic buyers. Changes in the hospital governance structure or in external regulation can bear on the power of each party within the hospital to affect resource allocation. Presumably, changes in tax policy, by affecting prices of inputs or outputs of the hospital, could also change its activities to some extent. As to the third set of interests (as expressed through regulation), society must change those regulations in order to affect the hospital. Some such actions have appeared on the hospital regulatory scene. For example, some hospital certificate-of-need hearings tie decisions about expansion or new construction of a hospital specifically to the past behavior or stated intentions of the petitioning hospitals regarding expenses for charity care. Rate-setting activity by state authorities, where allowed, also forms a natural forum for expressing societal views in general.

Beginning with the premise that some social goals for the hospital do indeed exist, then it is fair to ask how the hospital should finance them. Currently, the hospital finances those activities the same way it finances its own goals, by the use of cross-subsidies. To the extent that the goals of society correspond to those of the "enfranchised" parties within the hospital governance structure, no conflict arises. Introduction of charity care payments into rate-setting processes formalizes this activity legally.

Harris (1979) argued that the cross-subsidy patterns used by hospitals promote general social goals (in a particular sense), rather than conflicting with them. If true, then one must view this outcome as strictly fortuitous, for there is no reason in particular to expect that the desires of society will match, closely or even loosely, the outcome of the "sumo wrestling match" for use of hospital resources, an outcome that shapes the decisions of American hospitals. While the natural resource-control activities of the hospital might be altered somewhat through certificate-of-need or rate-setting procedures, this approach still must necessarily place the burden of payment for charity care on the shoulders of other sick persons.

When and if hospital and social goals might compete, the hospital must balance its own goals against those of the broader society, taking into account how effectively the social goals can be imposed, and how effective the enforcement of regulation might be. But in general, it appears that a small segment of society—those patients buying "unfavored" care—finances the "favored" activities of the hospital, whether those activities are favored by society in general or only by enfranchised parties within the hospital governance. At least for the resources needed to provide society's goals, it would seem mysterious, at best, to argue that this small segment of unfavored patients should shoulder the burden. A broader base of payment is surely more appropriate.

If parts of the customer base of the hospitals have sufficient market power to reduce their payments (on a basis other than cost differentials), one obvious effect is to shrink the base of customers buying "unfavored" services, and hence the financing of "favored" services. If it is undesirable to have the hospital's whole set of "unfavored customers" financing the social goals of the hospital, then *a fortiori* it is undesirable to have an even smaller set of customers carry the same burden.

Even if some public financial support arises for those activities that we as a society ask the hospital to accomplish, there will still be that set of cross-subsidies undertaken at the discretion of the hospital itself. There is no particularly obvious policy recommendation to make regarding these matters, for they will occur no matter what regulations we might pass to suppress them. Indeed, as hospital decisionmaking has been discussed, it appears that no regulation could be structured to deal meaningfully with the myriad cross-subsidies one might expect to find within the usual not-for-profit hospital and, to a lesser extent, in the for-profit hospital.

Clearly, competition in the hospital markets will limit, if not eliminate, the ability of not-for-profit organizations to function in this manner. (The competition could well be from other not-for-profits, as well as from for-profit hospitals.) As with other economic events, competition may prove the most effective policeman of all. The only relevant policy one might make is to promote competition. Certainly activities and regulations designed to reduce competition, whatever their intrinsic value, will foster economic conditions that continue to support the hospital-initiated types of cross-subsidies.

If monopoly power is indeed needed to sustain cross-subsidies, whatever their origin, then there should be less cross-subsidization where there is more competition. In that light, a useful new data base has been produced by Luft and Maerki (1984) describing, in effect, the number of hospitals geographically close enough to compete with any given hospital. While sheer numbers alone do not necessarily describe the nature of hospital competition, these data should produce fruitful studies of competition. One test is to follow the pattern of cross-subsidies initiated by the hospital and study the importance of buyer-induced cross-subsidy (monopsony) as competitive conditions vary.

There is no social or economic merit in continuing monopsony-generated cross-subsidies, particularly if the belief is accepted that general fund public payment is the most appropriate source for payment of currently uncompensated care. When the monopsonist is a government agency, then direct changes in public law and rules can resolve the matter. When the monopsony exists because of large private buyers, there appears to be no obvious direction for policy to take, except, again, to eliminate any artificiality in the markets involved.

Conclusion

Cross-subsidies arise in hospitals from several sources. The persons controlling the hospital's resources may choose a specific pattern of cross-subsidies for their own purposes. Groups of buyers (e.g., insurance plans, private or government) may try to impose cross-subsidies on hospitals by reducing payments made for care. Unless based upon true cost differences, these types of cross-subsidies seem only to exacerbate any undesirable aspects of other cross-subsidies within the hospital. One should expect to find a myriad complex of cross-subsidies in any American hospital, and it will probably prove impossible either to pinpoint the specific source of any single subsidy identified or to regulate such cross-subsidies out of existence. Since the magnitude of cross-subsidies must fall as hospital markets become more competitive (no matter what the source of the cross-subsidy), policies designed to increase competition should assist policymakers who wish to reduce or eliminate undesired cross-subsidies. However, since at least some of the cross-subsidies undertaken by the hospital clearly arise at the implicit or explicit request of society, we should proceed with caution if we move to eliminate such pricing behavior in the hospital.

Notes

Participants in the Vanderbilt University Conference on Uncompensated Hospital Care provided considerable valuable discussion. Frank Sloan provided excellent guidance not only in development of the paper but also in highly thoughtful comments on an early draft. However, the views expressed in this paper are mine only, and responsibility for errors obviously does not pass to those who have been helpful in the past.

1. The success or failure of raising prices to increase revenue depends upon how responsive the demand facing each hospital is to price. If wholly unresponsive to price (completely price-inelastic), the tactic obviously will succeed. If very price responsive, it will fail. The critical point is if use falls off 1 percent when price increases 1 percent (unitary demand-elasticity). Any larger price response facing the hospital makes the tactic a failure.

2. See Schwartz and Wilde (1982) and references cited therein for models of such hospital markets.

3. Health Insurance Association of America (1983).

4. This view most closely matches that of Sam Peltzman's model of the regulatory process (Peltzman 1976). Recent developments by Timothy Quinn (1983) provide useful extensions into the arena of environmental regulation, and it is this model which I am attempting to articulate briefly here.

5. I employ the word "capture" deliberately. In the theory of regulation, the same history of thought can be observed. Articles were written suggesting how each of the various parties involved in the regulatory process—the public, the regulated industry, and the regulators themselves—had "captured" the regulatory process for themselves. The Peltzman and Quinn writings essentially generalize that literature. This chapter gives a rough outline of how one might generalize the comparable hospital literature.

6. The Pauly and Redisch (1973) model presumes that physicians essentially capture this process. The Newhouse (1970) model views the administrator (or the board of trustees, embodied in the administration) as the victor of the struggle. Niskanen (1979) viewed the bureaucrat as a budget maximizer seeking to expand his own domain. Martin Feldstein (1971) suggested that the employees of the hospital are the winners, gaining

higher wages than might otherwise be the case. By ironic contrast, Yett (1975) viewed the employees, particularly the nursing staff, as victims of an exploiting monopsonist who pays them lower wages than otherwise because they have no alternative industries to which they might turn for employment.

7. One advantage in this approach is that it avoids a certain circularity that would arise if outputs of pencils and pens were weighted by their prices (or other measures of value). If one were trying to assess how prices differed from average (or incremental) costs in such a situation, one would obviously need some measure of costs that was independent of the prices charged before the concept would have any meaning. The concept proposed by Baumol and associates (1982) provides this independence.

8. Harris (1979) discussed how these groups might vie for control of hospital resources.

References

Baumol, William, Jon Panzar, and Robert Willig. 1982. *Contestable Markets and Competition*. New York: Harcourt, Brace and Jovanovich.

Becker, Gary. 1976. "Towards a More General Theory of Regulation: Comment." *Journal of Law and Economics* 19, no. 2 (August): 245–48.

Center for Health Policy Studies. 1984. *Massachusetts Payer Differential Study*. Final Report. Columbia, Md.: The Center, February 19.

Danzon, Patricia. 1982. "Hospital 'Profits': The Effects of Reimbursement Policies." *Journal of Health Economics* 1, no. 1 (May): 29–52.

Feldstein, Martin. 1971. *The Rising Cost of Hospital Care*. Washington, D.C.: Information Resources Press.

Ginsburg, Paul, and Frank A. Sloan. 1984. "Hospital Cost-Shifting." *New England Journal of Medicine* 310, no. 14 (April 5): 893–98.

Hadley, Jack, and Judith Feder. 1984. "Hospital Cost-Shifting: An Analysis of Hospitals' Markup and Financial Needs." Washington, D.C.: The Urban Institute, October. Mimeo.

Harris, Jeffrey. 1979. "Pricing Rules for Hospitals." *Bell Journal of Economics* 10, no. 1 (Spring): 224–43.

Health Insurance Association of America. 1983. *Hospital Cost-Shifting: Its Impact, The Solution*. Washington, D.C.: The Association, February.

Hoover, Mina, and Robert P. Mullen. 1979. "Blue Cross Contract Provisions." Chicago: American Hospital Association, December. Mimeo.

Jensen, Michael C., and William H. Meckling. 1976. "Theory of the Firm: Managerial Behavior, Agency Costs, and Ownership Structure." *Journal of Financial Economics* 3, no. 4 (October): 305–60.

Luft, Harold S., and Susan C. Maerki. 1984. "Competitive Potential of Hospitals and Their Neighbors." *Contemporary Policy Issues* 3, no. 2 (Winter): 89–102.

Newhouse, Joseph P. 1970. "Not-for-Profit Hospitals." *American Economic Review* 60, no. 3 (March): 64–74.

———. 1978. "The Erosion of the Medical Marketplace." Report R-2141-HEW. Santa Monica, Calif.: The Rand Corporation, December.

Newhouse, Joseph P., et al. 1981. "Some Interim Results from a Controlled Trial of

Cost-Sharing in Health Insurance." *New England Journal of Medicine* 305, no. 25 (December 17): 1501–7.

Niskanen, William. 1979. "Competition among Government Bureaus." *American Behavioral Scientist* 22, no. 5 (May–June): 517–24.

Pauly, Mark, and Michael Redisch. 1973. "The Not-for-Profit Hospital as a Physicians' Cooperative." *American Economic Review* 63, no. 1 (March): 87–99.

Peltzman, Sam. 1976. "Towards a More General Theory of Regulation." *Journal of Law and Economics* 19, no. 2 (August): 211–40.

Quinn, Timothy. 1983. "Distributional Consequences and Political Concern: On Design of a Feasible Market Mechanism for Environmental Control." In *Buying A Better Environment: Cost-Effective Regulation through Permit Trading*. Ed. Erhard F. Joeres and Martin H. David. Land Economics Monograph No. 6. Madison: University of Wisconsin Press.

Schwartz, Alan, and Louis L. Wilde. 1982. "Competitive Equilibria in Markets for Heterogeneous Goods under Imperfect Information: A Theoretical Analysis with Policy Implications." *Bell Journal of Economics* 13, no. 1 (Spring): 181–93.

Sloan, Frank A., and Edmund R. Becker. 1984. "Cross-Subsidies and Payment for Hospital Care." *Journal of Health Politics, Policy, and Law* 8, no. 4 (Winter): 660–85.

Walking, Ralph A., and Michael S. Long. 1984. "Agency Theory, Managerial Welfare, and Takeover Bid Resistance." *Rand Journal of Economics* 15, no. 1 (Spring): 54–68.

Yett, Donald E. 1975. *An Economic Analysis of the Nurse Shortage.* Lexington, Mass.: D. C. Heath.

SEVEN
Public Subsidies for Hospital Care of the Poor: Medicaid and Other Myths of Equity

Beverlee A. Myers

In the early years of this century, society, hospitals, and the poor had essentially congruent goals: the provision of needed medical care for those who could not afford to pay for alternative care. Hospitals were society's agents to care for the sick poor. According to Paul Starr,

> Few institutions have undergone as radical a metamorphosis as have hospitals in their modern history. In developing from places of dreaded impurity and exiled human wreckage into awesome citadels of science and bureaucratic order, they acquired a new moral identity, as well as new purposes and patients of higher status. The hospital is perhaps distinctive among social organizations in having first been built primarily for the poor and only later entered in significant numbers and an entirely different state of mind by the more respectable classes. As its functions were transformed, it emerged, in a sense, from the underlife of society to become a regular part of accepted experience, still an occasion for anxiety but not horror. (Starr 1982)

Today hospitals are unlikely to welcome and care for the poor unless there is a source of payment available (Feder and Hadley 1983). Rising hospital costs, availability of private and public health insurance, the decline of philanthropy as a source of payment for care, and the expectations of the public generally for high-quality, technology-intensive hospital care have all contributed to this change in goals and expectations.

Society, hospitals, and the poor no longer have common expectations. The poor would like to have access to the same hospital care as everyone else. Hospitals would like to have their full financial requirements met.[1] Society would like to assure equity among individuals, equity among third-party payers and taxpayers, and an efficient hospital system at an affordable price (President's Commission 1983).

These expectations lead to incompatibility of goals, pitting hospitals and the poor against each other when society appears unable or unwilling to pay the price. The problem involves how to structure an equitable and efficient system to share the burden of paying for needed hospital care for the poor. Are there models that can illustrate ways of sharing the burden more equitably and efficiently? What is known about how the burden is currently shared and with what effect?

This chapter addresses these issues by (1) formulating a concept of medical indigency; (2) summarizing sources of payment for indigent hospital care, drawing upon national Medicaid data, but particularly focusing on one state, California; (3) illustrating state and local variation in indigent care policy by comparing policies and effects in California with those in Maryland and Texas; and (4) suggesting options for national indigent hospital care policy. California has been selected for illustration primarily because of data availability and because persons in need of hospital care are highly likely to be able to obtain it in that state, being perhaps more likely to have access to needed hospitalization than persons in most other states.

Who Are the Medically Indigent?

Indigency is a local concept and definition. Each local government—which ultimately bears final responsibility for indigents—defines indigency in its own terms and with its own resources in mind (Stevens and Stevens 1974). Individuals move into and out of states and localities, not infrequently in search of hospital care. Persons move in and out of medical indigency as they need and use medical care, or as they are or are not covered by private insurance, or as they meet or do not meet various state or local indigency standards (Davis and Rowland 1983). Medical indigency has come to be the extent to which private or public health insurance in combination with any available personal, out-of-pocket resources is inadequate to cover the full charges for a hospital stay (Hadley and Feder 1983; Granneman and Pauly 1983).

A definition of medical indigency should encompass persons who are poor (i.e., having income and resources at or below a defined poverty level) and are Medicaid recipients receiving welfare grants (AFDC or SSI), or those who are not receiving welfare but who are medically needy and may or may not pay a share of medical costs. It should also include those who are not Medicaid recipients because in their state of residence Medicaid does not cover most of the poverty population (i.e., states having low welfare levels, no medically needy program, no coverage of unemployed-parent families, no coverage of pregnant women in first pregnancy, or no coverage of children in non-AFDC families). It should include, as well, persons not categorically or legally eligible for Medicaid, such as undocumented workers or illegal aliens, single adults or couples aged twenty-one to sixty-four without children, and jail inmates. Further, it should include those who are not poor (having incomes above the poverty level definitions) but who are Medicaid recipients, being eligible by having high medical care expenses and by "spending down" to the income and resources level necessary to qualify for Medicaid. Finally, it should include those who are not Medicaid recipients (not having applied or unable to qualify) but who have high medical expenses relative to their insurance coverage, income, and resources and who are unable or unwilling to pay out-of-pocket costs in the form of uncovered costs, deductibles, and coinsurance.

Medical indigency with respect to hospital care must therefore be defined in terms of a combination of person-oriented and payment-oriented factors: level of personal or family income and resources; adequacy of health insurance coverage; age, sex, and state and locality of residence; pregnancy status; Medicaid eligibility; ability or motivation to pay cost-sharing requirements; need for and use of medical and hospital care and resultant size of medical expenses relative to income; timing of medical expenses in relation to insurance coverage and income.

Any individual may at some time become medically indigent, depending upon individual circumstances. Some individuals for some episodes of hospital care are medically indigent in toto when the whole of their hospital expenses are not paid by personal resources or by health insurance. Other individuals are medically indigent only in part—for example, when they have some insurance and resources, but their expenses for hospital care are not fully paid by those resources.

Davis and Rowland (1983) estimated there were more than 25 million persons uninsured in 1977. However, only a small proportion of this total may require or be at risk for hospital care during the period of being uninsured. Similarly, Medicaid recipients would not be medically indigent for hospital care unless they were at risk or experienced hospitalization. Only 17 percent of Medicaid recipients were in fact hospitalized annually in 1980, a rate comparable to the general population (Sawyer et al. 1983).

Because of the complex nature of the medical indigency concept, this chapter will not provide an estimate of the absolute size of the medically indigent population. Such an estimate awaits fuller agreement on the definition of medical indigency and better data relating the population at risk for hospital care to the full or partial payment for such care.

Another way to analyze the problem of indigency in relation to hospital care is to focus on the sources available to pay hospitals for uncompensated care, and to estimate for each source its share of the burden of indigent hospital care. This approach carries the risk of making certain assumptions. Limiting the focus to the hospital necessarily ignores the essential role of primary care in total health care of the indigent and particularly in preventing the need for hospitalization. It also assumes that someone has to pay for hospital costs incurred, and does not question that reported hospital charges or costs approximate a reasonable level of payment. Finally, the substitution of payment sources for actual counts of indigents tends to understate the size of the medically indigent problem, unless one assumes that in our society all persons sick

Beverlee A. Myers

enough to need hospital care do in fact receive it. There is evidence suggesting this assumption is not necessarily true (Hadley and Feder 1983).

Indigent Hospital Care: Who Pays?

There are four major sources of payment for hospital indigent care: Medicaid, financed with federal, state, and local tax funds; other federal, state, and local tax-supported programs; private philanthropy; and hospital shifting of unpaid charges to private health insurers, called cost- or charge-shifting. Although the former term is more often used, this chapter uses the latter because it describes the phenomenon more accurately.[2]

Estimates of the proportion of indigent hospital care borne by each of these sources in California for 1983–84 are shown in Figure 7.1.[3] Total expenditures for indigent hospital care in California were about $3.4 billion in that year, or approximately one-fifth of all hospital expenses in California. Over half of all indigent hospital care expenses were paid by Medi-Cal, California's federal-state Medicaid program. About 50 percent of indigent hospital payments came from state government sources, 25 percent from federal government sources, 5 percent from local government, and the remainder from private sources, including 11 percent from charge-shifting. Each of these payment sources will be examined more fully, from a national and a California perspective, beginning with Medicaid.

Medicaid/Medi-Cal

Nationally, Medicaid is the largest single source of payment for indigent hospital care, paying for 30 million patient days at a cost of almost $6.5 billion in

Fig. 7.1.   Indigent hospital care in California in 1983–84 ($3.4 billion)

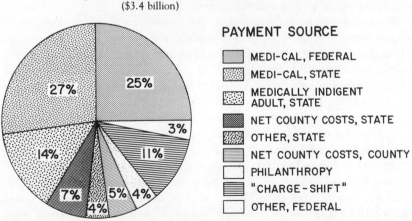

PAYMENT SOURCE

- MEDI-CAL, FEDERAL
- MEDI-CAL, STATE
- MEDICALLY INDIGENT ADULT, STATE
- NET COUNTY COSTS, STATE
- OTHER, STATE
- NET COUNTY COSTS, COUNTY
- PHILANTHROPY
- "CHARGE-SHIFT"
- OTHER, FEDERAL

1980.[4] There were 21.6 million Medicaid recipients nationally in 1980 (the most recent year for which estimates of actual recipients are available), down from a high of 23.5 million in 1976. It is estimated that the number of recipients in 1984 was below 20 million (Sawyer et al. 1983; Rowland and Gaus 1982).

Medicaid programs exist in fifty-four jurisdictions.[5] A major myth of Medicaid is that it can be described and analyzed as a single program or even as fifty-four separate programs (National Study Group 1983). Medicaid is a series of programs, funded by federal and state taxes, administered by each state, under policies determined in part by federal and in part by state decisions, to purchase some health services for some poor people.

There is evidence that Medicaid has achieved these equity goals, at least in part. The poor in general, and those eligible for Medicaid in particular, have increased their use of hospital care and of physician visits since the advent of Medicaid in 1966. Use of hospital care by the poor exceeds that of the non-poor, in large part because of higher need for such care. Greatly improved life expectancy rates and lower infant mortality rates since 1965 are attributed partly to Medicaid (Rogers et al. 1982; Aday and Anderson 1981).

But Medicaid is flawed in concept because it relies on tests of eligibility unrelated to need for medical care. Its variability from state to state and its inaccessibility to many poor people assure that it perpetuates, if not creates, inequities in access to hospital care. Inequities in the national program are further exacerbated in each state and locality with the presence or absence of public or private programs to complement or supplement Medicaid.

Classification of Medicaid Programs

Selected Medicaid program characteristics nationally and in California, Maryland, and Texas are compared in Table 7.1 to illustrate the wide variation among states and within program categories.

The major dimension for describing the various programs is the category of eligible person: welfare recipients or medically needy recipients. The welfare population—variously termed the cash-grant recipients or categorically needy—accounts for three-quarters of all recipients and about half of Medicaid vendor payments nationally. As shown in Table 7.1, the levels of income eligibility under welfare grants varied widely among the states in 1980, with a family of two, consisting of a mother and child or an elderly couple, granted an annual income of almost $5,000 in California, and less than $1,500 in Texas. Medically needy persons are eligible for Medicaid if they fit one of the welfare categories of Aid to Families with Dependent Children (AFDC) or Supplemental Security Income (SSI) but have medical expenses that bring their available income down to levels at or slightly above the welfare levels. Only thirty-four jurisdictions had medically needy programs, and the income eligi-

Table 7.1. Comparison of Medicaid programs, 1980

Comparison item	U.S.	California	Maryland	Texas
	Expenditures			
Maximum AFDC grant per year, 2-person family	—	$4,898	$2,532	$1,464
Annual net income protected for maintenance, 4-person family[a]	—	$9,612	$4,404	—
Mean Medicaid expenditure per recipient	$1,078	$ 798	$1,023	$1,426
	Percentages			
Recipients as % of poverty population	54.0	97.0	69.0	25.0
Recipients aged 65+	15.8	16.6	12.7	35.8
Expenditures for those 65+	37.8	27.4	35.7	50.4
Recipients on AFDC	65.1	62.0	76.2	52.6
Expenditures for AFDC enrollees	28.1	35.6	42.3	17.0
Distribution of Medicaid spending				
Inpatient hospital	27.0	35.1	41.4	17.6
Long-term care[b]	43.9	23.4	33.7	60.3
Physicians' services	8.0	16.8	6.5	10.2
Outpatient hospital	4.7	6.0	9.8	2.1
HIO/HMO[c]	2.3	5.5	3.8	24.3
Federal matching share	55.6	50.0	50.0	58.4
State-only program	21 states	yes	yes	no
Local assistance to state program	13 states	no	no	no

Source: Sawyer et al. (1983).

[a] Families classified as medically needy.

[b] Nursing-home, intermediate, or long-term care.

[c] HIO = health insuring organization.

bility levels vary from almost $10,000 per year for a family of four in California to less than $5,000 for a family in Colorado and other states.

Different Medicaid programs exist within each welfare or medically needy category.

The AFDC cash grant population is the largest recipient population, composing 55 percent of Medicaid recipients and 24 percent of expenditures. The group is composed principally of dependent children and their single parent. In twenty-four states both parents are included if both are unemployed. There are at least three distinct medical care programs for the AFDC population: primary care; episodic, acute hospital care; and health maintenance organization (HMO) arrangements.

Primary care includes the federally mandated early and periodic screening, diagnosis, and treatment program (EPSDT) for children and also the family planning, prenatal, and postnatal care that constitute a major part of the AFDC cash grant program.

Episodic, acute hospital care available for all AFDC/CG recipients is the most expensive part of the AFDC program. The proportions spent on hospital care vary from state to state depending upon the nature of Medicaid generally and the limits in amount, scope, and duration placed on hospital care. Eighteen states set limits on days of hospital care that will be covered: e.g., Maryland covers only twenty days per year, and Texas covers thirty days per episode. Other states leave the number of days unlimited but impose extensive prior, concurrent, and post utilization controls, like California, or eliminate payment for weekend admissions or other services, like New York. Each state also exercises options on payment methods and amounts: thirty-two states, including Texas, pay hospitals under the Medicare principles, while others, including Maryland, have prospective systems that control payments for Medicaid and other payers. California has had a per case prospective payment system which applied only to Medi-Cal and which, according to the California Health Facilities Commission (1982), paid only 82 percent of hospitals' full financial requirements. In 1983, California implemented a program to select hospitals to receive Medi-Cal contracts on the basis of negotiation of price, and range and quality of services.

HMO and risk-sharing arrangements are available in sixteen states that contract on a risk-sharing basis for some covered services for the eligible cash grant population. In most states, this consists largely of the AFDC group. For example, California contracts prospectively on a per capita basis for over 5 percent of its cash grant population with HMOs, with California Dental Services Corporation for dental care for the entire eligible population, and with different entities in five counties for all or part of the population for acute care services. As Table 7.1 indicates, in Texas almost 25 percent of the total Medicaid program is contracted on a risk-sharing basis (HIO/HMO); however, this is not an HMO arrangement but a risk contract with a computer firm for claims processing, with the state itself at risk primarily for the long-term care and drug problems.

The cash grant Supplemental Security Income (SSI) population accounts for 20 percent of recipients and 28 percent of expenditures in Medicaid. This population consists of welfare recipients who are aged, blind, or permanently and totally disabled. Their eligibility is generally determined by the federal cash grant program called Supplemental Security Income, although thirty-four states supplement the basic grant. This population participates in the acute hospital care program and the prepaid programs, but to a lesser extent than the AFDC population because of the crossover program.

The crossover program is available for about 15 percent of Medicaid recipients, including 84 percent of the elderly Medicaid recipients, also eligible for Medicare. States have the option of "buying-in" to Medicare for their cash-

Beverlee A. Myers

grant-eligible population and having the federal government match these payments. The state pays the premium, residual deductible, and coinsurance, and also provides any additional benefits, such as drugs, that are part of the regular Medicaid program. About 12 percent of Medicare Part B enrollees are enrolled in Medicaid, with the proportion of Medicare buy-in from 2 to 31 percent, depending upon the state (McMillan et al. 1983). The crossover program is identified as a separate program, since the crossovers are frequently treated more like Medicare than Medicaid patients by the states—e.g., crossover patients are not limited to contracting hospitals in California, unless they have used up all Medicare benefits.

Medically needy programs are available, as noted previously, in thirty-four jurisdictions. The federal government will share in the state costs of services for those persons not on cash assistance but in the same general categories of aged, blind, disabled, or families with dependent children, whose incomes and resources are above welfare levels but who incur costs of medical care beyond their means. On a national basis, 25 percent of Medicaid recipients are in the medically needy category, and this category consumes 48 percent of total expenditures because many in this category are in long-term-care institutions. The basic income levels that the medically needy are permitted to retain to meet their basic need vary widely in the same way as the welfare income levels. The maximum permitted by federal rules is 133 percent of the AFDC need levels in the state, which is the level established in California.

The "spend down," or share of cost, aspect of Medicaid is complex, misunderstood, and difficult to administer. It constitutes an income-related deductible and a monthly, quarterly, or semi-annual coinsurance. Persons in the medically needy category must divest themselves of nearly all savings and liquid or other assets except car and home, and then must allocate all their income above the need standard toward the costs of their medical care. About 220,000 persons in California were potentially eligible for Medi-Cal in 1980 if they met their monthly cost-sharing. In an average month, half of this population would meet that cost-share. For those who met their share of the cost, the median per person share was $199, with Medi-Cal paying the remainder of their medical bills for the month. Those eligible must meet the same amount of cost-sharing every month (California Department of Health Services 1983b).

Additional research on the issue of cost-sharing in Medicaid programs is needed and should address the nature of the "spend-down," its size and impacts, and its similarities and differences relative to more traditional cost-sharing methods of copayment, deductibles, and coinsurance.

Long-term-care programs for the aged and disabled, in cash grant and in medically needy categories, cover those in nursing homes and intermediate care facilities, as well as that small part of the population that receives home care. Two programs of long-term care can be distinguished: one for the sick elderly and physically disabled and another for the developmentally disabled of all ages. Nationally, nearly half of all Medicaid expenditures go to long-term care, but this varies among states (Sawyer et al. 1983, table 4.19).

State-only Medicaid-like programs are available in an estimated twenty-one states, providing some level of benefits to people not defined in the federal categories. Generally, persons ineligible for Medicaid as federally defined include poor adults on local general relief, those in the age range of twenty-one to sixty-four, single persons, childless couples, and persons not disabled. Many of these are the homeless mentally ill. Some are not poor, such as the recent widow suddenly without health insurance coverage who suffers the need for an expensive, uncovered hospital stay. In California between 1971 and 1982, the population not in the federal categories, called the medically indigent adults (MIAs), were covered on the same eligibility and benefits basis as the rest of the population, fully at state and local government expense. The only indigent persons ineligible for Medi-Cal in those years, theoretically, were undocumented aliens and jail inmates.

There is a wide range of choices open to the states in regard to overall Medicaid program concept and design, levels of eligibility, coverage of benefits, and cost and utilization controls. The many Medicaid programs are important not only in the positive effects they have had on equity of access to health care for the poor, but also in the way the states, under duress at times but at other times in a spirit of leadership, have used the programs to innovate and experiment with benefit packages, administrative controls, and eligibility (Rogers et al. 1982).

What Happens When Medicaid Is Cut?

In 1982, faced with a budget crisis of mammoth proportions, the California legislature joined with the governor to fashion major changes in Medi-Cal policies. Most of the attention has been placed on the hospital contracting conducted by the Medi-Cal czar. However, some sixty-five significant changes were enacted in Medi-Cal in 1982. The principal changes that affected hospitals were "cuts in eligibility levels for the SSI population; a very strict definition of medical necessity, particularly applied to elective hospital admissions; transfer of the state-only program for Medically Indigent Adults (MIAs) to county government, with a block grant of 70 percent of the state's estimated expenses; renewed emphasis on prepaid, capitation contracting; and the appointment of the Special Hospital Negotiator and selective hospital contracting."[6]

There are major problems in assessing the effects of contracting on hospitals in California. Several of the changes occurred simultaneously; lags in submission and payment of claims mean some recent and relevant data are unavailable; the hospital contracting program excluded the crossover population, psychiatric services, and emergency admissions.

Beverlee A. Myers

The largest impact on hospitals, and the greatest savings to the state budget, came from the MIA transfer, which meant that 270,000 high users of hospital care would be limited mostly to county hospitals. The next largest effect was reduced utilization of hospital care as a result of the eligibility reductions and, primarily, the medical necessity definitions and tightened utilization controls. Hospital stays per eligible AFDC and AFDC–medically needy client have declined by more than 5 percent, and the mean length of stay for this group has decreased by 9 percent, while the cost per day has increased by 14 percent (California Department of Health Services 1984). Thus the increases in price of hospital care have been more than offset by decreases in utilization. This suggests the tightened utilization controls may have been more effective cost controls than hospital contracting, which dealt primarily with negotiating a price per day.

In an effort to minimize shifting of charges from Medi-Cal to private health insurance, laws were passed permitting the private sector to emulate Medi-Cal—i.e., to contract selectively with health care providers. Private-sector preferred provider organizations appear to be flourishing in California, and most hospitals appear to be participating in developing or joining one or more such organizations (Trauner 1983).

The effect of all these changes on the sick poor is predictable: without a public source of payment for health care, access is limited and may disappear (Feder and Hadley 1983; Davis and Rowland 1983). What other programs are available for the poor if Medicaid is cut back or has limitations from its beginning?

Other State Government Funds

The next largest source of payment for indigent hospital care is other state government funds, accounting for one-quarter of the total for indigent hospital care in California (Fig. 7.1 and the Appendix to this chapter).

Medically Indigent Adults

MIAs were transferred in large part to the counties as part of the 1982 legislation. For the 270,000 persons transferred to county health services, the state continued to provide a block grant during 1983–84 which amounted to 14 percent of total funds for indigent hospital care. The MIA funds were allocated according to pre-1983 expenditures on the MIA population by county, with the requirement that eligibility levels be maintained at the former Medi-Cal levels at least through 1984. Most counties limited benefits to hospital and outpatient care and reduced or eliminated payments to private hospitals for emergency care for indigents, and many imposed cost-sharing. For example, clients in Los Angeles were advised that a minimum of $20 per visit would be required for each visit, although an ability-to-pay plan was to be developed if the client had no funds (Blum et al. 1983). Counties, overall, did not significantly increase their net county costs as a result of this transferred program.[7] Private hospitals experienced significant reductions in utilization (California Hospital Association 1983). There is evidence that chronically ill persons previously cared for through Medi-Cal suffered confusion and disruption in their care, could no longer identify sources of care, and experienced significantly higher levels of illness (Lurie et al. 1984). These reports support the view that both private and public hospitals ration their services to the poor when there is no additional or available source of public financing (Feder and Hadley 1983).

State Subsidy of Local Hospital Indigent Care

Subsidy by the state of indigent care may take several forms: state appropriations for particular city or county public hospitals, such as occurs in Arkansas and Colorado; operation or creation of catastrophic health insurance programs, like those in Hawaii, Rhode Island, and Alaska; creation of risk-sharing pools, such as those in Connecticut, Wisconsin, Indiana, Minnesota, North Dakota, and Florida; and state appropriations provided to local government for general indigent health care.

As of 1984, California state funds provided direct subsidy to the extent of an additional 7 percent of indigent hospital care.[8] The County Health Services Fund was created in California following passage of Proposition 13 as one state program to assist counties to continue essential services with greatly reduced property tax revenues. The state fund provideds a basic $4 per capita grant to each county and matches county funds with an average, statewide, of 56 percent of the net costs to the county for providing county health services. Net county costs were defined as expenditures less revenues for public health services and inpatient and outpatient hospital care for the indigent, exclusive of mental health, alcohol abuse, and drug abuse programs. A cap was placed on the fund, and counties were required to maintain effort at pre–Proposition 13 levels (California Department of Health Services 1983a). This fund primarily pays for urgent ambulatory and inpatient care of undocumented workers, jail inmates, and nonresidents not otherwise eligible for hospital care, and makes up the shortfall in Medi-Cal payments in meeting full financial requirements. Almost 70 percent of all births in the six county hospitals in Los Angeles in 1981 were to undocumented workers, costing almost $100 million per year from state and local funds (Beck 1984).

State Grants for Specific Diseases or Conditions

All states match federal Crippled Children's Service (CCS) funds, much of which pays for hospital treatment of poor, disabled children. In addition, some states target other conditions; e.g., Texas has a special kidney disease program, and South Carolina targets a special subsidy for indigent cancer patients. California extends its CCS program to adults with genetically handicapping conditions such as hemophilia and Huntington's disease, and also gives significant support to local mental health programs through what is called the Short-Doyle community mental health program.

Direct Operation of Public Hospitals

Some states may operate community hospitals directly and assume responsibility for indigent care. For the most part this is done through state university systems, with thirty-five states, including California, Maryland, and Texas, operating state university hospitals. The degree to which these hospitals have a responsibility for indigent care varies between states and within a state. The California Health Facilities Commission (1982) reports that the five University of California hospitals received 99 percent of their full financial requirements from patient care revenues. All five were in the top twenty-five hospitals in terms of the number of recipients served, and all received Medi-Cal contracts (California Department of Health Services 1983b). In addition, state tax funds provided support for clinical teaching programs to cover patients in the university teaching hospitals with no other source of payment.

Local Government

Local government is the payer of last resort for indigent health care. California's law, enacted in the early 1900s, is typical in defining this responsibility: "Every county and every city and county shall receive and support all incompetent poor, indigent persons, and those incapacitated by age, disease, or accident, lawfully resident therein, when such persons are not supported and relieved by their relatives or friends, by their own means, or by state hospitals or other state or private institutions" (California Welfare Code). Only three states—Vermont, Rhode Island, and Delaware—have no public community hospital. Most public hospitals are operated by city or county government in urban areas, or by special hospital districts in rural areas. The plight of these hospitals has been documented periodically. Public hospitals are most likely to provide a high volume of care to the poor and to be "stressed" financially. Public hospitals accounted for 23 percent of Medicaid-financed care and 43 percent of charity and bad debt in the early 1980s (Feder et al. 1983).

County governments in California, primarily through property taxes, provided 5 percent of total indigent hospital care in 1983–84, the county share of the net county cost calculation (Fig. 7.1 and the Appendix). In Texas, the burden on local government would appear to be much greater, with 26 percent of admissions being to public hospitals (Table 7.2), and with local government contributing over $1 billion toward expenses for health and hospitals. Only very small portions of federal grants and contracts awarded for health research,

Table 7.2. Community hospital statistics for three states, 1982

	California	Maryland	Texas
All community hospitals			
No. of beds	82,600	15,400	64,600
No. of admissions	3,155,800	551,200	2,560,600
Percent occupancy	68.5	81.9	72.0
Mean length of stay (days)	6.5	8.3	6.6
Total expenses (billions)	$12.3	$1.8	$5.8
Ave. expense per admission	$3,310	$2,743	$2,031
Ave. expense per day	$507	$329	$307
Public community hospitals[a]			
No. of beds	16,300	2,100	17,400
Percent of all community hospital beds	19.7	13.6	27.0
No. of admissions	599,200	53,800	662,500
Percent of all community hospital admissions	19.0	9.8	25.9
Total expenses (billions)	$2.6	$0.3	$1.5
Percent of all community hospital expenses	21.0	15.5	26.4

Source: American Hospital Association (1983).

[a] State and local government.

education, and service purposes would pay for indigent hospital care. Federal revenue sharing has become a locally programmed source of health care funds, although it is sometimes difficult to identify as such, since counties do not report such use on a uniform basis. In California, only 3 percent of indigent hospital care came from these sources in 1983–84.

Philanthropy

Philanthropy has diminished considerably as a resource for indigent patient care. California has three major hospitals which depend entirely on philanthropy. In addition, the California Health Facilities Commission (1982) reports that 0.4 percent of hospital expenses are attributed to charity. Only about 4 percent of total indigent hospital care in California in 1983–84 was attributable to philanthropy (Fig. 7.1).

Charge-Shifting

The extent and effect of charge-shifting is a matter of some discussion and controversy (Meyer 1983). A major problem is agreeing upon the definition of what constitutes appropriate payment. The California Health Facilities Commission in 1983 analyzed the extent to which hospitals shift charges to private payers to compensate for bad debts and the shortfall from Medi-Cal's lower payments (California Health Facilities Commission 1983). Using the concept of full financial requirements to define the level of appropriate payment, the commission allocated to each payer its own patient care costs plus its share of bad debts, charity, capital replacement, and working capital. The extent of charge-shifting in California was $376 million and accounted for 11 percent of total indigent hospital care in 1983–84 (Fig. 7.1 and the Appendix). This estimate is lower than it would have been if the Health Insurance Association of America (HIAA) method were applied; that method uses actual hospital net revenue as the estimate of appropriate payment and tends to overstate the size and nature of the shift (California Health Facilities Commission 1983; Schenker 1983).

Recent data from the California Health Facilities Commission (1984) indicate that charge-shifting may be increasing dramatically. The commission reported that 54 percent of the growth in average daily hospital charges was attributable to increases in uncompensated hospital charges during the summer of 1983. Uncollectible billed charges amounted to nearly one-fourth of the average charge per hospital day in California.

Social Policy Choices

States and localities are struggling with the problem of hospital care for the indigent and are serving as laboratories demonstrating different methods of addressing the problems.

The goal is to be fair to the poor, to hospitals, and to society. The objectives might be stated as follows.

1. All of the sick poor should have equitable access to needed hospital care without regard to extraneous criteria;
2. Hospitals should be paid their financial requirements for providing services to the sick poor; and
3. Society should assure that people are treated equitably in receipt of care for needed services, and should be assured that there is equity among payers and taxpayers in paying a fair price.

In the absence of a national health policy or programs to assure that these objectives are met uniformly throughout the United States, it remains for the states to devise policies and implement programs within their several political and economic frameworks. California, Maryland, and Texas illustrate a spectrum of choices available to states.

Unfortunately, data from Maryland and Texas do not permit an analysis comparable to that presented in Figure 7.1 for California. It would be desirable to conduct similar analyses on each state and particularly to compare per capita expenses on indigent hospital care and per capita expenses in relation to personal income. Some inadequate substitute comparisons are contained in Tables 7.1 through 7.3.

What can we say about these three public policies on indigent hospital care? California is able to meet the hospital needs of almost all the sick poor through a relatively generous but tightly controlled Medicaid program, supplemented by targeted state subsidies to public health care systems. At least in terms of infant mortality statistics (Table 7.3), California has the best record of the three states; however, the data in Table 7.3 do not reflect possible deterioration as a result of changes in Medi-Cal in 1982.

Private hospitals in California do provide care to the sick poor, mostly Medi-Cal patients, and do shift some of the associated bad debt to private health insurance. However, this charge shift accounts for less than 3 percent of total private hospital revenues in California. Reimbursements to private hospitals for patient care prior to the 1982 changes in Medi-Cal were 101 percent to 105 percent of full financial requirements. The current situation is apparently less positive, with both Medi-Cal and the private sector contracting with preferred providers. Hospitals with high Medi-Cal caseloads that did not negotiate contracts and teaching hospitals with Medi-Cal contracts where the state refuses to negotiate price increases appear to have been especially adversely affected. Some hospitals with contracts may find it necessary to cancel them.

California bears a heavier tax burden than other states in order to support its indigent poor (Table 7.3). It also has high hospital costs (Table 7.2), so that its health insurance premium payers, even without charge-shifting, are also paying a higher relative price for hospital care.

The new prudent purchasing of hospital care on the part of Medi-Cal and the private sector will tend to limit charge-shifting, as buyers negotiate for discounted prices and hospitals attempt to maintain particular markets. The ultimate effects of this on indigent hospital care are now unknown. As insured groups become more and more selective in their delivery and financing arrangements, hospital cost increases may be constrained, but the availability of

Table 7.3. Demographic and government fiscal data for three states, 1980 and 1982

	California	Maryland	Texas
1980 population (millions)	23.7	4.2	14.2
Percent of population under age 5	7.5	6.6	8.5
Percent of population over age 65	10.3	9.6	9.6
Personal per capita income (1980)	$10,929	$10,477	$9,528
Infant mortality per 1,000 live births (1982)	9.9	10.3	11.1
Revenue from state sources			
Per capita population	$1,172	$1,104	$806
Per $1,000 personal income (1980)	$202	$205	$172

Sources: U.S. Department of Commerce (1983); U.S. National Center for Health Statistics (1983).

Beverlee A. Myers

private-sector hospital care for the poor may become more and more limited to a few hospitals that specialize in the poor. Presumably, there may also be hospitals and financing systems that will specialize in the very rich, or in specific employed groups. Serious questions have been raised about equity in the distribution of quality care under a "separate but equal" medical care system (Wyszewianski and Donabedian 1981).

Maryland has a Medicaid program that is not overly generous, with eligibility levels about half that in California (Table 7.1) and limits on hospital days covered, and there does not appear to be a generous public subsidy of indigent care beyond Medicaid. Public hospitals constitute less than 15 percent of community hospital beds in the state, and have less than 10 percent of admissions (Table 7.2). However, studies suggest that the poor may have reasonably adequate access to care, in large part because of the hospital rate regulation system, which covers all payers (Hadley and Feder 1983). The system serves to redistribute resources from hospitals that serve charge-payers to hospitals that serve the indigent. Care for the indigent is financed in part by savings from rate-setting, which holds down costs.

Hospitals in Maryland appeared to be solvent as of the early 1980s. No hospital has an excessive load of Medicaid patients or bad debt. The state shifted costs from Medicaid to others by decreasing Medicaid coverage under the theory that bad debts generated by reducing Medicaid eligibility to twenty inpatient hospital days would be distributed to all classes of patients (Cohen 1982). Maryland has reduced the tax burden somewhat but at the expense of those who pay insurance premiums. Such a tax tends to be more regressive than a personal income tax. Maryland hospital costs are considerably less than those in California, and studies suggest that the rate regulation program is effective in constraining hospital rate increases (Sloan 1983).

Texas has a minimal Medicaid program, which reached only 25 percent of the poor in 1980. The poor must rely heavily on public hospitals, which contain 27 percent of the beds in the state and have 26 percent of the admissions (Table 7.2). Local government in Texas contributed over $1 billion annually to health and hospital care, suggesting that the property tax is a major source of funding. A recent report documents the plight of the leading public teaching hospitals in Texas. In the case of just four of the Texas public hospitals the uncollectible bills exceeded by almost 30 percent the amount paid by the Texas Department of Human Resources for Medicaid inpatient and outpatient hospital services for the entire state in 1981 (Anderson 1983).

Poor people are less likely to obtain needed care if they have no third-party source of payment. The sick poor in Texas probably frequently do without care, and/or the amount of charge-shifting or bad debt in hospitals is extensive. The access problem may well be reflected in the infant mortality rates in Texas, which are considerably higher than those in California or Maryland (Table 7.3).

Conclusion

A major policy issue is how to provide needed hospital care for the indigent while being fair to the poor, to the hospital, and to society. None of the three states meets the goal fully. In all three states, hospital beds appear to be in adequate supply, and, with the exception of some public hospitals, hospitals are in fairly good shape, either because they shift charges to paying patients or because they limit their clients to paying patients. The Urban Institute studies support this finding (Feder and Hadley 1983; Feder et al. 1983). California has met the needs of the poor with a generous Medicaid program and targets subsidies for public hospitals, although the evidence concerning recent state changes has not been fully evaluated. California taxpayers and premium payers pay a high price. Maryland has met the needs of the poor and controls hospital costs with all-payer hospital rate regulation which subsidizes the poor "off budget." But the burden is heavy, and perhaps inequitably so, on the health insurance premium payers. Texas has favored the taxpayers at the expense of the poor in need of hospital care and to the apparent distress of the public hospital system.

A universal national health program that treats all people and hospitals equally would meet the goal, and should not be forgotten as a potential solution even though the political climate is not particularly positive. Much of the inefficiency and inequity of the current system is due to the lack of political will in dealing with the issue in a universal, comprehensive, and equitable manner.

Lacking such a political will, a number of alternatives to a national health program are being discussed. These include the following plans:

1. Decategorizing and federalizing some of the Medicaid programs, which, depending upon the method, could remove some of the present inequities among categories of people and among states, but at a cost to the federal budget which seems unlikely, given present federal deficits;
2. Controlling hospital costs with revenue caps or mandated state rate review, perhaps on the Maryland model, which, as noted, has both positive and negative effects;
3. Providing targeted subsidies for high-risk populations or stressed hospitals, perhaps similar to the California county health services fund, which would have all of the advantages and disadvantages discussed in that plan;
4. Issuing vouchers and promoting system competition with increased consumer cost-sharing, which has potential for shifting burdens to the poor and creating inequitable multiple-tiered systems of care.

These alternatives are partial solutions that address only single aspects of a broader problem. All raise difficult issues of balancing public, private, and personal interests; federal, state, and local responsibility; and equality and efficiency generally. None will achieve the mutually intertwined goals of the three principals: society, hospitals, and the poor. But perhaps all will be tested and refined, singly and in combination, by state and local governments, with and without federal and private cooperation. Some combination must be found that works to balance all the interests and expectations.

It should no longer be denied that the public sector plays the pivotal and dominant role in our health care economy. Nor should one deny that individual demands for equal rights to the technology of medicine mean rising expectations for basic entitlements to health care. While society must achieve a balance between economic growth and equity, it should do so in the context of a concept of equity that will give everyone a sense of fairness (Bell 1984).

Appendix

Assumptions and Calculations for California Indigent Hospital Care Payment Sources Shown in Figure 7.1

Amount (in millions) and percentage	Payment source and basis for estimate
$3,370 — 100%	*Total indigent hospital care expenditure*
$832 — 25%	*Medi-Cal federal share:* Calculated from California Department of Health Services (1983c), subtracting state share.
$900 — 27%	*Medi-Cal state share:* Calculated from same source as above. Includes the state share of hospital inpatient and outpatient, both private and county, and 40% of expenditures for Redwood, prepaid health plans, county-organized systems.
$477 — 14%	*Medically indigent adult (MIA) program:* From Governor's Budget (1984), report of expenditures and budget for the Office of County Health Services.
$250 — 7%	*Net county costs, state share:* 1983–84 County Health Services fund totalled $368 million, of which 68%, or $250 million, is estimated to be the state share for inpatient/outpatient services, as opposed to public health services. Personal communication, Office of County Health Services.
$30 — 1%	*Crippled children services:* Estimated from Governor's Budget (1984) and Annual Report on Maternal and Child Health Block Grant, California Department of Health Services. This amount reduces the total $54 million from the federal fund by $5 million, includes the genetically handicapped persons program, and assumes that 75% of expenditures for treatment services are for inpatient and outpatient hospital care.
$79 — 2%	*Short-Doyle mental health programs:* Estimated from Governor's Budget (1984). The total expenditures in 1983–84 Short-Doyle community programs were $44 million. The Department of Mental Health, Office of Community Programs Statistics (personal communication), reports that 23% of Short-Doyle is spent on inpatient hospital care.
$47 — 1%	*University of California:* The Governor's Budget (1984) indicates expenditures from state general funds of $47 million by UC

(*continued*)

		teaching hospitals for clinical teaching support; this amount is allocated to pay for services not otherwise reimbursed.
$165 —	5%	*Net county costs:* Based on submitted county budgets which amounted to $483 million for inpatient/outpatient care in 1983–84. Subtracting the $250 million for the state share and the $90 million for federal revenue sharing leaves $143 million. Adding in $13 million for the county share of CCS and $9 million for the county share of Short-Doyle mental health programs gives $165 million.
$120 —	4%	*Philanthropy:* California Health Facilities Commision (1982) reports that 0.4% of hospital reimbursements for most hospitals in California derived from "subsidized charity." Assuming a total hospital expense in 1983–84 of $15,000 million, as estimated by the commission (1984a), this calculates to $60 million. In addition, three major charity hospitals—City of Hope and the Los Angeles and San Francisco Shriners' hospitals—are estimated to have annual combined expenses of $60 million, totally from philanthropic contributions (CHFC reports).
$376 —	11%	*Private charge-shifting:* The California Health Facilities Commission (1983) estimated that the extent of charge-shifting in 1979–80, based on the concept of full financial requirements, amounted to $233 million. The commission also reported that public hospitals tended not to charge-shift, in large part because of the lack of private payers. Assuming that all the charge shift can be attributed to private hospitals would overstate the estimate somewhat. However, the full financial requirements test is considerably lower than the $425 million estimated by the HIAA, which is based on total hospital revenues. The $233 million is inflated to 1983–84 on the basis of the commission's hospital inflation estimates per year, which are as follows: 16%, 16%, 9%, and 9%.
$94 —	3%	*Other federal programs:* Counties estimated that federal revenue sharing amounted to $90 million of their net county costs (California Department of Health Services 1983a). In addition, $4 million of the federal block grant for CCS is estimated to go for indigent hospital care.

Notes

1. The term "full financial requirements" is derived from work done by the California Health Facilities Commission (1982) and includes patient care costs plus bad debt and charity costs, capital replacement costs, and working capital.

2. The term "cost-shifting" has come into vogue largely through a well-advertised and publicized campaign by the Health Insurance Association of America.

3. The Appendix to this chapter identifies sources of data, assumptions, and calculations.

4. Unless otherwise noted, data on state Medicaid programs cited in this discussion are for 1980 and derive from Sawyer et al. (1983).

5. Fifty states (including Arizona under a special waiver program), the District of Columbia, Guam, the Virgin Islands, and Puerto Rico.

6. Johns, Derzon, and Anderson (1983). See also Governor's Office (1983). The hospital contracting program has been discussed elsewhere.

7. Personal communication from A. Oppenheim, California Department of Health Services, Office of County Health Services. Net county costs are defined as the difference between county expenditures and revenues in the form of fees, third-party payments, grants, and subventions, for county public health and inpatient and outpatient care. Or, in another view, net county costs are the subsidy from local and state tax sources necessary to meet fully the cost of providing county health services.

8. In 1983–84, the state provided $250 million to the counties to pay for that part of net county costs for indigent inpatient and outpatient hospital care.

References

Aday, LuAnn, and Ronald M. Anderson. 1981. "Equity of Access to Medical Care: A Conceptual and Empirical Framework." *Medical Care* 19 (Supplement), no. 12 (December): 4–28.

American Hospital Association. 1983. *Hospital Statistics: 1983 Edition.* Chicago: American Hospital Association.

Anderson, R. J., et al. 1983. "Critical Issues Confronting Public Teaching Hospitals in Texas." *Texas Medicine* 79 (April): 54–59.

Beck, Melinda. 1984. "Costs and Benefits." *Newsweek,* June 25, p. 23.

Bell, Daniel. 1984. "The Public Household." *Public Interest* 39 (Fall): 29–68.

Blendon, Robert, and Thomas Moloney, eds. 1982. *New Approaches to the Medicaid Crisis.* New York: The Free Press.

Blum, H., et al. 1983. *Impact of the Medi-Cal Reforms in California.* Berkeley: University of California, Institute of Governmental Studies, California Policy Seminar, March.

California Department of Health Services. 1983a. *County Health Services Reports for 1980.* Sacramento: The Department.

———. 1983b. *Medi-Cal Fact Book.* Sacramento: The Department.

———. 1983c. *Medi-Cal Quarterly Statistical Report, July–September 1983.* Sacramento: The Department.

———. 1984. *Medi-Cal Quarterly Statistical Report, January–March, 1984.* Sacramento: The Department.

California Office of the Governor. 1984. *Budget for the State of California, 1984–85.* Sacramento, January.

California Health Facilities Commission. 1982. *Prospective Reimbursement Systems for Hospitals.* Sacramento: The Commission.

———. 1983. *Hospital Charge-Shifting: The California Experience Examined.* Commission Report. Sacramento: The Commission, August 15.

———. 1984a. *Economic Criteria for Health Planning.* Sacramento: Commission, January.

———. 1984b. "Hospital Cost Rise Continues to Slow." *CHFC Bulletin,* April.

Cohen, Harold. 1982. "State Price Controls." In Blendon and Moloney 1982, pp. 125–38.

Davis, Karen, and Diane Rowland. 1983. "Uninsured and Underserved: Inequities in Health Care in the United States." *Milbank Memorial Fund Quarterly* 61, no. 2 (Spring): 149–76.

Feder, Judith, et al. 1983. "Poor People and Poor Hospitals: Implications for Public

Policy." Working Paper 3179-06. Washington, D.C.: The Urban Institute, October.

Feder, Judith, and Jack Hadley. 1983. "Cutbacks, Recessions, and Care to the Poor: Will the Urban Poor Get Hospital Care?" Working Paper 144-03. Washington, D.C.: The Urban Institute, September.

Governor's Budget. 1984. *See* California Office of the Governor.

Governor's Office of Special Health Services (California). 1983. *First Annual Report to the Health Care Financing Administration.* Sacramento: State of California.

Grannemann, Thomas W., and Mark V. Pauly. 1983. *Controlling Medicaid Costs: Federalism, Competition, and Choice.* Washington, D.C.: American Enterprise Institute.

Hadley, Jack, and Judith Feder. 1983. "Hospitals' Financial Status and Care to the Poor in 1980: Executive Summary." Working Paper 379-02. Washington, D.C.: The Urban Institute.

Johns, L., R. A. Derzon, and M. Anderson. 1983. *Selective Contracting for Health Services in California: First Report.* Washington, D.C.: National Governors' Association, Center for Policy Research, December.

Lurie, N., et al. 1984. "Terminations of Medi-Cal: Does It Affect Health?" *New England Journal of Medicine* 311 (August): 480–84.

McMillan, Alan, et al. 1983. "A Study of the Crossover Population: Aged Persons Entitled to Both Medicare and Medicaid." *Health Care Financing Review* 4, no. 4 (Summer): 19–46.

Meyer, Jack A. 1983. *Passing the Health Care Buck: Who Pays the Hidden Cost?* Washington, D.C.: American Enterprise Institute.

National Study Group on State Medicaid Strategies. 1983. *Restructuring Medicaid: An Agenda for Change.* Washington, D.C.: Center for the Study of Social Policy, January.

President's Commission for the Study of Ethical Problems in Medicine, Biomedical, and Behavioral Research. 1983. *Securing Access to Health Care,* vol. 1, *Summary of Recommendations.* Washington, D.C.: The Commission.

Rogers, David E., Robert J. Blendon, and Thomas W. Moloney. 1982. "Who Needs Medicaid?" *New England Journal of Medicine* 308 (July): 13–18.

Rowland, Diane, and Clifton Gaus. 1982. "Reducing Eligibility and Benefits: Current Policies and Alternatives." In Blendon and Moloney 1982, pp. 19–46.

Sawyer, Darwin, et al. 1983. *The Medicare and Medicaid Data Book, 1983.* Pub. No. 03156. Baltimore, Md.: Health Care Financing Administration, December.

Schenker, David. 1983. "HIAA Fallacies: No Case for Cost-Shifting." Paper presented at the Blue Cross-Blue Shield Association, 1983 Annual Meeting, April 20.

Sloan, Frank A. 1983. "Rate Regulation as a Strategy for Hospital Cost Control: Evidence for the Last Decade." *Milbank Memorial Fund Quarterly* 61, no. 2 (Spring): 195–217.

Starr, Paul. 1982. *The Social Transformation of American Medicine.* New York: Basic Books.

Stevens, Rosemary, and Robert Stevens. 1974. *Welfare Medicine in America.* New York: The Free Press. Chapter 1.

Trauner, J. B. 1983. *Preferred Provider Organizations: The California Experiment.* Institute for Health Policy Studies Monograph Series. San Francisco: University of California.

U.S. Department of Commerce. 1983. *Statistical Abstract of the United States, 1982–83.* Washington, D.C.: U.S. Government Printing Office.

U.S. National Center for Health Statistics. 1983. "Births, Marriages, Divorces, and Deaths." *Monthly Vital Statistics Report* 31, no. 12 (March).

Wyszewianski, Leon, and Avedis Donabedian. 1981. "Equity in the Distribution of Quality of Care." *Medical Care* 19 (Supplement), no. 12 (December): 28–56.

EIGHT

Underwriting the Uninsured: Targeting Providers or Individuals

Gail R. Wilensky

Earlier chapters have presented evidence about the magnitude of uncompensated care as well as its concentration among particular types of hospitals. While this evidence may be the subject of some dispute, the emergence of the concerns prompted by the evidence as a significant policy issue is not. This chapter discusses and assesses four specific policy options concerning uncompensated care. The first option is to do nothing—that is, to continue forcing hospitals to finance uncompensated care implicitly by "cost-shifting" to nongovernment patients or by consuming funds in reserves.[1] A second option is to target providers: hospitals could be compensated directly by factoring the costs of uncompensated care into the routine reimbursement for services, or indirectly by granting a lump sum determined by need and taken from a pool of funds. The third is to target individuals: those likely to generate uncompensated care could be provided with catastrophic or some other type of insurance. A fourth is to make grants to states (or local governments) and allow them to develop programs appropriate to their particular circumstances.

Which of these four approaches—and which particular policy within that approach—provides the most attractive means of targeting the relevant populations and minimizing health care expenditures? On the following pages, technical, administrative, and political considerations are presented to help answer this question. Because most of these options require new dollars, attention is also given to various proposals for raising additional revenues. Unfortunately there is a paucity of *direct* information about the characteristics of individuals who generate uncompensated care. More is known about the types of hospitals that experience uncompensated care and the populations associated with those hospitals. Specifically, the hospitals with the greatest concentrations of uncompensated care are the urban public teaching hospitals, followed by other teaching hospitals and voluntary hospitals.[2] These hospitals treat disproportionate numbers of patients who are uninsured and low-income.

As discussed in Chapter 2, the individuals most likely to generate uncompensated care are uninsured or "self-pay" patients, although, to an unknown extent, they may also be individuals with low levels of insurance coverage. Unlike the data on uncompensated care population, much is known about the uninsured population. (See Kasper et al. 1980; Wilensky and Walden 1981; and Davis and Rowland 1983.) Some of the economic and demographic characteristics of the uninsured are shown in Table 8.1.[3] Overall, 8.7 percent of the population are consistently uninsured, and an additional 7.6 percent are unin-

Table 8.1. Health insurance status of the U.S. population by selected characteristics

Population characteristics	Total population (thousands)	Always insured (%)	Insured some of the time (%)	Always uninsured (%)
Total population[a]	212,098	83.7	7.6	8.7
Age in years				
Less than 6	18,179	80.0	11.4	8.6
6 to 18	50,626	83.3	7.7	9.0
19 to 24	22,307	69.3	14.5	16.2
25 to 54	78,505	83.6	7.5	8.9
55 to 64	20,203	87.2	4.6	8.2
65 or older	22,278	99.2	*0.5	*0.4
Sex				
Male	102,602	83.2	7.3	9.5
Female	109,496	84.1	7.9	8.0
Ethnic/racial background				
White	147,239	85.8	7.1	7.1
Black	19,573	76.4	13.4	10.1
Hispanic	8,821	74.2	12.2	13.6
Income adjusted per family size				
Poor	26,534	71.9	13.6	14.5
Near poor	9,320	74.6	11.4	14.0
Other low income	34,270	77.8	9.9	12.3
Middle income	78,455	86.0	6.4	7.6
High income	63,519	90.4	4.8	4.9
Perceived health status				
Excellent	93,935	85.0	7.1	7.9
Good	78,902	83.2	8.0	8.8
Fair	22,046	82.0	8.5	9.4
Poor	7,100	84.6	6.5	8.9
Employment status				
Employed all year	85,147	83.7	7.3	8.9
Employed part year	22,606	78.4	9.9	11.7
Never employed, younger than 65	36,209	80.8	8.3	10.9
Never employed, 65 or older	15,872	99.4	*0.4	*0.1

Source: National Center for Health Services Research, National Medical Care Expenditure Survey household data, United States, 1977.

[a] Includes all other ethnic/racial groups not shown separately and persons with unknown ethnic/racial background and with unknown perceived health or employment status.

* Relative standard error equal to or greater than 30 percent.

sured at some time during a year. Among the entire population, certain groups are much more likely to be uninsured than other groups. These include young adults aged nineteen to twenty-four, minorities, the poor and other low-income populations, and those who are employed part of the year or were never employed.

For purposes of recommending public policy, however, it is important to distinguish between the relative likelihood of belonging to a particular group and the characteristics of the group in terms of absolute numbers. For example, even though the poor and near poor are two to three times more likely to be uninsured than the average citizen, half of those who are consistently without insurance (9 million) are middle-class or higher. This happens because there are many more people defined as middle-class and above (i.e., with an income at least twice the "poverty line") than as poor or low-income. Similarly, although people who work all year are less likely to be consistently uninsured, the majority of those uninsured over the age of sixteen are in fact employed all year.

Because our perceptions of a group are frequently determined on the basis of relative frequencies rather than absolute numbers, it is necessary to remember during policy formulation that many of the uninsured are neither poor nor unemployed. Policies appropriate to the problems of inadequate and nonexistent insurance may well be different for these various groups. Furthermore, the kinds of care that go without reimbursement are also variable. As discussed in Chapter 3 by James Perrin, not all uncompensated care involves "big-ticket" items such as catastrophic care associated with neonatal services, accidents, and burns; much can be attributed to "little-ticket" items such as normal deliveries, circumcisions, and the like. Given the large number of young adults among the uninsured, it is not very surprising that pregnancy-related expenses represent an important component of uncompensated care.

Assessing the Options

Although there may be some disagreements about specifics, most will agree that any program dealing with uncompensated care should

1. Cover the uninsured;
2. Minimize coverage of the uninsured;
3. Minimize substitution with private insurance;
4. Promote cost containment;
5. Encourage innovation and competition;
6. Be administratively feasible; and
7. Account for political reality.

The rationale for the first three criteria is that the program should target only the relevant group and not provide incentives that would increase the size of

Gail R. Wilensky

the target population. Restricting the program to only those individuals generating uncompensated care and avoiding incentives which increase the target
population will help minimize program costs. The fourth, fifth, and sixth
criteria reflect desirable characteristics of any insurance or direct coverage
program, although the fifth is less relevant for a limited program than for the
health care system as a whole. The last criterion needs to be treated with some
caution, as political reality can shift with surprising speed, as seen in the
passage of the Omnibus Budget Reconciliaion Act (OBRA) in 1981 and the
Tax Equity Fiscal Responsibility Act (TEFRA) in 1982. Two examples of
provisions which would have been regarded as politically infeasible a few years
earlier are the restrictions on "freedom of choice" and the introduction of cost-
sharing for Medicaid beneficiaries.

Targeting Providers

The first set of options considers targeting providers, either by reimbursing
them directly through an all-payer system, or indirectly by granting lump sums
to hospitals from a fund of pooled resources.

Direct Reimbursement via All-Payer Rate Setting

As described by Jack Meyer in Chapter 9, a few states reimburse providers of
uncompensated care directly through all-payer rate-setting systems. There are
several advantages to an all-payer system relative to the criteria described
earlier. It is an effective way to limit expenditures to those who are without
insurance and who would otherwise generate uncompensated care, particularly
if there are requirements that hospitals demonstrate reasonable effort in collecting bad debts. It also appears that directly compensating providers for
uncompensated care does not encourage individuals to forego insurance they
would otherwise carry. The substitution for private insurance is not likely to be
an issue at least as long as the favorable tax treatment of employment-related
insurance continues. This approach is likely to be less costly than policies
which cover individuals since it pays only for users of the system rather than
providing coverage for all uninsured. The use of an all-payer system also fares
well on the last two criteria: administrative and political feasibility. Experience
to date suggests it is administratively feasible, especially in states prone to
regulating health care. This approach also has considerable political appeal,
both to insurers and to state legislators. Insurers, particularly commercial
insurers, favor this approach because all payers of health care contribute a
stated share of the cost of uncompensated care rather than only those payers
(i.e., commercial insurers) who cannot shift it to another party. Legislators
also find this approach attractive relative to paying for uncompensated care by
direct budget appropriation.

An all-payer system has at least four disadvantages. First, it provides little incentive for competitive innovation and reinforces existing relationships between payers and hospitals. Second, while it focuses on price, it does not control utilization. Third, it pays for care at whatever hospitals individuals use, as opposed to providers' directing these individuals to the most efficient hospital. Finally, some states may not have political climates receptive to such involved government regulation. There is an additional negative attribute of all-payer systems not related to the criteria being used here. Including compensation in the reimbursement system is likely to appeal to legislators because it keeps the payment out of the state budget, but it also obfuscates the size and scope of the program and may result in higher levels of expenditures than what might be appropriated if the transfers were more explicit. Many students of government regard this as an undesirable way to implement policy.

Pooling Revenue

A second means of targeting providers is to grant providers a lump sum from a common pool of revenues. For example, New York, an all-payer state, does not include allowances for bad debt and charity in the reimbursement rates set for hospitals. Instead, hospitals are reimbursed for charity care and bad debt from revenue pools financed by surcharges on the rates paid by third-party payers.

In general, the use of revenue pools is subject to the same advantages and disadvantages as direct reimbursement by all-payer systems. Both systems compensate hospitals according to their specific patterns of utilization, irrespective of whether those patterns reinforce an efficient delivery of care. Although this tactic has not yet been tried, revenue pools could be used to encourage competitive innovation by reimbursing cost-effective providers at a higher rate (dollars reimbursed/dollars uncompensated care) than less efficient providers.

An interesting modification of the revenue pool concept for financing indigent care was under consideration by the state of Florida (Eckels et al. 1984), although the legislation actually passed was far less innovative than the initial proposal. The proposal was directed at the uninsured poor, near poor not on Medicaid, individuals with catastrophic expenses, and others whose income is under 150 percent of the poverty line, i.e., the indigent care portion of uncompensated care.

A pool was to be established and financed by hospitals, counties, and the state. Hospitals were to be taxed a percentage of their net patient revenue, counties would be taxed according to a per capita rate based on their ability to pay (with a maintenance-of-effort provision to make sure they continued their current commitment to indigent care programs), and the state would match county contributions at a specified rate. The pool was to fund the nonfederal match of a medically needy program and an expanded Medicaid program and also to reimburse hospitals for indigent care. The expansion of the Medicaid program would have included children below the Aid to Families with Dependent Children (AFDC) cash assistance level and families with unemployed parents below the case assistance level. In addition, families of the unemployed and others slightly above the case assistance level could be included in the medically needy program. Hospitals were to receive payment for charity care at 80 percent of the Medicaid rate. Charity care would be determined by uniform standards and would be based on the individual's income and assets.

The original Florida revenue pool proposal is a particularly attractive option because it is one element of a larger attempt to provide for indigent care, and the method is particularly suited to the state's needs and political climate. It does not rely on either general revenues (which would raise taxes) or a tax on insurance premiums (which would exclude the large number of self-insured groups in Florida from contributing to the fund). In addition, it is not an all-payer system of reimbursement and therefore may be attractive to states which would not accept the degree of regulation inherent in all-payer systems. It does share, however, the basic advantages and disadvantages, discussed earlier, of programs which target providers, perhaps the most serious disadvantage being that it provides no incentive for consumers to be cost-conscious in their choice of hospitals or providers of care.

Targeting Individuals

A second general strategy to reimburse hospitals for the supply of presently uncompensated care is to target individuals—in other words, to make sure that individuals without insurance acquire some sort of coverage so that they can pay their bills. Six options of implementing this strategy are to provide catastrophic illness insurance only, a state risk-sharing pool under which high-risk individuals can be insured, insurance for the unemployed, insurance for the indigent, voucher systems, or grants to local governments. Since these options differ substantially in size and scope, their advantages and disadvantages are best discussed and assessed individually.

Catastrophic Illness Programs

Catastrophic illness programs differ in scope and benefits, but their common purpose is to protect individuals and families from being ruined financially by very large medical expenses. They generally cover all out-of-pocket medical bills in approved categories, which include a long list of medical and hospital services. Typically, the individual faces a deductible and co-insurance based on income, assets, or both. Individuals must also be residents of the state and generally must have incurred the expenses while residing in the state.

Several states have enacted catastrophic illness programs, but only Alaska, Maine, and Rhode Island currently have operational programs.[4] The funding for the Minnesota program ceased in 1981; New York's enacted program was contingent on being integrated with the Medicaid program and has not been implemented. Eligibility in Alaska depends on income, family size, and assets. The minimum deductible is $1,000, but the deductible and co-insurance increases rapidly with income and assets. A family of four with an income of $16,000 and no liquid assets would have a deductible of $5,550 and be liable for 75 percent of its income above $16,000. Maine's deductible is $7,000, plus 30 percent of pretax income, plus 10 percent of assets over $20,000. In Rhode Island, the deductible and co-insurance vary with the family's income and with the type of insurance the individual has purchased. The deductibles are lower if the individual's insurance coverage is more comprehensive. The deductible varies from $500 plus 5 percent of income above $10,000 for individuals with Medicare and private insurance (the "highest-quality coverage") to $5,000 or 50 percent of allowable income for individuals with no health insurance (the "lowest-quality coverage"). These programs typically pay 100 percent of expenses above the deductibles but do not cover all psychiatric or nursing home care. Most do not cover extended nursing home stays.

The intent of the catastrophic illness programs is to make the state a payer of last resort and to serve only the small number of persons who experience catastrophic expenditures. In 1982, for example, Alaska paid for 160 persons, Maine 1,107, and Rhode Island 901. The average cost per case varied greatly: $12,376 in Alaska, $1,560 in Maine, $2,813 in Rhode Island. States with these programs have introduced cost controls—utilization controls in particular—as well as more stringent eligibility criteria because the cost of the programs has risen rapidly.

There are drawbacks to such a program. Insofar as those generating uncompensated care are those with enormous bills, catastrophic illness insurance will cover the targeted population. However, because much of uncompensated care is not associated with enormous bills (see Chap. 3 by Perrin), this would not be a comprehensive solution. Also, if coverage eligibility does not consider whether or not the individual holds some other insurance, some individuals outside of the immediate target population may be covered.

The program measures well, judged by several of the other criteria. Catastrophic illness insurance is unlikely to substitute for private insurance because out-of-pocket expenses are set very high. For the same reason, competition will be encouraged by consumers' searching for a cost-efficient site of care. The effect of cost containment is unclear: competition will encourage savings, yet the volume of very expensive services may increase if neither the hospital nor the patients are at risk for catastrophic expenditures. The program has been proven to be administratively feasible and has the political advantage of appearing to cater to a "deserving" needy group, the very ill. A catastrophic insurance program would be more attractive if it were part of a larger package which more accurately covered the target population.

Gail R. Wilensky

Risk-Sharing Pools

Six states (Connecticut, Minnesota, Wisconsin, Indiana, North Dakota, and Florida) have adopted risk-sharing pools made up of insurance companies that provide comprehensive insurance to high-risk individuals who would otherwise have trouble obtaining coverage. The programs are similar in most aspects, although Connecticut has opened its plan to all state residents, whereas other states have limited it to high-risk individuals.

These programs involve tension between the goal of affordable premiums and sufficient total revenues to fund the program. To the extent that this tension is resolved in favor of affordable premiums, there may be a tendency for private insurers to turn to a supplementary source of revenues—such as cost-shifting to other insurance clients—to keep the program solvent. If this occurs, then employers may consider self-insuring rather than paying these higher premiums, resulting in an inequitable situation in which employers who self-insure bear less of the costs of the state risk pool than other employers. Should self-insurance become commonplace, cost-shifting would be rendered ineffective as a means of producing supplementary revenues. Among the programs now in operation, state risk pools have addressed only a fraction of uncompensated care, indicating that premiums probably have been set at high rates.

The effects of risk-sharing pools depend greatly on how the premiums are set. If they are kept high, then much of the target population may remain covered. If they are set low, either the state will have to subsidize the program or else there will be substantial pressure on private insurers to absorb part of the costs with the attendant cost-shifting problems just described. Setting the rates low may encourage some substitution with private insurers, particularly for individuals who purchase insurance entirely or mostly on their own. Cost-containment features and incentives for innovation will depend on the co-insurance rates, deductibles, and other features associated with these policies. The program may be useful—if premiums are kept relatively high—as an insurance option for nonindigent high-risk individuals.

Insurance for the Unemployed

Another policy issue dealing indirectly with the question of uncompensated care is insurance for the unemployed. Because most private health insurance for the non-aged is employment-related, the sharp increase in unemployment during 1982–83 brought with it concern about a potentially large-scale loss of health insurance coverage. As a result, a number of legislative proposals were introduced in Congress in the spring of 1983 to protect the unemployed from the loss of health insurance coverage.[5]

Assessment of insurance for the unemployed in terms of incentives for efficiency, cost containment, and innovation will vary according to the specific legislative proposal being considered. A couple of proposals, for example, included various provisions which should stimulate cost consciousness on the part of the beneficiary; proposals which primarily extend Medicaid coverage would do little to make beneficiaries cost-conscious.

Two major concerns with all these plans, however, are whether or not they would reach the relevant target population, and whether or not they are likely to substitute for private insurance. Research conducted at the National Center for Health Services Research (NCHSR) indicates that a program of insurance for the unemployed would cover many individuals who retain or buy insurance, thus failing the first criterion, and would also substitute for private insurance, failing the second criterion. It was found that a relatively small proportion of the unemployed—8 percent in 1977 and 13 percent in 1982—lost health insurance as a result of being unemployed and that unemployed workers with health insurance did not experience a decline in medical care use. The 13 percent unemployed translated to 1.4 million unemployed workers and represented about 3 million individuals including dependents.

These data also indicate that the lack of insurance coverage, rather than unemployment per se, is the greater barrier to care. Since it was estimated that the majority of those over the age of fourteen who lacked insurance coverage were employed throughout the year, any attempt to define a policy option in terms of unemployment will fail to account for most uncompensated care. Furthermore, there may be substitution with private insurance if the 75 percent of the unemployed who maintained their old insurance coverage are tempted to switch into a new program of insurance for the unemployed.

The validity of the NCHSR data has been questioned by the Congressional Budget Office (CBO), which estimated that as of February 1983, 5 million workers, rather than 1.4 million, had lost health insurance coverage as a result of being unemployed. While part of this difference is due to the increase in the unemployment rate between March 1982 and February 1983, at least part of the difference is due to different estimates of the association of insurance loss with unemployment. At issue is how many more of the unemployed lost their jobs involuntarily between 1982 and 1977 (60 percent versus 45 percent) and how much this difference affected the estimates of the number of unemployed who are also uninsured. Also at issue is the correlation between job loss and the lack of insurance.

While the NCHSR estimate may be a little low because of the increase in involuntary job loss between 1977 and 1982, there is reason to believe that the NCHSR data basically are more relevant to this issue than the CBO estimate. The NCHSR collected data over several points in time and so was able to assess directly the pattern of the relationship between changes in employment and insurance coverage, whereas the CBO only considered data from a single point in time. This meant that the CBO estimates are based on average relationships rather than the insurance coverage resulting after a change in employment status.

Insurance for the Indigent

Another set of options involves providing insurance for some or all of the indigent. This could include either an expansion of state medically needy programs or a more fundamental change in the Medicaid program.

Several states have considered adapting or expanding their medically needy programs, at least in part, as a way of covering some of the uncompensated care generated by the indigent. The legislative package put together for Florida, for example, included a medically needy program limited to basic acute care services and expansion of the basic Medicaid program to families below the current Florida Aid to Families with Dependent Children (AFDC) cash assistance level (Lewin and Associates 1983).

An example of a more fundamental change in Medicaid which would cover some of the indigents not currently covered by Medicaid can be found in the 1984 recommendation of the National Study Group on State Medicaid Strategies, a bipartisan group of state health officials. They recommended that Medicaid be split into two separate programs: a basic health care portion with uniform national eligibility standards and benefits, and a long-term care portion for nursing home residents and the mentally retarded. The basic portion would be financed entirely by the federal government; the long-term care part would be financed jointly by the federal and state governments. The report did not specify which services would be covered, but they would probably include hospital care, physician care, prenatal care for pregnant women, and well care for children. Unlike Medicaid, there would be no automatic link between the program and cash assistance programs: all persons with income below 55 percent of the poverty line would be eligible. The report estimated that this plan would add about 11 million poor people to the Medicaid eligibility roles. Care under the basic plan would be provided by prepaid provider groups rather than groups on a fee-for-service system. It was estimated that the new system would cost only $1 billion to $2 billion more than the existing system as of 1992, primarily because of the savings produced by the reorganization of providers into a prepaid group.

The primary advantage of an expanded Medicaid and medically needy program with respect to the funding of uncompensated care is that the indigent population would be more consistently covered in every state. Even so, there may be some difficulty in designing eligibility requirements that qualify only the uninsured, and if the coverage is generous enough, it might begin to substitute for private insurance as well.

Major expansions of Medicaid programs should present no difficulties in terms of administrative feasibility, since there is a long history of experience in this area. Political feasibility will vary from area to area and also according to the level of government being considered. At the state level, many states would find this a relatively attractive way to finance uncompensated care, since it uses state dollars to leverage additional federal dollars into the area. (On average, the federal government finances 56 percent of the costs of Medicaid.) States which are adamant about not increasing program costs would not find this a very attractive option, nor is the federal government, which has been working actively to reduce expenditures for Medicaid in particular and social programs in general, likely to embrace this approach.

There are several disadvantages to the use of expanded Medicaid programs as a funding mechanism for uncompensated care. First, it would not address the lack of coverage for a large number of the uninsured: all of those who are middle- and high-income and many of those who are low-income but not at or near the official poverty line. Second, the current construction of the Medicaid program produces incentives for beneficiaries to reduce work effort, and this incentive is likely to increase as the program is expanded. The problem is the "all-or-nothing" character of Medicaid coverage—i.e., persons are either qualified for Medicaid and therefore fully covered for all Medicaid services in their state or they are not qualified and therefore not eligible for any services. The fact that Medicaid beneficiaries lose their coverage when their income reaches certain levels produces a strong incentive not to earn so much income as to be disqualified for Medicaid.

The impact on costs and the incentives for competition, innovation, and cost containment are ambiguous and in part will depend on the particular program being considered. Medicaid programs which cover some portion of the indigent population will cost more than programs restricted only to users, as is true for programs which target payments to providers. Medicaid itself, however, has experienced a slower rate of expenditure increase than other health care programs, despite its reputation to the contrary. Medicaid has been regarded as a program with few incentives toward cost containment and efficiency because prior to the Omnibus Budget Reconciliation Act (OBRA) the beneficiaries faced no cost-sharing whatever, and providers were typically paid on a fee-for-service basis. As a result of the increased autonomy provided states to experiment with modifications in Medicaid through the waiver process, many states are now introducing a variety of cost-containment measures, including case managers, capitation reimbursement, prudent buyers, and lock-in provisions.[6]

It is too early to assess what effects these various innovations in the delivery of services will have on costs (or quality) of health care, but it appears that many of the criticisms of the current Medicaid system regarding insufficient incentives toward cost containment can be addressed. However, there may be other ways to incorporate the advantages of these innovations besides expanding the Medicaid program—as, for example, with the use of vouchers.

Gail R. Wilensky

Voucher Systems

A voucher system is an alternative means of covering indigent uninsureds by providing them with the opportunity to purchase a health care plan. It is a key aspect of many competitive plans because it allows consumers to make periodic choices among competing plans using a specific amount of funds provided by the government (or by employers, if used by the private sector). The amount of the voucher for the lowest-income individuals should be set at a level at which a low-cost provider would agree to provide a given set of services. The value of the voucher could be adjusted according to actuarial expectations, such as age, sex, and the income of the individual. Beneficiaries would be allowed to supplement the amount of the voucher so they could choose higher-priced providers if they desired. Similarly, if the beneficiaries chose lower-priced providers, they would receive the difference between the voucher amount and the premium in the form of cash.

There are several major advantages to the use of vouchers. First, they are effective instruments for targeting particular subgroups of the population. Second, they provide consumers with strong incentives to be cost-conscious both in their use of health services and in their choice of providers. As a result, a voucher system could be expected to encourage competition among providers as well as the adoption of innovative delivery systems such as HMOs, primary care networks, and the like. There would not be substitution with private insurance directly because the vouchers would be used to buy private insurance; indeed, if the voucher system replaces a government program such as Medicare or Medicaid, then the demand for private insurance may increase. There may, however, be some subsidization of low-income individuals who currently buy their own insurance. One of the most important advantages of this system is that it can be used to partially subsidize low-income individuals who need some assistance but not the full assistance of indigent individuals; it thus avoids the "notch" effect (the all-or-nothing feature) of Medicaid.

While many characteristics of vouchers make them a desirable policy instrument, several others cause concern. The one most frequently cited is adverse and preferred-risk selection. This occurs when individuals can predict their future expected use (and insurers cannot) and choose their plans accordingly. The result of adverse selection is that bad risks—i.e., high users—tend to choose the same health plan, thereby driving up the premiums and producing an unstable situation. Vouchers based on actuarial expectations, however, should be able to avoid the most serious consequences of this problem. Concern has also been raised about high selling costs and about the requisite assumption made about voucher systems, that consumers have, or can be given, enough information about competing insurance plans to make rational choices. Structured vouchers (that is, a limited choice among a prespecified set of plans which meet federal requirements) could eliminate many of these problems; while they also take away some consumer options, they are far less restrictive than prudent buyer lock-in arrangements by which the state negotiates with a low-cost provider and locks the Medicaid beneficiary in to this arrangement.

One final concern about vouchers involves the changing eligibility patterns associated with many Medicaid recipients. A sizeable portion of the Medicaid population is eligible for Medicaid for only part of the year. Unless the voucher covered a period of at least six months to one year, it would be difficult to use it in purchasing insurance coverage.

Grants to Local Governments

A final option is to let each respective state or local government decide what type of program it wants. They would be given matching or block grants, with the amount of the grant based primarily on the number of individuals below the poverty line. An adjustment could be made for unusually high levels of unemployment as well. The state or local government would then be allowed to decide whether to reimburse hospitals directly (either through all-payer rate setting or through lump sums from pooled revenues), or whether to attempt to provide the uninsured with insurance for the unemployed, expanded insurance for the indigent, or a voucher system. Such a program would supersede Medicaid except for those over sixty-five and those receiving long-term care.

Conceptually, it would be preferable to have the grant directed to local governments. That is probably not feasible, however, because of variations in the levels of local government responsible for the provision of services for the needy across the United States.

A more administratively feasible alternative would be to give the funds to the states and have them distribute the funds to local governments on the basis of the poverty population and unemployment rates in the local jurisdictions. As long as states allow local jurisdictions to be given the choice as to how the funds are distributed, the primary advantages of local decisionmaking would remain. State or local governments presumably would have to make their programs and expenditures public and demonstrate that the funds were being used for health care of the poor (and unemployed uninsured). If the funds are distributed in the form of a block grant, rather than a matching grant, serious consideration should be given to a maintenance-of-effort provision or at least a mandatory state contribution; otherwise, there could be a substantial substitution of federal funds for currently provided state and local funds. A maintenance-of-effort clause should be included with a block grant if the federal government is concerned that the funds be used specifically for uncompensated care. Unlike a matching grant, which makes state dollars spent on the matching program more potent than dollars spent on any other program, a block grant does not make an increase in state efforts for funding indigent care "cost" any less to the state; it merely replaces front-end state funding (see Grannemann and Pauly 1983).

The major disadvantage of such a program is that there would be higher direct costs and higher administrative costs than for one limited to providers and therefore reflecting only current users. Its major advantages, however, are that it can be used to channel funds to needy individuals, it does not establish a new entitlement program for individuals, it reflects both needs and desires of local communities, and it grants local communities the autonomy to determine their own levels of competition and innovation.

Raising Revenue

Several of the programs discussed would increase public expenditures on health care. In moving to a system of explicit financing of uncompensated care, public policymakers must consider the types of taxes that would be used to support additional expenditures. The most likely options include general revenue financing, a tax on insurance premiums, an excise tax on the hospital bills of insured patients, an excise tax on alcohol and tobacco, and a ceiling on the size of an employer's tax-free contribution to an employee's health insurance plan (i.e., a tax cap).

General Revenue

There are many varieties of general fund financing mechanisms that could be used to pay for such a program. These include a consumption tax, a surcharge on the income tax, or a general revenue contribution. A consumption tax is a means of raising general revenues by taxing not total income but consumption, defined to be income minus savings. This mechanism raises tax revenues while maintaining savings incentives. Since savings increase with income, concern has been expressed that consumption taxes are not progressive. In fact they can be made progressive through the use of a progressive rate structure, if that is desired. Alternatively, a surcharge on the income tax could be used. This would increase contributions of all taxpayers by a fixed percentage of their current contribution. It thus contains all the advantages and disadvantages of our current progressive income tax system. Finally, the general funds of the federal government, rather than specific funds, could be used to finance the additional expenditures to be provided by the federal government. Given our current federal deficits and impending fiscal problems with Medicare, reliance on either general revenues or specific broad-based taxes seems unrealistic.

Excise Taxes

An excise tax on health insurance premiums represents a natural extension of our current mechanism for financing uncompensated care: cost-shifting. The reason is that cost-shifting affects the hospital bills of private patients, in turn raising the premiums for private hospitalization insurance. A tax on health insurance premiums would be a formalization of cost-shifting and would show similar patterns of incidence—that is, the same general groups of people would ultimately pay the bill. A premium tax would be slightly progressive, since we know that employer contributions show a small positive correlation with family income and that total premiums both for the aged and non-aged rise with income (Wilensky and Taylor 1982), but it would be much less so than the income tax. Furthermore, a tax on insurance premiums could be regarded as recovering some of the subsidy currently provided by the tax exclusion for employment-related insurance, although this rationale is less applicable for the aged, who pay for a large part of their private insurance premiums themselves.

The main problem with the premium tax is that employers who self-insure would be exempt and therefore would not contribute taxes to the fund for the uninsured. This not only would result in an inequity, with some employees funding care for the indigent and other employees not, but would also provide a powerful incentive for employers to self-insure and ultimately make the tax unproductive as a revenue raiser. The difficulty with taxing the self-insured is not a technical one: that is, the self-insured could be taxed according to the amounts paid out plus an average charge for administration. The exclusion is a legal one: the Employee Retirement Income Security Act (ERISA) exempts the self-insured from state regulation, including state taxation. While some exceptions to this provision have been granted, they have been of a limited nature with specific indication that the exception could not be generalized.[7] Nonetheless, challenges are continuing.

A tax on the hospital bills of privately insured patients is an alternative to the premium tax that would gain increasing interest if the legal issues regarding ERISA and the self-insured cannot be resolved. Such a tax would be equivalent to a price increase for hospital services that would be spread among all households with private insurance in the form of higher hospitalization insurance premiums. Since insurance premiums are somewhat correlated with income, this again would result in a mildly progressive tax but one less progressive than the income tax. There is, however, a psychological difficulty with such a tax in that it would be perceived as a tax on the sick. This type of tax is very similar to the tax being used in New York, which is based on inpatient hospital revenues.

Excise taxes on alcohol and tobacco are frequently cited as potential revenue raisers for health care. The rationale for using the proceeds of such a tax to finance health expenditures is that the consumers of these products also consume greater than average quantities of medical services and should therefore pay a larger share of the national health care bill. These taxes are also quite easy to administer and their revenues can be earmarked for special use. Opponents of these taxes argue that not all consumers of alcohol and tobacco are heavy health care users and that these products are already taxed heavily. Also, increasing the excise tax on alcohol is not as straightforward as it appears. However, the main concern is that excise taxes on alcohol and tobacco are already being considered as a way to resolve the financing problem of the Medicare trust fund and for other potential uses as well.

Tax Cap

Another financing mechanism which has been frequently discussed for health care is the taxation of employers' contributions to employee benefit plans when these contributions exceed a predetermined amount. This has been called a tax cap because the amount of premium contribution that escapes income tax is "capped." Economists have been almost unanimous in advocating tax capping because it not only raises revenue but should also reduce both the quantity and the cost of health services consumed. The lowest income groups would be unaffected by a tax cap because these individuals typically pay little or no taxes and/or receive employer contributions under most caps. Middle-income groups tend to pay slightly larger shares than upper-income groups. Overall, the tax cap can be shown to be more progressive than the use of an excise tax on hospital bills, but less progressive than the general income tax (Meyer 1983).

Proposed Policy Directions

Although there is not detailed information on who generates uncompensated care, there is evidence to suggest that they are people with no insurance or with limited insurance. More data are available on the uninsured, and these make clear that many of the individuals without health insurance are not poor. This suggests that direct financing of uncompensated care is more than a problem of financing care for the indigent. Financing care for the indigent, however, is an important component of uncompensated care.

Recognition that uncompensated care reflects a heterogeneous population suggests a two-pronged approach. Although care for the indigent can be financed through many policy options, the most promising is the use of grants to state governments with funds passing through to local governments. While there are many attractive features to the use of vouchers—including the incentives for choosing efficient health care plans, targeting funds for the neediest individuals, and giving limited assistance to those who need only limited assistance—local governments should also be allowed the option of expanding medically needy programs or directly targeting reimbursement to providers. This would allow communities to assess their own particular circumstances and decide whether vouchers, direct reimbursement to providers, an expansion of Medicaid or medically needy programs, or some other program would be best for them.

Those individuals who are not poor but are uninsured need to have insurance made available to them, perhaps through the formation of risk pools. The risk pools should be subsidized by federal and state governments on the grounds that these individuals—unlike the vast majority of non-aged individuals, who have employment-related insurance—are not currently receiving any subsidy from the tax exclusion accorded employment-related insurance. Additionally, without some limited subsidization such insurance is likely to be prohibitively expensive. There is a danger, however, that if the subsidy is substantial, some employers might encourage their employees to get their insurance from the risk pool, although this is not likely to be a serious danger unless a tax cap is set very low.

These two programs should be financed by a combination of tax capping to support risk pools and excise taxes on either insurance premiums or hospital revenues to support additional financing of indigent care.

This two-pronged approach is not without potential problems. Grants to state governments might not always result in the proper distribution to local governments; grants to local governments may be difficult to implement because of differing local governmental structures. Given options, some state and local governments will adopt more equitable or more efficient mechanisms than others, thus leaving some of the indigent population better off than others. Furthermore, not all eligibles may take advantage of the risk pool: some may be willing to engage in "free rider" behavior, particularly if they know that grants are being made to finance uncompensated care. While it could be required that individuals carry some form of major medical insurance, such a requirement would be difficult to police. Finally, some of the care currently being provided as uncompensated care would not be covered by this type of insurance. Despite these problems, the two-part program suggested here is a way of addressing what is currently a major policy issue, and it does so in ways that may be politically acceptable because it would not require major disruption of the entire health care delivery system.

In summary, a general tax such as a consumption tax or the income tax may be attractive as a source of revenues, but in the current era of high federal deficits and pending Medicare fiscal insolvency, it is politically unrealistic. Excise taxes on alcohol and tobacco are less desirable and are subject to the same concern. An excise tax on premiums is an acceptable approach to supplement or entirely finance uncompensated care. A tax on hospital revenue financed by private payers is a less preferred variant on the excise tax on insurance premiums. The tax cap, if it is not earmarked for other purposes, is a desirable revenue source for funding the risk pool and perhaps a portion of indigent care. However, any of the above explicit taxes is preferable to the current method of financing uncompensated care through cost-shifting.

Gail R. Wilensky

Notes

The author would like to thank Larry Lewin of Lewin and Associates, Jack Meyer of the American Enterprise Institute, and Sam Mitchell of the Federation of American Hospitals for their valuable advice; David Crozier, Project HOPE, for numerous suggestions; and Steven Chapman, Project HOPE, for research assistance and editorial help.

1. The issue of cost-shifting is covered in greater depth in Chapter 6, by Charles Phelps.

2. A more detailed discussion of the association between hospital type and the amount of uncompensated care is presented in Chapter 2, by Sloan and co-authors. Also see Feder, Hadley, and Mullner (1984) on the findings of the AHA 1980 Survey of Hospitals in large cities.

3. While these data are now substantially out of date, comparisons with the 1980 population by aggregate insurance status indicate little change between 1977 and 1980, the latest year for which insurance information is currently available. The body of data from 1977 to 1980 is also probably not a bad proxy for 1984 data, although in many respects it will not adequately represent the recessionary 1982–83 period.

4. A more detailed explanation of these programs is available in Lewin and Associates (1983), which is the basis of the information provided here.

5. One set of proposals (Dole S. 951 and Waxman H.R. 2552) in 1983 provided that benefits related to state Medicaid programs would be financed by a combination of federal matching funds, premiums, and beneficiary cost-sharing. Employers were also required to open enrollment so that the unemployed could obtain coverage by attaching to the policy of a working spouse. Other proposals (Walgren H.R. 1823 and Reigle S. 307) offered temporary coverage under the Medicare program for the involuntarily unemployed, but also encouraged the formulation of state reinsurance pools supported by contributions from employers, the unemployed, and the federal government.

In the summer of 1983, the House passed a $4 billion program of health insurance for the unemployed. It included giving block grants to participating states to cover the unemployed. These grants would have carried the stipulation that employers who provide health insurance must offer a thirty-day open enrollment period for the recently unemployed to join the policy of their spouse; employers would have been required to offer continued health insurance coverage for ninety days to laid-off workers, and to allow them to switch from group to individual policies, thereby retaining private insurance at individual rates.

No action was taken in the Senate. This was due in large part to the dramatic drop in unemployment which occurred between September 1983 and February 1984, making the issue moot, politically. In addition, new information challenging earlier estimates of the number unemployed who became uninsured raised questions about the desirability of such a policy (Monheit et al. 1984). Nonetheless, the interest in this proposal was sufficiently intense to warrant its evaluation as a policy option in this chapter.

6. Under case management, an individual is assigned responsibility to manage the Medicaid beneficiary's utilization of medical care and particularly the referral patterns of physicians used by the beneficiary. The manager may be a nonphysician receiving a fee for the management service or a physician who is partially placed at risk for the expenditures incurred by the beneficiary. Under capitation reimbursement, a preset amount is paid to a provider to cover all of the care for an individual, as in the case of an HMO or

other prepaid group practice. Under the prudent buyer concept, the state receives bids from various providers who agree to provide all or some services at preset prices. The state can then choose the low-cost bidder. With "lock-in," the beneficiary who chooses or is assigned a case manager, a prepaid group, or a low-cost provider must remain with that arrangement; medical services provided outside the preset agreement will not be reimbursed by Medicaid.

7. A pre-ERISA state statute in Hawaii mandating benefits for the self-insured was challenged in court post-ERISA, with ERISA being ruled to take precedence over the state statute (Standard Oil Co. v. Agsalud, 633 F.2d 760 [9th Cir. 1980]). Hawaii requested and received an exemption from Congress. The language of the exemption clearly stated, however, that this was not to be a precedent for other states.

References

Davis, Karen, and Diane Rowland. 1983. "Uninsured and Underserved: Inequities in Health Care in the United States." *Milbank Memorial Fund Quarterly* 61, no. 2 (Spring): 149–76.

Eckels, Timothy, Lawrence Lewin, and Dale Roenigk. 1984. "Health Care Financing for the Medically Indigent in Florida: A Proposed System." Prepared for the Florida Task Force on Competition and Consumer Choice in Health Care, January 4.

Feder, Judith, Jack Hadley, and Ross Mullner. 1984. "Falling through the Cracks: Poverty, Insurance Coverage, and Hospital Care for the Poor, 1980 and 1982. *Milbank Memorial Fund Quarterly* 62, no. 4 (Fall): 544–66.

Grannemann, Thomas W. and Mark V. Pauly. 1983. *Controlling Medicaid Costs: Federalism, Competition, and Choice.* Washington, D.C.: American Enterprise Institute.

Kasper, Judith A., Daniel C. Walden, and Gail R. Wilensky. 1980. *Who Are the Uninsured?* National Health Care Expenditures Study. Data Preview 1. Hyattsville, Md.: U.S. Department of Health and Human Services.

Lewin and Associates. 1983. "State Options for Addressing Catastrophic Health Expenses." Synthesis and Dissemination of Health Services Research for State and Municipal Health Leaders, prepared for the National Center for Health Services Research, January 14.

Meyer, Jack A. 1983. *Passing the Health Care Buck: Who Pays the Hidden Cost?* Washington, D.C.: American Enterprise Institute.

Monheit, Alan, Michael Hagan, Marc Berk, and Gail Wilensky. 1984. "Health Insurance for the Unemployed: Is Federal Legislation Needed?" *Health Affairs* 3, no. 1 (Spring): 101–11.

Wilensky, Gail, and Amy Taylor. 1982. "Tax Expenditures and Health Insurance: Limiting Employer-Paid Premiums." *Public Health Reports,* September–October, pp. 438–44.

Wilensky, Gail, and Daniel Walden. 1981. "Minorities, Poverty, and the Uninsured." Paper presented at the 109th Meeting of the American Public Health Association, Los Angeles, November.

NINE

Financing Uncompensated Care with All-Payer Rate Regulation

Jack A. Meyer

everal states have adopted "all-payer" rate-setting programs to deal with rising hospital costs and with the differential amounts various insurers pay for hospital care. Uncompensated care is an important reason for the payment differentials these programs address. This chapter examines the common elements and variations in the ways that these state regulatory programs channel funding to certain hospitals judged to have a disproportionately high incidence of free care and bad debt—the two basic elements of uncompensated hospital care.

The evaluation sections address two issues. First, the different aspects and features of all-payer systems in four different states are compared and assessed. Second, alternatives to the all-payer rate-setting approach to uncompensated care are compared to the rate-setting models. Thus, this chapter compares individual all-payer systems at the state level with each other and contrasts the all-payer approach as a whole with a more market-oriented strategy.

In recent years, state governments have faced rapidly rising health care costs (both in Medicaid and as employers), diminished federal support, and a shortfall in revenues associated with sluggish economic activity. Since most states are prohibited by law from running deficits, they have been forced into a painful choice between higher taxes and lower benefits.

In an effort to avoid tax increases, as well as eligibility restrictions and cutbacks in covered health services under Medicaid, many states have been experimenting with innovative payment systems (Sullivan and Gibson 1983). Some states are enacting legislative changes that encourage their state health departments to act as "prudent purchasers" (e.g., California and Arizona). Other states are establishing primary care networks and case management programs for Medicaid recipients. In these last programs, internists, general practitioners, pediatricians, and obstetricians serve as gatekeepers who take responsibility for referrals to specialists and incur some measure of financial risk in return for a case management fee or a share of potential savings (e.g., New

Jersey, Tennessee, and Santa Barbara County, California). Some states are modifying or eliminating laws that effectively preclude preferred provider organizations (California), while others are adapting the recently implemented diagnostic-related group (DRG) system under Medicare to their state Medicaid programs (e.g., Utah and Ohio).

A number of states have adopted all-payer rate regulation in an effort to control hospital cost escalation and to apportion the burden of uncompensated care among all payers doing business in the state (e.g., Maryland, New York, Massachusetts, New Jersey, and, more recently, West Virginia and Maine). Other regulatory measures include strict limits on the number of hospital beds (Michigan, Wisconsin).[1] In Wisconsin, a hybrid package of both market-oriented *and* regulatory reforms was enacted in 1983.

Thus, many states are now experimenting with a range of cost-containment efforts involving either market-based incentives, government limits on allowable cost increases or bed growth and capital spending, or a combination of these measures. From this vast and highly differentiated terrain of new experiments, this chapter selects for review one prominent feature—all-payer rate regulation—with a special focus on the treatment of uncompensated care.

Prior to the implementation of all-payer rate-setting programs, charity care and bad debt were reimbursed in varying amounts according to the type of payer. Medicaid, in accordance with federal law, did not contribute to the cost of providing uncompensated care. Medicare and Blue Cross paid only for the bad debt associated with their own copayments and deductibles, and in some states, Blue Cross paid an additional amount toward care for uninsured patients. As a result, commercial insurers often paid a disproportionate amount of the uncompensated care costs (charity care and bad debt) that were included in or "cost-shifted" into their hospital charges (Meyer 1983).

The all-payer systems that several states have adopted are aimed at alleviating the financial burdens of the hospitals, establishing more equity among payers, and assuring access to care for the indigent. The four states that have either the most established systems or the most comprehensive and visible systems are Maryland, Massachusetts, New York, and New Jersey. Each state's all-payer system is different from the others. For this reason, each system will be briefly described, with the focus on the provisions in each state for dealing with uncompensated care. These programs are, however, very complicated and complex and cannot be comprehensively summarized in a few pages. The descriptions, therefore, capture the main features of each program according to the information available in mid-1984.

All-Payer Systems in Four States

Massachusetts

All-payer rate-setting in Massachusetts originated as a prospective hospital payment contract between the Massachusetts Hospital Association and Mas-

Jack A. Meyer

sachusetts Blue Cross. The financing provisions of the contract, HA-29, were extended to other payers in the state for six years under Chapter 372.[2] The law, which went into effect in October 1982, was passed with the support of the Massachusetts Business Roundtable and the commercial insurance industry.

Chapter 372 provides that a limit on revenue, a maximum allowable cost (MAC), is to be determined for each hospital by the state's rate-setting commission. Hospitals then set their rates at levels that will allow them to reach, but not exceed, their revenue limit. If hospitals keep their costs below the limit, they may keep the balance as "discretionary profit." If a hospital's costs exceed the revenue limit, the hospital must absorb the loss, and if a hospital collects more revenue than its MAC figure, the difference can be subtracted from the MAC set for the following year.

The MAC is based on a hospital's state-approved revenue from the previous year, adjusted for inflation. The MAC is further adjusted for changes in volume, increased costs caused by hospital construction and capital expenditures, and a "productivity factor." The productivity factor, which is adjusted annually and varies according to the payer, is used to reduce hospitals' projected revenues 7.5 percent over the first six years of the program by lowering the annual inflation adjustment by an average of 1.25 percentage points.[3] It is applied on the assumption that hospitals can actually improve operating efficiency in line with the estimated gain in productivity. As Massachusetts hospitals reduce their costs to levels closer to the national average, the productivity factor will be phased out.

If a hospital increases its total inpatient days from the previous year by more than 4 percent, it will be reimbursed for the days exceeding the 4 percent threshold at rates below the marginal cost of that care. If a hospital decreases its inpatient utilization up to 7 percent per year, there will be no reduction in authorized revenue. Thus, a hospital can profit by reducing the volume of care provided—up to a certain amount. A hospital that experiences a dramatic increase or decrease in volume can appeal to the rate-setting commission in mid-year to readjust its MAC figure.

Before the all-payer system was initiated, the various public and private insurers paid different rates for similar care at the same hospitals, although the amount of the payment differential varied from hospital to hospital. When the all-payer system began, the rate-setting commission froze the payment differentials attributable to each payer. However, beginning in October 1984, a common and fixed differential was applied to every hospital.

The Blue Cross payment rate is used as the standard for calculating the rates paid by other payers. Included in this standard rate is an amount for the Blue Cross share of bad debt and charity care costs. Commercial insurers, by contrast, pay an average of 109 percent of the Blue Cross rate, although the exact differential varies by hospital. The Medicare payment averages approximately 95 percent of the Blue Cross rate.[4] Again, these differentials varied across hospitals until October 1984.

Federal law prohibits Medicaid and Medicare from paying for care given to people not eligible for those programs, including charity care. Massachusetts applied for and was granted waivers from the U.S. Department of Health and Human Services (HHS) that allow Medicaid and Medicare to contribute to the cost of charity care under the Massachusetts prospective payment program. (The waivers do not, however, allow Medicaid and Medicare to contribute to bad debt costs.) Under the waiver, Medicaid will pay its share of charity care only in hospitals where 68 percent or more of gross patient service revenues is attributable to Medicare, Medicaid, other government subsidies, bad debt, and charity care. According to the rate-setting commission, four hospitals qualified for Medicaid payments under this stipulation in 1984. Boston City Hospital, which collects 95 percent of the Medicaid payments to Boston for charity care, received over $12 million more from Medicaid in 1983 than it did in 1982.[5] The amount Medicare can contribute to charity care costs is limited to 1.4 percent of total reimbursable costs statewide. A limit was set because the Health Care Financing Administration (HCFA) was concerned that some bad debt would be shifted to charity care costs, and the waiver does not allow payment for bad debt. The 1.4 percent figure was based on the ratio of charity care costs to total hospital payments at ninety-nine hospitals in 1982. The Massachusetts Hospital Association and Blue Cross believe this figure inaccurately reflects the cost of charity care because municipal hospitals were not included in the calculations. According to MHA and Blue Cross, 2.15 percent is the percentage of total costs attributable to charity care in 1982 when municipal hospitals are included (Alpha Centerpiece 1983).

Beginning with the fiscal year starting after October 1984, all of the costs of bad debt and charity care not paid by Medicare and Medicaid are paid on a proportional basis by Blue Cross and charge payers, up to 125 percent of their basis of payment (National Health Law Program 1984). This provision, in effect, reimburses hospitals for uninsured care at the private sector rate, a rate higher than the Medicaid reimbursement rate, thereby making it more desirable for a hospital to treat uninsured patients than to treat Medicaid patients. Legislation has been proposed and is expected to pass that will neutralize the effects of this provision by creating an incentive for hospitals to maintain their current levels of Medicaid patients.

Massachusetts has also established a Hardship Relief Fund to provide funds to hospitals that experience financial difficulty during the six-year period that Chapter 372 is in effect. Hospitals have been assessed an amount, not to exceed 0.5 percent of their Blue Cross payment, to finance the $17 million placed in this fund (Alpha Centerpiece 1983). To be eligible for these funds, a hospital must have had operating deficits in 1982 that threatened its financial viability or operating deficits in 1983 attributable to the Medicare waiver. This does not seem like a significant amount for all hospitals experiencing financial difficulty over a six-year period, but an MHA representative noted that it is unlikely that hospitals will show deficits attributable to the Medicare waiver in 1986 or 1987.

Maryland

The Maryland Health Services Cost Review Commission (HSCRC) was established in 1971 to determine prospective rates for all nonfederal short-term general hospitals and all nongovernmental long-term and specialty hospitals. In 1977, rate reviews were completed for all hospitals under the jurisdiction of the HSCRC, and a federal waiver was obtained to include Medicare and Medicaid in the prospective reimbursement program.

The HSCRC initially conducted a budget review for each hospital and developed a set of mean charges for each hospital department based on total approved revenue. Included in the approved revenues were allowances for a payer differential, for capital facilities, and for bad debt and charity care. The hospital rates may be increased annually under the voluntary inflation adjustment system (IAS) that adjusts for inflation, changes in volume and case mix, and some pass-through costs such as minimum wage increases mandated by the state or federal government. Only hospitals passing a case-mix-adjusted cost per case screen are eligible for the IAS. A hospital can also request a detailed rate review if it feels the IAS is not allowing adequate increases in revenues.

In addition to the payment system based on the unit of service (e.g., payment per operating room minute), a number of Maryland hospitals with approximately 80 percent of the inpatient hospital revenues in the state are reimbursed under a guaranteed inpatient revenue (GIR) system, an additional constraint which sets revenue limits on a per case basis.[6] The GIR freezes hospital revenues at the base period level, and annual increases are limited to an allowance for inflation plus 1 percent. Some hospitals categorize their case mix according to DRG groupings, but most hospitals use a much more detailed case mix measure split by age. The GIR is calculated according to the hospital's own experience, and the case mix adjustment is added at the end of the year. Thus, patients in all hospitals are billed on a per unit of service basis, thereby avoiding the possibility that a self-pay patient, as a result of averaging the cost of procedures within a DRG, will be confronted with a disproportionately high bill for a minor procedure (as might occur under the New Jersey all-payer program). In addition, the money that a hospital saves under the GIR system by reducing the average length of stay and ancillary services can be used at the hospital's discretion.

Reimbursement for bad debt, which in Maryland includes charity care, is figured into both of the hospital payment rates (per unit of service and per case). The Health Services Cost Review Commission uses regression analysis to predict a reasonable limit to or expected amount of bad debt. The variables used in the regression analysis—the percentage of Medicaid revenue, the percentage of commercial and self-pay patients, urban location, and the presence of an emergency room—were found to be the most predictive of bad debt and charity care delivered by a hospital. Other variables considered but found to be less predictive include suburban setting, weighted unemployment rates for a hospital's service area, and the percentage of Medicare and Blue Cross care (Health Services Cost Review Commission 1983). If a hospital's bad debt is more than the predicted amount, the hospital assumes the loss. The reimbursable amount of bad debt is calculated as a percentage of gross patient service revenues, and therefore is not adjusted every year. Hospitals can, however, appeal the reimbursement amount set by the commission and offer additional information substantiating the need for a higher rate of payment. Reimbursing hospitals only for the predicted amount of bad debt encourages them to continue reasonably aggressive payment collection procedures.

If a hospital's actual bad debt experience is less than the predicted amount, the hospital will be reimbursed for the actual amount. The commission has concluded that hospitals with bad debt costs below their predicted amounts should be commended but not rewarded beyond their actual bad debt costs.

The HSCRC must also account for payer differentials in setting hospital reimbursement rates. Maryland allows a 1 percent discount to any payer for payment within thirty days. A 2 percent discount is given to any payer who pays upon discharge. Medicare, Medicaid, and Blue Cross each receive a 6 percent discount, including a discount for prompt payment and for the increased risks they assume for insuring their respective populations.[7] Commercial insurers are ineligible for this additional discount because they can be more selective in their coverage. The HSCRC established a Differential Committee to determine if the existing differentials were equitable in 1984.

New York

New York was the first state to adopt prospective payment in 1966, although only for Blue Cross and Medicaid. By 1980, all payers except Medicare were subject to the rates set by the Office of Health Systems Management (OHSM). In January 1983, Medicare was included in New York's rate-setting program under a three-year waiver from HHS.

The OHSM determines per diem reimbursement rates and a limit on the amount of total revenues a hospital can collect from all sources. The prospective inpatient revenue cap is based on each hospital's 1981 allowable costs. Adjustments are made for inflation, changes in case mix, service intensity or volume, and "reasonable" cost increases, such as those related to labor costs.

The bad debt and charity care allowances are included in the rates calculated and published by the OHSM, but the allowances are not usually paid directly to the hospital. In most cases, the allowances added to the rates paid by third-party payers are paid directly to bad debt and charity care pools established on a regional basis within the state. The dollar amount of the allowance, based on a region's amount of bad debt and charity care, varies by region, but in 1983 it averaged 2 percent of total hospital operating costs. The allowance was to increase to 3 percent in 1984 and 4 percent in 1985 (New York Department of Health 1983). The differences in the regional allowances, however, are calculated to allow hospitals statewide to be reimbursed the same percentage of their need. The allowance is placed into an escrow account that is forwarded to the pool. The pool administrator then distributes the pool revenues to hospitals in the region.

Some payers, such as worker's compensation and self-pay patients, pay the allowance directly to the hospital as part of the total rate rather than having to pay the hospital one amount and the pool a separate amount. Hospitals must account for the allowance revenues paid in this manner and must return the amount in excess of their entitlement.

The revenue in these pools is allocated separately to major public hospitals and all other hospitals, including voluntary nonprofit, private proprietary, and all other public hospitals. In 1983 the eight regional bad debt and charity care pools collected $143 million.[8] Major public hospitals (defined as all general hospitals operated by the state or by the New York City Health and Hospital Corporation and all public general hospitals with more than $25 million in annual inpatient operating costs) receive an amount based on their percentage of the statewide public hospital inpatient reimbursable costs. In 1983, $29 million was allocated to the pools that reimburse the state's twenty-one major public hospitals.

All other hospitals (those not defined as major public hospitals) receive a proportional amount of the revenue remaining in the regional pools based on their actual bad debt and charity care need (New York Department of Health 1983). Hospitals received $0.39 for each $1.00 spent on uncompensated care in 1983, $0.60 for every $1.00 spent on uncompensated care in 1984, and $0.80 for every $1.00 spent in 1985. Hospitals are required to maintain reasonable collection procedures in exchange for their shares of the regional pool funds. The commissioner of health reviews changes in the proportional amounts of uncompensated care and adjusts the distribution of the pool funds accordingly.

In addition, New York has established regional pools that provide additional funds only to financially distressed voluntary nonprofit and proprietary general hospitals. (Public hospitals are not eligible for funds from this pool.) The $21 million available in these pools in 1983 was financed by another allowance equal to 0.25 percent of a payer's hospital reimbursement rate. This allowance is paid and administered like the allowance for the regional pools. Hospitals must apply to the commissioner of health for access to these funds, and selection criteria are based on the financial condition of the institution and the bad debt and charity care that is unmet by the other regional pools. Eight hospitals had qualified for and were receiving funds from this pool in May 1984.

The inclusion of Medicare in the state's prospective reimbursement system and shifts in payer liability were expected to cause financial hardship for a number of nonpublic hospitals that have a disproportionate share of Medicare patients. To assist these hospitals, regional transition pools were created, funded by a 0.33 percent allowance added to the reimbursement rates for nonpublic hospitals. This allowance is also paid and administered like the bad debt and charity care regional pool allowance. The funds are distributed to hospitals that apply for assistance and meet certain criteria. One hundred and five hospitals had qualified for these funds in 1983.

Finally, a discretionary allowance has been added to each payer's rate. This allowance is paid directly to hospitals and may be used at the discretion of the hospital's governing board. Acceptable uses of this allowance include, but are not limited to, retiring long-term, noncapital debt, purchasing new technology, and meeting the costs of bad debt and charity care not met by the regional pools. The allowance was 1 percent in 1983, 2 percent in 1984, and will remain at 2 percent for voluntary and proprietary hospitals in 1985; it will increase to 3 percent for public hospitals.

New Jersey

New Jersey's all-payer system is quite different from the systems previously described. From 1976 to 1980, New Jersey had a prospective payment system based on a per diem rate. The current system, which pays hospitals a prospectively determined amount per case based on diagnostic-related groups (DRGs), was implemented in 1980.[9] Under this system, referred to as Chapter 83, hospitals' total revenues and charges, as well as reimbursement per case, are regulated.

A preliminary cost base (PCB), a prospective determination of what the hospital's reasonable costs of operation should be, is established for each hospital. After adjustments are made for inflation, patient volume, and local and regional variations in wages, as well as for fixed costs such as capital facilities and working capital, the PCB data is used to calculate statewide and hospital-specific payment rates for the DRGs and for outpatient charges. If a hospital's total revenue exceeds the limit, the excess is subtracted from the next year's PCB. If a hospital's revenue is less than the allowed amount, perhaps because its uncompensated care costs were higher than anticipated, the next year's PCB will be increased accordingly.

As in other states, the cost of uncompensated care in New Jersey was a major concern of hospitals and payers. To address this concern, New Jersey's prospective payment system allows for a percentage increase in a hospital's payment rate by an amount approximating the hospital's own ratio of uncompensated care to gross revenues. In fact, this approach seems to have alleviated the financial distress of most hospitals with large uncompensated care costs. New Jersey hospitals received over $190 million for the cost of uncompensated care in 1983 (National Health Law Program 1984).

Under a waiver granted from HHS in 1979, Medicare and Medicaid pay the same rate for uncompensated care as other payers. Thus, each payer pays a proportional share of uncompensated care costs. All payers, however, do not pay the same overall rate. Payment differentials still exist, although they are much smaller than before the implementation of Chapter 83, when Blue Cross's differential was 30 percent. As of 1984, the Blue Cross differential was 6.18 percent, the Medicare differential 2.66 percent, and the Medicaid differential 2.65 percent.[10] Commercial insurers are reported to be satisfied with this system because it more evenly allocates the costs of uncompensated care to all payers, thereby reducing the amount of the costs shifted to them.

To be eligible for uncompensated care payments, however, hospitals must follow certain procedures to prove that reasonable efforts were made to collect payment for services delivered. Patients must be screened prior to admission to assess insurance coverage or ability to pay, except in emergencies. In addition, a patient's file must document that at least three bills and follow-up letters were sent to the patient and that telephone and telegram contacts were attempted. Other collection procedures must also be pursued unless there is no likelihood that payment will be recovered.

Comparison of the Four All-Payer Rate-Setting Models

The alternative approaches to the treatment of uncompensated care implemented in the four states differ in important ways. This brief evaluation of the alternative state models of all-payer systems focuses on those aspects of the four plans that relate to uncompensated care.

Risk Pools Versus Adjustments to Allowable Revenue Increases

There are two major alternatives for funding uncompensated care under an all-payer system. First, the state rate-setting authorities may add an amount to the allowable rate of increase in revenues that hospitals may receive to compensate them for bad debt and/or charity care. Second, payers may be assessed a surcharge on the amount they pay hospitals, with the extra amount flowing into a fund or pool. Then, administrators of this pool apportion the funds to selected hospitals on the basis of their proportionate share of the indigent care burden. All-payer systems in New Jersey, Maryland, and Massachusetts follow the first model, while the New York program follows the second model.

The New York model appears preferable because it establishes a more explicit, earmarked approach to financing care for those who cannot afford to pay. Instead of burying the subsidy in the overall revenue cap, this approach approximates the preferable method of an explicit tax. Indeed, if one could uncouple the risk pool approach to uncompensated care in New York from the rate-setting apparatus, the risk pool would have some of the same features and advantages of an excise tax on payers. Either an excise tax or a risk pool earmarked for uncompensated care is preferable to the formula-cap adjustment approach. In this sense, the lines between a regulatory and a more incentive-based approach to helping the economically disadvantaged can become blurred (though, in other important respects, there are still sharp differences that, in my view, favor incentives).

The New York pool approach also is more effective in assuring the financial stability of hospitals with many nonpaying patients. The pool approach equal-izes rates *across* hospitals rather than only equalizing the rates for all payers *within* hospitals. The rate-setting programs in Maryland, New Jersey, and Massachusetts specify an amount in hospital rates specifically allocated to pay the costs of the uncompensated care delivered in that hospital. If a hospital delivers a substantial amount of uncompensated care, the rates it charges all of its payers will be high, although the differentials among the rates paid by different payers will have been significantly reduced. If a hospital delivers a small amount of uncompensated care, its rates will include a small amount for uncompensated care and will therefore be lower for all payers.

This approach leaves the hospital with few nonpaying patients with a signifi-cant competitive advantage. Payers will want to avoid hospitals with higher rates, which will in turn limit the hospital's ability to spread costs over a wide payment base, thereby creating a spiralling effect. The New York approach avoids this problem by charging the same allowance to all payers in the same region and paying all hospitals in the state the same amount per dollar of uncompensated care delivered. Because hospitals are not paid the full amount of the uncompensated care they deliver, hospitals that deliver a substantial amount of uncompensated care may still be at some disadvantage, but not so much as similar hospitals might experience in other states. The pool approach also allows New York to recalculate the amount of revenue distributed to public hospitals if nonpublic hospitals begin to "dump" indigent patients on the public hospitals.

Although an explicit approach to uncompensated care seems preferable, even within the context of selecting one of several *regulatory* structures, there is also a possible drawback. By making the subsidy explicit, as Schuck notes in Chapter 4, it may become more political and vulnerable to opposition. The hidden tax, and corresponding hidden subsidy, though less desirable in some respects, could shield the uncovered poor from the reduction or elimination of a subsidy. In other words, economic rationality and political feasibility do not always coincide.

Thus, although a policy that funds uncovered beneficiaries directly and not providers appears preferable (as outlined in the next section), the risk pool/excise tax model is attractive as a second best solution. It is possible that the availability of funds in a pool will lead to political deals and legislative logrolling regarding the distribution of the funds. But this process is conducted by a greater number of people with greater public accountability than would be a set of determinations by a handful of state regulators who can make the revenue cap adjustments largely removed from public view. Allocation of funds from a pool may be sloppy and at times political, but it is likely to be visible; the subsidy is there for people to see. Under the revenue cap adjustment model, the subsidy is ensnared in a thicket of complex calculations and is difficult to isolate. It is worth noting that the best way to conduct the risk-pool model would be to have one pool instead of the series of pools described above in the New York model. The use of three types of pools, as well as regional instead of statewide pools, could make the ultimate allocation more arbitrary.

Method Used to Allocate Monies from Pools

The preferable way of allocating money from the pools to individual hospitals would involve a blending of the extent of uncompensated care and the overall cost experience and performance or quality of the hospital. Funding should be provided for disproportionately large shares of uncompensated care, but in a way that does not prop up inefficient hospitals. Considering only the amount of unpaid care could inadvertently reward inefficiency. To the extent possible, factors such as the degree of unpaid care or relative efficiency should be valued in gradations, as opposed to all-or-nothing determinations.

Against this criterion for distributing funds, the Massachusetts model seems undesirable. In Massachusetts, Medicaid does not contribute toward charitable care unless 68 percent or more of the hospital's revenue is accounted for by Medicare, Medicaid, other state and local subsidies, and uncompensated care. This arrangement presents a classic "notch problem" in public policy. A hospital with 67 percent of revenues from these sources does not obtain any payment from Medicaid for charity care, while a hospital with one percentage point more in any of these categories gets a large chunk of assistance—hardly a sensible policy. This 68 percent requirement also creates an incentive for hospitals that do not meet the requirement to send indigent patients to Boston City Hospital or one of the other three hospitals that qualify for Medicaid charity care payment. These hospitals, however, are public hospitals that are already financially stressed and understaffed.

It would also be undesirable to allocate money solely on the basis of efficiency, without regard to the degree of indigent care. This would clearly bypass the original intent of the risk-pool strategy.

The blended approach recognizes that a hospital's financial problems may be caused by factors other than uncompensated care, including poor management and inefficiency. This approach would help to avoid entrenching high-cost facilities at the same time that it compensated for the public service aspect of providing unpaid care.

The Desirability of Including Bad Debts in the Reimbursement of Uncompensated Care

An argument for paying hospitals for their charity care, but not for their bad debt, as is the case with Medicare and Medicaid in Massachusetts, is that including bad debt could dampen the incentive of hospitals to collect from those incurring the bad debts. This is a legitimate concern, but it could be addressed through other means, as in New Jersey, where the program requires stringent collection efforts on behalf of hospitals. Thus, one does not need to ban bad debt reimbursement to avoid encouraging bad debt. In fact, even states that do reimburse bad debt—New Jersey, New York, and Maryland—do not pay for the full amount, so an incentive remains for hospitals to be diligent in their collection efforts.

An Assessment of the All-Payer Approach

Access to health care for the indigent is a very real problem in this country, and the mechanisms for funding unpaid care established under all-payer systems represent one well-intentioned way to try to improve access and to distribute the financial burden more fairly. Even if one favors the programmatic concepts adopted by all-payer systems, however, one could oppose the hospital rate-setting apparatus that has been inextricably bound up with these provisions. In other words, rate setting and a solution to the problem of indigent care do not have to go hand in hand. To fix the rates at which all payers reimburse hospitals in the name of fixing the indigent care problem is a classic case of regulatory overkill.

Rate setting is justified as a means of thwarting cost-shifting among payers. Yet, rate setting is basically another form of cost-shifting. It shifts the cost of care either back to Medicare or onto hospitals. In the former case, the reverse private-to-public cost-shift merely hastens the day of Medicare's looming insolvency. In the latter case, rate setting threatens the quality of and access to care by squeezing hospital operating margins, which average about 3 percent of revenues (ICF 1983). If payers seek a regulatory license to "gang up" on hospitals and collectively underpay them, some hospitals will go bankrupt, while others delay necessary repairs and modernization or cut back services. Society as a whole will pay if the hospital sector is squeezed.

This is not to suggest that there are no inefficiencies in hospitals that could be ferreted out without adverse side effects. Rather, the magnitude of such inefficiencies has been greatly overdrawn, and in any case, a regulatory device is not likely to provide a mechanism for separating waste from need. If society says to hospitals, "Here's the target, start cutting," it will have to be prepared to sacrifice both fat and lean.

Some observers have attempted to justify all-payer systems of rate regulation on grounds of fairness, but the wrong concept of fairness is employed. The real problem of fairness in health care is that the government subsidizes a select group of those in need on a very discriminating basis. Yet the government also subsidizes many people who are *not* in need, thereby inflating the cost of care. While pumping up costs with open-ended subsidies, the government has tried to decelerate cost escalation with one new regulatory scheme after another.

Ironically, most of these regulatory measures are actually roadblocks to long-term cost relief, as they stifle potentially cost-saving innovations and protect inefficiency. Advocates of all-payer systems have brushed aside proposals that would cap subsidies flowing mainly to middle- and upper-income households, redirecting the revenues to the uncovered poor. Instead, such advocates have focused on what may be considered to be a lesser problem of fairness—fairness among payers. Sadly, another layer of regulation would be placed on an already heavily regulated industry to address a decidedly secondary problem while the essential inequity lingers.

In fact, in recent years both higher unemployment and tightened eligibility criteria under welfare programs have increased the number of low-income households without health insurance coverage. These people are not concerned about a "level playing field" for insurers. They are not even in the stadium.

Neither all-payer rate setting nor an antitrust exemption for commercial insurance carriers is the appropriate response to developments such as the rise of self-insurance or the disparate treatment of commercial insurers and Blue Cross regarding state taxes and state regulation. For example, if premium tax exemptions for Blue Cross are judged to be unfair, one should change these policies at the state level instead of asking government to fix prices in a compensatory action.

Review of the Evidence

Even this shorter-term goal of an immediate deceleration in cost increases has proven to be more difficult to achieve than a first look would suggest. When state rate-setting programs are examined as a group, the results suggest that the programs have been instrumental in achieving an average annual reduction of 2 to 3 percent. But the work of Morrisey and associates (1983) suggests that assessing the impact of a hypothetical average program can be misleading, falsely suggesting that all the state initiatives are having some effect. A careful disaggregated analysis shows that the programs have by no means been equally effective. Indeed, the small overall effect on costs seems to result exclusively from a fairly significant effect in two states—New York and New Jersey. Programs in Maryland and Massachusetts appear to have been ineffective in cost containment (Morrisey et al. 1983; Sloan 1981). Coelen and Sullivan (1981) found some favorable impact of rate setting in Maryland and Massachusetts, but the data on which their study was based extended only through 1978.

While there is considerable ambiguity about the effect of state rate-setting on overall health costs, there is evidence that Medicare loses money by participating in such programs (Morrisey, Sloan, and Mitchell 1983, p. 46). This poses a troubling dilemma for the public sector: a gain in the form of a slight deceleration in overall costs (if indeed this gain can really be achieved) may be purchased at the expense of a loss in the hospital insurance trust fund. In view of the large deficits looming in the next decade for this fund, the dangers involved in squeezing Medicare further should not be taken lightly.

Funding Indigent Care: An Alternative to All-Payer Systems

The alternative to a rate-setting solution for indigent care is an approach that raises revenues through explicit, progressive taxation and distributes the money to individuals in need, not to hospitals in need. The public policy goal should be the fair coverage of those excluded from assistance through arbitrary categorical restrictions, financed by those who can best afford it.

Under a voucher approach for low-income health coverage, beneficiaries would be given a voucher for the purchase of any qualified private health plan in their area. If the premium of the plan selected were lower than the voucher amount, the beneficiary would receive the difference in cash from the government, while those choosing plans with higher premiums would pay the extra amount themselves. The value of the voucher could vary according to factors such as age, sex, and local medical costs.

The voucher approach to either Medicare or Medicaid would breathe life into recent federal Medicare legislation calling for prospective payment and fair compensation for health maintenance organizations (HMOs). It would do this by including incentives to reduce admissions to hospitals and by broadening the range of alternatives to traditional fee-for-service medicine beyond HMOs, including primary care networks (PCNs), preferred provider organizations (PPOs), and independent practice associations (IPAs).

To the extent that competition among HMOs, PCNs, PPOs, Blue Cross, Blue Shield, and commercial insurers for taxpayers' dollars yields lower costs for a given package of services, a voucher plan offers a way to meet the health needs of both our growing elderly population and lower-oncome households in an environment of increasingly scarce federal dollars. A voucher approach, however, would not yield immediate savings. In fact, there could be a small increase in outlays initially as the more cost-effective plans are reimbursed at a community-wide average level that may exceed their costs. Also, a voucher might have to promise continuous coverage for a block of time, such as six months or a year, irrespective of the actual maintenance of Medicaid eligibility. This factor could raise costs although it would assure a steadier "safety net."

In comparing a voucher/tax increase approach to the rate-setting/indigent-care-aid-to-hospitals approach, it is important to ask who wins and who loses from the choice society makes (Meyer 1983).

The rate-setting approach to financing indigent care gives too much emphasis to the direct needs of a subset of hospitals and to the state itself, at the expense of the needs of recipients and taxpayers. It features a hospital-specific subsidy that will eventually subsidize some needs of the hospital that extend beyond insufficient compensation for bad debts or free care. This does not mean these other needs are not real, but they do not necessarily merit public subsidy.

In subsidizing hospitals instead of people, society will inevitably prop up some relatively inefficient hospitals. This creates a public license to provide services inefficiently in the name of helping the indigent. To the extent that this occurs, these hospitals are winners; other, more efficient hospitals are put at a competitive disadvantage, and the taxpayer and the patient lose in two ways. First, it takes more tax dollars than need be to help a given number of patients. Second, the quality of health services may decline as efficient hospitals are effectively penalized.

In addition to entrenching and possibly rewarding inefficiency, an all-payer system sidesteps a fundamental force driving health care spending—increased utilization. In other words, an all-payer system can be faulted not only for what it *does*, but for what it *fails to do*. With proper safeguards, incentives for consumers and providers to weigh the benefits and costs of services can make an important contribution to health care cost control. Indeed, many people believe that without such incentives, lasting cost savings will necessarily be elusive.

The issue of utilization involves not only a volume dimension (the number of tests, procedures, and admissions) but also the dimension of technological break-throughs and innovation. The all-payer system tries to address these questions by striving to shrink the system according to the preferences of government planners. These preferences are likely to discount the importance of technological advance and the need to replace and modernize facilities, subordinating the goal of assuring a fully adequate future delivery system to the shorter-term objective of immediate cost deceleration.

Who Are the Desired Beneficiaries?

The problem of indigent care is a problem of certain individuals having insufficient money to obtain care. It is easy to transform the dialogue to depict the problem group as one set of sellers—in either the hospital industry or the insurance industry—believing that they need a government subsidy to meet the competition. This recasting of the problem makes arbitrary winners of one group of companies at the expense of other groups.

Government also wins when aid to the poor is channeled through a government-to-industry indirect subsidy route. Along with the role of rechanneling funding to aid those in need, government absorbs the extra power to set industry prices. Indeed, one difference between the two approaches contrasted here is that under a more market-oriented plan with vouchers, each payer bargains individually with hospitals, who face an array of diffuse power bases. Under the rate-setting model, the industry faces a government monopoly. The former is better suited to strike a proper balance between the cost of care and its quality than the latter.

When the power lies with payers, there is a much clearer responsibility for outcomes than when it lies with government. Moreover, while government power may look formidable, it is subject to outcomes ranging from legal evasion of controls and gaming to outright capture.

The argument for subsidizing needy households instead of needy (or supposedly needy) providers has an analogue in many other social services. Traditional program designs have often favored providers of services as much as (or even at the expense of) recipients of services. Thus, in housing programs, the interests of home builders and bankers were reflected in the bias toward new construction that governed housing policy for over four decades. Instead of directly assisting people with inadequate resources, the federal government has funneled money to local housing authorities for public housing projects and to builders through mortgage subsidies.

The "68 percent rule" for hospital assistance in Massachusetts mentioned earlier typifies another basic problem with the rate-setting/all-payer system approach to financing indigent care: the tendency in government policy to congregate all the needy in certain facilities. Indeed, under this scheme, hospitals must become a kind of "government mill"—or two-thirds of one—in order to get any aid. The analogy to housing policy is again germane. Through the public housing program the public has offered rent subsidies to those poor people who would congregate in a specific building, while others who would not (or could not because of long waiting lists) obtained no aid. By contrast, an admirable feature of the food stamp program is that it does not require needy households to patronize government-supported grocery stores in order to obtain assistance. Needy individuals pass through the same checkout line as those who can afford to pay.

This distinction not only involves efficiency; it is also a matter of dignity. Society should not foster policies whose effect—intended or not—is to herd low-income individuals into a select group of facilities serving the poor. An often overlooked advantage of the voucher approach to public policy is that it

Jack A. Meyer

is a kind of anonymous subsidy: you can get it without declaring yourself to be poor by utilizing separate facilities.

Notes

The author would like to thank Marie Hackbarth for a very valuable contribution to all aspects of this paper. Nancie Krieger provided additional research assistance, and Marion Ein Lewin and Samuel A. Mitchell offered numerous helpful suggestions.

1. *Michigan Public Health Code,* act 368, secs. 22154 and 22156 (1978); *Wisconsin Statutes,* ch. 150, subch. 3, as repealed and recreated by 1983 Wisconsin Act 27 and *Wisconsin Administrative Code,* ch. HSS 123.

2. *Massachusetts General Law,* ch. 6A, secs. 31 and 50–72, amended by Chapter 389 of the Acts of 1983.

3. Conversation with Dennis Beatrice, associate director and senior research associate at the Health Policy Center at Brandeis University and former assistant commissioner for Medicaid in Massachusetts.

4. Conversation with John Chapman, director of the Hospital Bureau of the Massachusetts Rate-Setting Commission.

5. Remarks delivered by Dennis Beatrice at an American Enterprise Institute conference, "Changing Social Welfare Policies," March 20–21, 1984.

6. Conversation with John Colmers, chief of Methodology Development, Maryland Health Services Cost Review Commission.

7. Ibid.

8. I am indebted to a conversation with Bob Barnett, director of the Bureau of Health Economics and Systems Development, Albany, New York, for the data on New York revenue pools and hospitals in this paragraph and the following paragraphs.

9. Ch. 83, P.L. 1978, *New Jersey State Acts,* 26:2H-1 et seq.

10. Conversation with Joel May, president of Health Research and Education Trust of New Jersey.

References

Alpha Centerpiece. 1983. "Indigent Care under Prospective Payment: The New York and Massachusetts Experiments." *Alpha Centerpiece,* April.

Coelen, Craig, and Daniel Sullivan. 1981. "An Analysis of the Effects of Prospective Reimbursement Programs on Hospital Expenditures." *Health Care Financing Review* 2, no. 3 (Winter): 1–40.

Health Services Cost Review Commission. 1983. "Background Policy Paper: Uncompensated Care Policy." February, updated October 1983.

ICF. 1983. "Background Data on Changes in Hospital Expenditures and Revenues, 1971–1981." Washington, D.C.: January.

Meyer, Jack A. 1983. *Passing the Health Care Buck: Who Pays the Hidden Cost?* Washington, D.C.: American Enterprise Institute.

Morrisey, Michael A., Frank A. Sloan, and Samuel A. Mitchell. 1983. "State Rate-Setting." *Health Affairs* 2, no. 2 (Summer): 36–47.

National Health Law Program. 1984. "Access to Hospital Care for the Poor under Prospective All-Payer Systems." Los Angeles.

New York State Department of Health, Office of Health Systems Management. 1983. "New York's Prospective Hospital Reimbursement Methodology." Albany: New York Department of Health, April.

Sloan, Frank A. 1981. "Regulation and the Rising Cost of Hospital Care." *Review of Economics and Statistics* 63, no. 4 (November): 479–87.

Sullivan, Sean, and Rosemary Gibson. 1983. *Restructuring Medicaid: A Survey of State and Local Initiatives.* Washington, D.C.: American Enterprise Institute.

Book title

TEN
Conclusion

Frank A. Sloan

9130 JS 185–189

Uncompensated Hospital Care: A "Hot" Policy Issue

Uncompensated hospital care has become a "hot" policy issue for several reasons. First, the hospital industry has become large; in 1982, payment to hospitals represented $136 billion, or 42 percent of total spending on health care services (Gibson et al. 1983). As a consequence of both the level and growth of expenditures, hospitals have become subjects of special scrutiny by policymakers, the media, and the public alike.

Second, there have been cutbacks in public programs providing cash and in-kind benefits to the poor and near-poor, both in the health field and more generally (see Chap. 7 by Myers). There is some debate in the mid-1980s about the extent to which these cutbacks have adversely affected low-income groups. Given the special status of health care and the importance of hospital care to persons with catastrophic illnesses, part of the public discussion has focused on new barriers the financially disadvantaged may face in obtaining hospital care.

Third, because of the high unemployment rates in the early 1980s and the fact that insurance coverage for the middle class, nonelderly in the United States is job-centered, much concern has been expressed about the access of the unemployed and their families to hospital care and other health services.

Fourth, competitive pressures are mounting in the health field, and as Chapter 6 by Phelps emphasizes, competition is inconsistent with cross-subsidization. Some hospitals once could shift unpaid bills onto the bills of charge-paying patients, but this practice will become increasingly difficult under competition, since charge-paying patients and their surrogates will purchase services from hospitals offering the lowest price for a given service or quality of service. If charge-paying patients are no longer to be a source of the subsidy, what other group will fill the gap?

Fifth, state and local governments are facing fiscal stresses of their own in the 1980s. In some cases, they face eroding tax bases. All face the threat that high taxes will adversely affect the business climate in their communities. Thus, although state and local governments are concerned, they will not readily provide additional funding to compensate for funding decreases from federal and private sources. In fact, one manifestation of the fiscal problems hospitals face are cutbacks in Medicaid programs, which in turn may have exacerbated the uncompensated care problem (Chap. 7).

Sixth, the structure of ownership and control in the U.S. hospital industry is changing rapidly. One major change is the growth of investor-owned and not-for-profit chains (Ermann and Gabel 1984). A persistent question arises from the community when a previously independent hospital is acquired: "Will you care for the indigent in our community, and, if so, on what basis?" At some stage, to achieve further growth, the chains will have to provide satisfactory assurances on this score.

The total value of uncompensated hospital care in 1982, $6.2 billion, amounted to less than 5 percent of payments to hospitals in that year (Chap. 2 by Sloan, Valvona, and Mullner). This is about a third as much as Medicare, Medicaid, and other payers obtained from hospitals in the form of contractual allowances or discounts in the same year. Also, uncompensated care is *not* a reason for hospital closings but only one of many reasons for some hospitals' adverse financial condition. Much of the policy debate has occurred without reference to data. Now that the volume of uncompensated care has been documented and seen to represent a relatively small proportion of total hospital spending, should policymakers now regard this as a "nonissue"? Probably not. Although the *average* citizen, hospital, and locality may face a small burden, a prominent feature of uncompensated hospital care is its maldistribution (Chap. 2). The value of care foregone because uninsured and low-income individuals believe hospitals and other health care providers would not accept them for treatment or otherwise embarrass them has not yet been documented in this book or elsewhere. Lacking the empirical evidence, it would be foolhardy to venture a guess as to what this number would be. Increased competition in the hospital industry and further reductions in public budgets to reduce deficits may increase the uncompensated care burden.

Larger Societal Issues

Uncompensated hospital care should be placed in a larger context, as several chapters in this book have done (see, in particular, Chap. 1 by Reinhardt, Chap. 4 by Schuck, Chap. 5 by Blumstein, and Chap. 7 by Myers). At issue is the level and nature of hospital care to which each individual is entitled and who should pay for the entitlement. Reinhardt emphasized that there is an inherent conflict among these goals: (1) equitable distribution of health care services; (2) freedom from regulation for health care providers; and (3) budgetary control or cost containment. He argued that it is possible to satisfy at most only two of these objectives and remarked that we in the United States have been almost uniquely generous in granting health care providers the freedom to practice and, to a certain extent, charge what they wish.

Certainly, at first glance, it would appear that, if there must be a sacrifice, it should be at the provider's discretion. Why not solve the problem of uncompensated care by requiring that each hospital take a certain number of nonpaying patients and/or by including a tax to pay for uncompensated care as part of a mandatory hospital rate-setting program? Mandatory provision does not make the hospital pay for such care. The hospital derives virtually all of its funds from patient revenue. Ultimately, citizens pay for mandatory coverage (Chap. 6, Phelps; Chap. 5, Blumstein). There is some concern that all-payer rate-setting may stifle innovation (Chap. 8, Wilensky; Chap. 9, Meyer). Thus, although society may ultimately decide to deal with uncompensated hospital care by regulating hospitals, it should consider the potentially adverse side effects of such a decision.

No one opposes "equality" as a general concept; rather, disagreement occurs when it is operationalized, as it must be, explicitly or implicitly, when specific public policies are implemented. Moreover, society's definition of equality changes. The finding by the President's Commission for the Study of Ethical Problems in Medicine and Biomedical and Behavioral Research that "adequacy" rather than "equality" constituted "equity" is symptomatic of the thinking of the 1980s, not the 1930s or the 1960s. Although the authors of the chapters in this book do not attempt to operationalize the concept, they, like society more generally, would probably not agree about specifics. Yet, there is some agreement that competition in health care is fundamentally inconsistent with a one-tier system (see, in particular, Chaps. 1 and 5, by Reinhardt and Blumstein). If competition is to be achieved by fostering a health care marketplace, there will be a need for specific public policies to protect the access of disadvantaged persons to health care.

Policy Options

As shown by Schuck's comprehensive and general framework (Chap. 4) and by Myers', Wilensky's, and Meyer's discussions of specific public policies (Chaps. 7, 8, and 9), a wide range of options is available for financing uncompensated hospital care. Even though providing coverage for uncovered individuals has some attractive features (Meyer), providing a new entitlement for individuals also has important deficiencies (Schuck, Wilensky) and, in any case, appears inconsistent with the climate of the 1980s. If there is to be an entitlement, it is more likely to be linked to an existing program such as Medicaid than to a new one which would require establishing an administrative apparatus *de novo*.

Individual authors have suggested specific policies (see, in particular, Wilensky and Meyer), but, except possibly for espousing the virtues of explicit rather than hidden financing, there appears to be no general consensus among the authors about how uncompensated hospital care should be financed and what the level of public support should be.

Our reluctance to arrive at a consensus is both understandable and defensible. Empirical evidence on uncompensated care is still meager. Final choices among options necessarily are value-based, and we policy analysts as individuals have values as individuals, but we are not justified in placing ours above those of others. On the other hand, an important task of policy analysis is in making implicit values explicit. Policymakers can then make the normative calculations. Finally, while there is some merit in a federal solution, the United States is diverse (Schuck), and the proper solution for one geographic area may be inappropriate for another.

Financing options have received most attention in this book and elsewhere, but there is reason to pay attention to delivery options as well. First, why should the hospital continue to be the "health care home" for the indigent? Might some hospitalizations be prevented if there were a point of first contact other than the hospital emergency room or outpatient clinic? In some cases, too much rather than too little hospital care may be provided. Options should encourage rather than discourage the use of a less costly substitute for hospital care when substitution can be made without undue sacrifice of quality. Second, specific delivery options should be evaluated for diagnoses and procedures for which nonpaying patients are particularly concentrated. Judging from available data, a disproportionate number of uncompensated care cases are maternity- or accident-related (Chap. 2, Sloan and coauthors; Chap. 3, Perrin). A few low-birth-weight infants accounted for a relatively high proportion of total uncompensated care at one tertiary care hospital. Where concentration occurs, society should weigh the advantages and deficiencies of concentrating delivery of care in a few sites. Relevant issues in this regard have been reviewed by Perrin.

Research Agenda

The lack of a sound conceptual and empirical knowledge base works to the detriment of sound policy formulation in any area, and uncompensated hospital care is no exception. At one level, there is a need for more basic research on the distributional issues raised by the topic of uncompensated care. At another, there is a need for empirical research. The latter should range from fact-gathering of the type found in Chapters 2, 3, and 8, to empirical behavioral research, some of which is contained in Chapter 2. To date, the only national data on the characteristics of uncompensated care patients are really on hospitalized patients whose expected source of payment at the time of discharge was "self-pay" or "no-charge." Although hospitals properly regard such patients as poor credit risks as a group, such patients paid over 70 percent of hospital charges in a recent year (Ginsburg and Sloan 1984). More direct evidence on patients with unpaid bills is collected by hospitals, but is not published. The data from Vanderbilt University Hospital for 1982–83 assembled by Perrin (Chap. 3) provide the most recent and comprehensive description publicly available anywhere. However, the Vanderbilt data are from only one hospital, and it is a tertiary care institution, a minority group among hospitals, and located in the South, where uncompensated hospital care is high on average (Chap. 2). The data on insurance coverage presented by Wilensky (Chap. 8) are for 1977. There has been no support from either public or private sources for an on-going survey of health insurance coverage. Without more comprehensive and recent data, policymakers concerned about uncompensated care will have to work essentially blindfolded.

Knowledge of important behavioral relationships is also lacking. Answers to the following types of questions would be useful: Under what circumstances is care of the nonpaying patient cross-subsidized? What determines health care–seeking patterns of patients without health insurance? (This question encompasses types of providers selected as well as patients' geographic choices, such as the decision for rural residents to seek care at a hospital in a large city.) Under what circumstances are employers likely to provide extended coverage in the event of a job loss? Why are some employed persons uninsured? Finding answers to these questions should occupy researchers as well as policymakers for years to come.

References

Ermann, Dan, and Jon Gabel. 1984. "Multihospital Systems: Issues and Empirical Findings." *Health Affairs* 3, no. 1 (Spring): 50–64.

Gibson, Robert M., Daniel R. Waldo, and Katherine R. Levit. 1983. "National Health Expenditures, 1982." *Health Care Financing Review* 5, no. 1 (Fall): 1–31.

Ginsburg, Paul, and Frank A. Sloan. 1984. "Hospital Cost-Shifting." *New England Journal of Medicine* 310, no. 14 (April 5): 893–98.

Notes on Contributors

JAMES F. BLUMSTEIN is professor of law, special advisor to the chancellor for academic affairs, and senior research associate at the Institute for Public Policy Studies, Vanderbilt University.

JACK A. MEYER is resident fellow in economics at the American Enterprise Institute, Washington, D.C.

ROSS MULLNER is associate director of the Health Information and Data Services, American Hospital Association, Chicago.

BEVERLEE A. MYERS is professor and head of the Division of Health Services, School of Public Health, University of California, Los Angeles.

JAMES M. PERRIN is assistant professor of pediatrics, director of the Primary Care Center, and senior research associate at the Institute for Public Policy Studies, Vanderbilt University.

CHARLES E. PHELPS is director of the Public Policy Analysis Program and professor of political science and economics, University of Rochester, Rochester, N.Y.

UWE E. REINHARDT is James Madison Professor of Political Economy, Woodrow Wilson School, Princeton University.

PETER H. SCHUCK is professor of law at Yale University.

FRANK A. SLOAN is Centennial Professor of Economics and director of the Health Policy Center, Institute for Public Policy Studies, Vanderbilt University.

JOSEPH VALVONA is research associate at the Health Policy Center, Institute for Public Policy Studies, Vanderbilt University.

GAIL R. WILENSKY is vice-president of the Domestic Division, Project HOPE, Millwood, Virginia.

Index

Davis, Karen, 128
Debts. *See* Bad debts
Delaware, 137
Deliveries, 32, 33
Demoralization problem, 97
Denver Children's Hospital, 61
Diagnosis-related groups (DRGs), 110, 112, 116, 171, 174
Diagnostic categories, technology and, 55–60
Discounting, 111
Discriminant analysis, 19, 52
Drug abuse, 55, 57

Early and periodic screening, diagnosis, and treatment program (EPSDT), 131
Economic privilege, 6
Efficiency: subsidized hospital care and, 77–78, 82, 83; technology and, 62–63, 64, 67–68
Employee Retirement Security Act (ERISA), 162
Entitlements, 13, 187; approaches to, 96–97; closed-ended subsidies versus, 83–87; justice theory and concept and, 6–10. *See also* Grants
Equality, 7, 94, 95
Equity: of access to health care, 94, 95; adequate health care and, 95–96; free choice and indigent care and, 11, 12, 13; health care and, 10–13; level of care and, 186–87; subsidized hospital care and, 82
"Equity of Access to Health Care" (Daniels), 11

Feder, Judith, 116
Financial issues: hospital status and uncompensated care, 18, 25–26, 38; investment in technology, 69; the poor, 72
Florida, 136, 152, 153, 155, 157
Food stamps, 85

Governance, hospital resource distribution and, 120–21
Government: cutbacks by, 185; subsidized hospital care and level of, 78–80. *See also* Local government; State government
Grants, 127; to state and local government, 148, 160–61, 163, 164. *See also* Entitlements

Hadley, Jack, 116
Harris, Jeffrey, 120, 121
Hawaii, 136
Health care: "adequate," 2; egalitarian distribution of, 8–9; equity and adequate, 95–96; equity and freedom and, 10–13; equity of access to, 94, 95; goals of, 10;

justice and, 7–10; level and nature of present, 186–87; a poor individual's access to, 72
Health Care Financing Administration (HCFA), 170
Health insurance. *See* Insurance
Health Insurance Association of America (HIAA), 12
Health maintenance organizations (HMOs), 11, 91, 159, 180; enhancement policies and, 75; Medicaid and, 131; states and, 132; vouchers and, 76
Hill-Burton Act, 16, 72, 77, 87; current regulations of, 102–4; enactment of, 98–99; hospitals and indigent care and, 3; policy and, 104–6; regulatory development of, 99–102; subsidies and, 81, 82, 89, 90, 91
Hospital Discharge Survey: Denver Study comparisons and, 61–62; patient characteristics and, 29, 30, 38–39; as source of data, 18
Hospitals: barriers to care at, 39–40; care in public, 65–66; causes of cost-shifting and, 110–11; challenges to, 87; charity care and not-for-profit and investor-owned, 5; closing of, 26–27, 38; compensation and, 12–13; decentralized (Hill-Burton), 105; distribution of uncompensated care among, 36–37; efforts to reduce uncompensated care and, 27–29; financial responsibility for uncompensated care and, 2–6; financial status and uncompensated care and, 25–26; Hill-Burton and obligations of, 97–106; insurance and type of, 148; payment to, 185; politics and public, 66; rate regulation and, 12; resource distribution and, 120–21; statistical analysis and type of, 20–24, 32; use of cost-shifting and, 120–21
Hospital Survey and Construction Act. *See* Hill-Burton Act

Independent practice associations (IPAs), 180
Indiana, 136, 155
Indigent adults: defining, 127–29; states and, 134, 135–36, 143
Indigent care, 152; all-payer rates and, 180–81; data and, 16–17, 18; defining indigents, 127–29; financial responsibility for, 2–3, 4, 5; free choice and equity questions and, 11, 12, 13; insurance and, 157–58; limits on, 27–28; right to health care and, 94; technology and, 4. *See also* Bad debts; Poor individuals; Uncompensated care
In-kind benefits, 76–77
Insurance: barriers to hospital care and, 40–

41; business firms and, 4–5; catastrophic illness programs, 153–54; characteristics of, 149–50; characteristics of uninsured and, 149–50; direct reimbursement and, 151–52, 163–64; employment-related, 58; excise taxes and, 161–63; grants to states and local governments, 148, 160–61, 163, 164; hospital type and, 148; indigent and, 157–58; individuals and, 14, 153–61; middle-class families and, 3; policy options and, 148, 149, 163–64; pooling revenues and, 152–53; providers and, 148, 151–53; public, 9; risk-sharing pools and, 155; tax cap financing and, 163, 164; unemployed and, 155–57, 163; voucher system and, 159–60

Justice: concept of, 7–10; theory of, 6–7

Liberty, 7, 9
Liquidity, 18, 25
Local government, 137–38, 141–42, 143, 186; insurance and, 148, 160–61, 163, 164
Luft, Harold S., 122

Maerki, Susan C., 122
Maine, 153, 154
Management, hospital closings and quality of, 26–27
Maryland, 130, 137, 139, 141; all-payer rates and, 171–72, 175, 176, 178, 180
Massachusetts, all-payer rates in, 168–71, 175, 176, 177, 178, 180, 182
Means tests, 88–89
Medicaid, 19, 77, 91, 96, 186, 187; all-payer rates and, 167, 168, 170, 172, 175, 177, 178, 180, 181; charge-shifting and, 110; cutbacks in, 36; Hill-Burton and, 98, 99, 100–101, 106; indigent and, 3; in-kind benefits and, 76; insurance and, 152, 153, 154, 156, 157–58, 159, 160, 164; neonatal reimbursement and, 61; patient characteristics and, 30; states and, 127, 128, 129, 130–35, 141, 142; subsidies for poor and, 79–80, 85, 87, 90
Medi-Cal, 129, 130–35, 136, 137, 138–39, 140
Medically indigent adults (MIAs), 134, 135–36, 143
Medical Tribune, 9
Medicare, 60, 96, 186; all-payer rates and, 168, 169, 170, 172, 174, 175, 177, 178, 180; charge-shifting and, 110, 111–12, 116; free choice and, 11; Hill-Burton and, 98, 99, 100–101, 106; hospital allowances and, 29; indigent and, 3; in-kind benefits

and. 76; insurance and, 154, 159, 161; subsidies for poor and, 79, 80, 85, 90
Middle-class families, medical costs and, 3
Mill, John Stuart, 6
Minnesota, 136, 153, 155
Morrisey, Michael A., 179

National Center for Health Statistics, 18
National Hospital Discharge Survey. See Hospital Discharge Survey
National Medical Care Expenditure Survey (NMCES), 40
Neonatal care. See Newborn care
Newborn care, 34–35, 57, 58, 60–63, 68, 70
Newhouse, Joseph P., 109
New Jersey, 174–75, 176, 178, 180
Newsom v. Vanderbilt University, 102–3, 104
New York, 153; all-payer rates and, 172–74, 175–76, 178, 180
New York City Health and Hospital Corporation, 173
North Dakota, 136, 155

Occupational Safety and Health Act, 79
Omnibus Budget Reconciliation Act (OBRA), 151, 158

Patients: costs and class of, 116–19; lack of standing to challenge hospitals and, 87; statistical analysis and characteristics of, 18, 29–33, 38–39; technological services and, 55–60; technology and random distribution of, 67
Pauly, Mark, 109
Payment-in-kind benefits, 76–77
Peltzman, Sam, 114
Physicians, egalitarian doctrine and, 12
Policy: health-care, 10; Hill-Burton, 104–6; insurance and, 148, 149, 150, 163–64; services and, 2; social, 63; states and social, 139–41, 143; uncompensated care and public, 187–88
Politics: health care and, 10; public hospitals and, 66; regulation and, 111; right to health care and, 2; subsidies and, 82–83, 86, 89
Poor individuals, 119; access to health care and, 72; appropriate scope of assistance for, 88–90; assumptions concerning, 127–29; defining, 127; entitlements versus closed-ended subsidies for, 83–87; explicit versus concealed subsidies for, 80–83; forms of subsidies for, 75–78; government and, 78–80; means testing and, 88–89; publicly financed health care for, 72; reasons for subsidizing, 73–74. See also Indigent care

Preferred providers organizations (PPOs), 11, 76, 110–11, 180
President's Commission for the Study of Ethical Problems in Medicine and Biomedical and Behavioral Research, 11, 94–96, 105, 187
Price discretion, 108
Price discrimination, 12–13
Pricing: causes of cost-shifting and, 110–11; distortions in, 120; historic background on, 108–10; monopoly, 119
Primary care networks (PCNs), 11, 180
Prospective payment, 1

Quality of care, technology and, 68

Race, 32
Rates, 108; regulation of, 12; vouchers and, 76. See also All-payer rate setting
Ratio of costs to charges, applied to charges (RCCAC), 111
Reagan administration, 72, 84
Redisch, Michael, 109
Regression analysis (statistical analysis of uncompensated care), 18, 24, 38–39, 41–52
Regulation: cross-subsidies and, 122; hospital costs and theory of, 112; of rates, 12. See also All-payer rate setting; Hill-Burton Act
Reimbursement: direct, 151–52, 163–64; neonatal, 61–62; retrospective, 1. See also All-payer rate setting
Research (uncompensated care), 188–89
Revenue pooling: all-payer rates and, 175–78; provider, 152–53
Rhode Island, 136, 137, 153, 154
Risk-sharing pools (state), 155; all-payer rates and, 175–78
Rowland, Diane, 128

Schroeder, Steven A., 55, 58
Schwartz, William B., 69–70
Services: political policy and, 2; technology and organization of, 63, 64
Short-Doyle mental health programs, 143
Sloan, Frank A., 65, 118–19, 120, 123
Social policy, 63, 139–41, 143
Social security, 79, 80, 84–85, 86
South Carolina, 137
Specialized treatment centers, 63–65, 66
State government, 186; insurance and, 148, 160–61, 163, 164; medically indigent adults (MIAs) and, 135–36; Medicaid and, 127, 128, 129, 130–35, 141, 142; risk-sharing pools and, 155; social policy and, 139–41, 143; subsidized hospital care and, 78–80. See also All-payer rate setting

State regulation programs. See All-payer rate setting
Statistical analysis of uncompensated care: aggregate amount of uncompensated care and, 19, 35–37; barriers to hospital care and, 39–40; current interest in uncompensated care and, 40–41; data source and, 17–18; defining uncompensated care and, 16; distribution of uncompensated care and, 36–37; financial issues and, 18, 25–26, 37–38; hospital efforts to reduce uncompensated care and, 27–29; hospital type and, 20–24, 32; methodology and, 18–19; patient characteristics and, 18, 29–33, 38–39; regression analysis variables and, 18, 24, 38, 41–52; Vanderbilt Hospital and, 34–35
Subsidies, 182; alternatives to cross-subsidies, 120–22; costs and, 114, 115, 116; entitlements versus closed-ended, 83–87; explicit versus concealed, 80–83; forecasting trends in, 122–23; forms of (for poor individuals), 75–78; major issues with cross-subsidies, 119–20; measuring of cross-subsidies and charge-shifts and, 116–19; reasons for, 73–74
Sullivan, Daniel, 180
Supplemental Security Income (SSI), 127, 131, 132
Supreme Court, 87
Surgery: technology and, 60; uncompensated care and patient characteristics and, 29, 33

Tax cap (insurance financing systems), 163, 164
Tax deduction (health care assistance), 74, 75–76, 78, 91
Tax Equity Fiscal Responsibility Act (TEFRA), 111, 151
Taxes: all-payer rates and, 167; insurance and excise, 161–63
Tax exemptions, 119
Technology: classes of uncompensated patients and, 54; compensation and future, 69–70; competition and, 69; defining, 54; diagnostic categories and, 55–60; efficiency and, 62–63, 64, 67–68; forecasting direction of, 67–70; indigent care and, 4; investment in, 69; newborn care and, 57, 58, 60–63, 68, 70; public hospital care and, 65–66; quality of care and, 68; random distribution of patients and, 67; rationing of, 69–70; services and, 63; social policy and, 63; specialized treatment centers and, 63–65; tertiary care centers and, 66; uncompensated care and, 38–39, 40

Tertiary care centers, 66
Texas, 130, 137, 139, 141, 142
Treatment centers (specialized), 63–65, 66

Uncompensated care: defined, 1, 16; financial responsibilities for, 2–6; limits on, 27–28; research and, 188–89; social perspective on, 2; total value of, 186; at Vanderbilt Hospital, 34–35. *See also* Bad debts; Indigent care; Statistical analysis of uncompensated care
Unemployed, 185; health insurance for, 155–57, 163
Unemployment insurance, 85

Uninsured, underwriting of. *See* Insurance
Urban areas, uncompensated care load distribution and, 36, 37
U.S. Department of Health, Education and Welfare (HEW), 102, 103

Vanderbilt Hospital, 34–35, 55–56, 58, 61, 189
Vanderbilt University, 102–3, 104, 123
Vermont, 137
Vouchers (health care assistance), 76, 90–91
Voucher system (insurance), 159–60

Wisconsin, 136, 155

The Johns Hopkins University Press

Uncompensated Medical Care

This book was composed in Goudy Old Style text and Serifa display type by The Composing Room of Michigan, Inc., from a design by Chris L. Smith. It was printed on S. D. Warren's 50-lb. Sebago Eggshell Cream Offset paper and bound in Holliston Roxite A by BookCrafters, Inc.